AF269777

JACK
HAWKINS

JACK HAWKINS

A BIOGRAPHY

NATHAN MORLEY

FONTHILL

Fonthill Media Language Policy

Fonthill Media publishes in the international English language market. One language edition is published worldwide. As there are minor differences in spelling and presentation, especially with regard to American English and British English, a policy is necessary to define which form of English to use. The Fonthill Policy is to use the form of English native to the author. Nathan Morley was born and educated in England; therefore British English has been adopted in this publication.

Fonthill Media Limited
Fonthill Media LLC
www.fonthillmedia.com
office@fonthillmedia.com

First published in the United Kingdom and the United States of America 2024

British Library Cataloguing in Publication Data:
A catalogue record for this book is available from the British Library

Copyright © Nathan Morley 2024

ISBN 978-1-78155-917-8

The right of Nathan Morley to be identified as the author of this work has been asserted by him in accordance with the Copyright, Designs and Patents Act 1988.

Typeset in 10.5pt on13pt Sabon
Printed and bound in England

Acknowledgements

There is no way I could have written this book without the help and contributions of the following people: Virginia MacKenna, Carolyn Seymour, Sir Michael Parkinson, Robert Henrey, Derren Nesbitt, John Woodvine, Harriet Cruickshank, Dr Stanley Taub, Susan George, Peter McEnery, Dame Joan Collins, Ian Ogilvy (who kindly let me reproduce a passage from his autobiography), Michael Jayston, Susan Cooper Cronyn, Lawrence Douglas, Peter Asher, Peter Medak, Joyce Bulifant, Richard Chamberlain, Muirne Mathieson, Jonathan Aitken, Barry MacGregor, Elizabeth Rees-Williams, Christopher Witty, Nanette Newman, Roger Ordish, Petula Clark, Bernard Morley, Desmond Carrington, Dame Vera Lynn, Britt Ekland, and Joe Brown. I am greatly indebted to Josh Greenland at Fonthill for his thoughtful copy editing of the manuscript. I am also thankful to the estate of Ray Galton and Alan Simpson for allowing me to read the original shooting script of Jack's episode of *Hancock's Half Hour*.

CONTENTS

Introduction by Robert Henrey

The shooting of *The Fallen Idol* was coming to an end in what to me, an inquisitive and restless eight-year-old, was a magically evocative set at Shepperton Studios that had been built to evoke the magnificence of an embassy's great hall. Many of the scenes were being shot against the background of a grand sweeping staircase. I could not help sensing, though, that the plot had darkened. I was being interrogated by three men whose job, I was told by Carol Reed, was to be ponderous and intimidating. What I remember quite clearly is that they wore imposing overcoats, that my hero Baines (Ralph Richardson) was most obviously in trouble, that his relationship with his presumed niece (Michèle Morgan) was somehow an intriguing complication, and that I had caught sight for a fleeting moment of Mrs Baines's body (Sonia Dresdel) rolling down the very staircase on which I was being interrogated. Detective Ames was one of the three.

In hindsight, it occurs to me that these must have been among *The Fallen Idol*'s most challenging sequences to direct. This was Carol Reed making the very best of the deft subtlety of Graham Greene's script. Consummate actors—among them Ralph Richardson, Michèle Morgan, and, yes, Jack Hawkins—were all being asked to interact anxiously with an over stimulated and disarmingly unpredictable child apparently holding the key to solving a life-or-death puzzle.

It took me a very long time to come to terms with how very lucky I had been that chance events had led me as a child to be associated with so capable and talented a group of professionals. So, yes, I had first met Jack Hawkins on that famous staircase, as it were, but not really. Meeting a fellow human being takes maturity and reflection. So, my encounter with Jack Hawkins came much, much later. Not, alas, a Jack Hawkins alive and exuberant who, generous as he was, would surely have greeted me warmly and no doubt offered me a drink. No, this was the Jack Hawkins brought to life by my watching *The Cruel Sea*, *The Bridge on the River Kwai*, and *Ben-Hur*.

Memory is a subtle and wondrous thing. The longer we live, the more opportunities we have to build it up. It is a much-layered aspect of our consciousness. Thanks to Nathan's love of history, his meticulousness, and his admirable desire to narrate Jack's life, it is a profoundly human story. Further still, I have been given the opportunity to further enrich my own life. I am awed that it all goes back to what was, after all, a chance encounter at Shepperton Studios in the early months of 1948.

I had, of course, learned much later that Jack Hawkins had died of cancer, but it is thanks to Nathan that I have become aware of the depth of his love for his family, and, yes, the further depth of the tragedy of a life cut short. It was, though, a life well and intensely lived and, yes, tragedy is, one way or another, part of our common human experience. Perhaps one of our greatest challenges is to learn to let hope shine through it. Jack's life resonates, so to repeat, I am thankful.

1

Making an Entrance

So many decades have passed, so many trends in the entertainment business have flourished and withered, that it might seem outrageous to us that we are still watching—and enjoying—the films of Jack Hawkins. With his barrel-chest and raspy voice, Jack was the living embodiment of British ruggedness, resilience, straightness, and compassion. In the theatre, he dominated every stage he took, and film success brought him even closer to his audience. As the late Sir Michael Parkinson remarked to the author, nobody could mimic Jack's unique sense of restraint: 'He was a formidable presence in the British film industry and later became one of those trustworthy stars who an audience loved because he made them believe that everyone was as decent and brave as Jack Hawkins.'

John Edward Hawkins, or Jack as everyone called him, was delivered in the master bedroom of 45 Lyndhurst Road, a modest Victorian terraced house in the tight north London community of Wood Green on Saturday 10 September 1910. Born just months after the death of King Edward VII, he was very much a child of the Edwardian era, a time brimming with prudish conservatism, prosperity, and opportunity.

On the day after he was born, Jack weighed 7 pounds. At three months, he weighed 9 pounds. He began to crawl at twelve months and showed every sign of becoming a gripping chap just like his father, Thomas George Hawkins, the local master builder, and a man of good standing. His mother, Phoebe Hawkins (*née* Goodman), kept the house meticulously clean, and Jack remembered how the noises of tradesmen calling, horses' hoofs, and school kids playing on the cobblestones provided the soundtrack of his youth. His visual memory—like his father's—was remarkable. He never forgot the family assembling in the sitting room to listen to readings, poetry recitals, and join in singsongs at the piano. To the outside world, the Hawkins family represented the model of upstanding Edwardian people, leading a decent, clean living and industrious life. His earliest recollections were of women—his mother, teenage sisters, Florence and Gladys, and two religious-minded grandmothers (both Victorian widows) given to overt displays of affection. 'I was the afterthought!' he once joked. 'Everything revolved around the family. Our home was our orbit; my older brother Tom was a playmate—it was a happy place.'

Photos taken during his childhood show a self-confident, attentive, bright-eyed, cheerful boy; his memories were dominated by church, school, and family. One of his earliest recollections was emerging from his home in 1916 and watching a policeman race along Lyndhurst Road warning residents that German Zeppelins were literally on the warpath. As the story is usually told, he stood open-mouthed at the spectacle as the airship was shot down and fell with a terrific wallop across a street in Potters Bar. Except this, the war made no sudden or shocking interruptions to his life. In fact, Jack's father dreamed of being a soldier, but failed his army medical due to 'TB on the lung'—a condition which remained dormant, and he managed to live into his late eighties.

In early in 1918, as the First World War entered its final phase, Jack was enrolled at the Trinity County School under the watchful eye of headmaster Dr E. E. Jones. Outdoor life held his interest more than classrooms did, and he discovered fishing and the joy of idling away hours casting a net at Pymmes Brook, the New River, and Moselle, the three most abundant tributaries near Wood Green. On balmy summer afternoons, sport dominated play times, and although he was slim (weighing just 130 pounds), he hurled himself around the pitch in the football team and owned the loudest voice at St Michael's parish choir where Reverend Midwinter—a pensioner with salt-and-pepper grey hair—pressed the message of decency and obedience. These were gentler times than we know today. Every week, Midwinter dispensed a programme of sacred solos and thundered at the organ during rousing renditions of 'Onward, Christian Soldiers'. 'Everything circled around marriage, the church and the vicar,' Jack explained, 'choir practice usually closed with the Benediction. As well as being in the choir, I was a boy scout...'

It is hardly surprising his flair for performing was apparent at an early age. 'I came into acting via the choir's Gilbert and Sullivan operas. At the time they seemed splendid,' he laughed when telling how—heavily made-up and in costume—he exploded onto the school stage with 'dreadful self-assurance' as the youngest performer. 'Some great friends of the family suggested it would keep me out of mischief. I was a maid of all work in a grey wig in *The Pirates of Penzance*! It's the contralto part you know! It was a shattering performance, but I enjoyed myself.'[1]

Once adolescence set in, the changes in Jack were quite dramatic. He occasionally spent time in his father's workshop, where he was allowed to have a go at using the tools but never enjoyed carpentry or metalwork nor had talent for technical things. Instead, it was anything theatrical which aroused his keenest interest. He spent more time with his sister Florence and shared her passion for opera. Her fiancé often charmed the family on Sunday afternoons with popular melodies, including a stirring rendition of Fred E. Weatherly's 'Thora', a crowd-pleaser of the day.

> *Come! Come! Come to me, Thora,*
> *Come once again and be*
> *The child of my dream, light of my life,*
> *Angel of love to me!*

Urged on by Florence, he joined a local children's concert party, 'The Redcaps', where his ambition was unleashed performing at church halls and fetes. It was a constructive nudge and Jack said, 'it strengthened my determination to become an actor'.[2] His dramatic abilities must have seemed especially remarkable to his parents, whose only connection to the performing arts was applauding vaudeville 'turns' at the local theatre as enthusiastic audience members. His association with the 'The Redcaps' led to an interview and elocution test (to show-off his rounded vowels) at the Italia Conti Academy of Theatre Arts, an institute famed for 'training stage and screen stars', or as Jack later described her: 'The famous teacher and agent of child actors, dancers, and other such monsters'. From a building in central London, Conti supplied adolescents to West End and provincial producers, and when it came to juvenile actors, her banner fluttered high. Students included the vivacious Gertrude Lawrence and a gifted teenager named Margaret Lockwood—both of whom created a terrific buzz.

In his Conti debut (as a frog) on 26 December 1923, Jack joined a young cast in *Where the Rainbow Ends* acting out the story of St George and the Dragon. 'Master Hawkins' was a 'natural actor', fellow student Sydney Bromley remembered: 'He had this contact with the audience. He was aware of his position on the stage, of his ability and personality. He knew it was all working'. From his earliest years, he loved singing and stagecraft, and lapped up the hum and bustle of the Conti school, a grand old pile opposite the Great Ormond Street Hospital.

When *Rainbow* closed, he successfully auditioned for the role of 'page boy' in George Bernard Shaw's first production of *Saint Joan* where he found himself treading the boards with Sybil Thorndike, one of the outstanding figures in British theatre. In later years, he often regaled friends with stories of Shaw, who was on hand to oversee rehearsals and upset everyone with his rough tongue. He remembered there was a furious disagreement between the Scottish actor John Laurie and the elderly playwright about the pronunciation of the word 'Skoon.' 'Shaw,' Jack recounted, 'was a red bearded gentleman who jumped up and down and seemed rather ridiculous.'[3]

Encouraged by the artistic opportunity in front of him, Jack was grandly announced in the 1924 theatrical yearbook and, soon after, moved permanently to the Thorndike-Casson company, where he would perform for the next three years. He received 30 shillings a week (a decent sum of money) and toured in Shakespearean repertory, playing boy parts. Thorndike's distinguished husband, Lewis Casson, was determined that his young charge should be properly educated and arranged for Maisie East, a strong-minded and efficient guardian, to take care of his private tuition. 'She was a perfectly splendid woman,' Jack reflected years later, looking back with nostalgic affection. 'During my early years—those impressionable ones—I managed to pick up a good bit of stage know-how in Thorndike's company.'[4]

> I had a marvellous apprenticeship, painting scenery, playing boys parts, doing everything. I wasn't originally a public-school type, but because during so many of my school years I was touring. I was brought up in the theatre and it imposed an almost military discipline on its players. It did not matter whether you were the humblest stagehand, walk-on actor or the star of the show, the play was the most important thing.

Though he barely intertwined with his parents or siblings during this period, and only occasionally came home for weekends, their relationship remained warm.

Nevertheless, Ms East assumed the role of a good-natured aunt, she was never a coddler but nurtured his imagination and encouraged self-reliance. Nothing missed her beady eyes, especially the occasional unwelcome glance her pupil received from the 'considerable homosexuals' in the cast. Jack liked to point out to interviewers that East was not only a guardian of morals but also helped him achieve constantly high grades in English and arithmetic. Nevertheless, despite the attention and encouragement that came with this personal schooling, he was never academically accomplished nor received any formal qualifications.

That was not important. His future on stage was almost assured when James Agate, the most popular and respected drama critic of his generation, opined that Jack was blessed with just the right combination of charm, talent, technique, and versatility: 'It is possible that in Master Hawkins we have a very fine actor in the making. I have certainly never seen a boy player of so much promise'.

Jack cannot have failed to see his stock rising as he stood beside Thorndike and basked in the spotlight. Over the coming years, he appeared in a variety of plays and roles of varying importance—and interestingly, it was from Thorndike he learned never to mention illness to anyone as rumours spread and producers heard them, meaning opportunities could be missed (instead, he always worked harder at his recovery and kept generally fit). He also remembered the remarkable personality of Thorndike's husband, Louis Casson, during a period when the company faced financial calamity during the 1926 General Strike. The largest industrial dispute in Britain's history lasted nine days and saw attendances plummet and the cast playing to a handful of people. Despite enduring great losses, Casson (a committed socialist) drove TUC leaders to their regular meetings with the government. Around this time, Jack's education included learning vast chunks of Shakespearean dialogue, including all the notable soliloquies. 'I moved up all the way through and at 18, I played St George,' he reminisced. Before that, he had acted in *Macbeth*, *Henry VIII*, and the 1926 production of Shelly's tragedy *The Cenci*, widely regarded as the play which 'introduced' two promising young actors to the London stage. Laurence Olivier appeared as Orsino's servant and Jack's portrayal of Bernardo was hailed as 'a distinct success' (*The Stage* remarked the part was 'acted affectingly by young Jack Hawkins'). In three years with the Casson-Thorndike company, he became a disciplined actor, receptive to criticism and grateful for advice. He stayed with the company until he was seventeen, and when he left, there was a brief period of unemployment in late 1927, when he walked out of a play called *Interference*—an incident he recounted on *Desert Island Discs*:

> I was heartily disliked by the stage-manager of the play I was touring in. So, I gave in my notice and gave up the princely salary of £3 which I was getting, and which I badly needed—and went to London to look for another job. I was walking down St Martin's Lane, as debonair as any other young actor who hasn't got two half-crowns to rub together and looking at the bills in front of the theatres, wondering if I'd ever have a chance in the West End, when I was hailed by a manager, who took me straight into Basil Dean's office. I was immediately engaged for a new play, which turned out to be *Young Woodley*.

Although he was established in a modest way, Basil Dean changed everything. A sarcastic and highly strung individual—later famed for making Gracie Fields a star—Dean cast Jack as Ainger, the head prefect in *Young Woodley* by John van Druten about a sensitive public-school student who cultivates an 'impossible infatuation' with the house master's wife. Having caused something of a sensation after the censor banned it from mainstream theatres, Dean staged it for one night at the '300 Club', and then to limited audiences at the 'Arts Theatre', a members-only club for the performance of unlicensed plays, from 13 February 1928. The unexpected lifting of the ban prompted a move to the Savoy on 5 March, where bookings rocketed. Curiously, Jack's performance was remarked upon in *Further Letters from a Man of No Importance*, the iconic bestseller written anonymously by 'a personal friend of Royalty and of nearly all the leading figures in politics and society both in London and in Paris.' In an entry from 8 March 1928—three days after the Savoy opening—the unknown scribe noted:

> Very young Lawton plays young Woodley with exquisite freshness and restraint and remarkable knowledge of his business, but the boy Jack Hawkins, who acts 'Charles, the friend,' makes so much out of a comparatively small part that I think he may eventually go the further of the two.[5]

Watching from the stalls, a young actor named John Mills was also impressed—even awed—by what he saw: 'Anyone who was anyone' came to see it. After the first act, there was a feeling in the audience that they were 'witnessing a sensational success'.[6] Behind the scenes that night, cast member Henry Mollison remembered Dean's frightful temper and the appalling treatment he meted out to various actors during the intermission—a ploy designed to keep his young cast on their toes. 'This was Dean's *modus operandi*,' according to actor Stuart Granger, who recounted a similar episode, though in a different production:

> I played the juvenile lead—more juvenile than leading. Basil Dean had the reputation of being the rudest, most sadistic, and sarcastic producer in the business and, by God, he lived up to his reputation. Once when I became very upset by his attacks, Leslie Banks tried to console me by telling me Dean wasn't just picking on me—he did it to everyone. After a verbal thrashing during rehearsals one day, Leslie had become so angry that he had fainted. The whole cast was horrified, but Dean simply walked up on to the stage, nudged Leslie with his foot and said, 'Break for lunch.' This made me feel a little better, but not much.[7]

As always, Dean's eruptions paid off, and if he took any joy or pride in the success, he hid it well. *The Stage* praised *Young Woodley* as being 'at times even beautiful', while Jack was singled out in *The Era* for his 'fine study' of Ainger.[8] Despite Dean's insults, humiliations, and self-absorption, Jack praised his mastery of the stage, extolling him as one of the 'greatest directors in British theatre'. In his memoirs, he hailed *Woodley* as a 'turning point', which ended his juvenile period. In fact, his friends were dazzled to see the seventeen-year-old splash-out £60 on a gleaming plum-coloured Fiat convertible, but he kept domestic arrangements modest, despite his princely salary of £10. In an effort to build up savings, he lodged at a boarding house on Charing Cross Road and spent weekends in Wood Green, fussed over by his mother.

When it ended, the whiff of scandal that clung to *Young Woodley* ensured the production was witnessed by over a quarter of a million people over 350 performances. In an attempt to repeat the *Woodley* success, Dean put 'Master Hawkins' on contract and cast him as second male lead in *Beau Geste*, alongside Lawrence Olivier in the title, who by then was already a young but seasoned actor.

Telling the story of three brothers' adventures in the French foreign legion, the play had all the elements of high drama: adventure, power struggles, gun fights, all set in exotic desert locales. 'Christ,' Olivier recounted, 'I was the envy of all London, all the young actors there were.' In typical fashion, Dean set about toughening up his leading men by sending them to join troops at a local army base for drills. Within a week, the cast was thoroughly fed up. 'I remember Basil Dean screaming at me,' Olivier lamented. 'I mean directions that were impossible for anyone to follow.' Dean also handed him meticulous notes explaining the tone he wanted for each scene. Jack later noted that Olivier, at this point, delivered nothing to suggest of the greatness to come. Indeed, when *Beau Geste* debuted at His Majesty's on Saturday, 26 January 1929, it was more noteworthy than *Young Woodley* for the wrong reasons. Jack remembered the play's main problem—despite its rich scenery—was excessive dialogue and gimmicky special effects, including real gunshots and a funeral pyre, which terrified audiences and threw the production off-kilter:

> It opened up with a background of real smoke, which swept across the stage. Unfortunately, it not only choked the actors, getting right down their throats and making it difficult for them to speak, but also the wind from the wings swept it across the footlights and into the auditorium. Half-asphyxiated members of the audience coughed and spluttered and fought to get outside.[9]

In the end, critics were overwhelmingly hostile, deeming it too brittle for a public that had experienced first-hand the brutalities of war. Harris Deans, from the *Illustrated Sporting and Dramatic News*, complained of a lack of authenticity: 'The trouble was these three musketeers failed to make their presence felt sufficiently both physically and theatrically, they were a little too frail to hold the attention on so large a stage as His Majesty's'. He continued: 'To take a minor detail, not worth mentioning were it not that it illustrates what I mean, the scene where the men disrobe for the night. They strip to snowy singlets, and pants so white, they would have graced the members of a Polytechnic Athletic Club giving their annual display'.[10] It was hardly surprising that *Beau Geste* lived a short life, folding after just thirty-nine performances. While Olivier took the media flak, Jack was touted as 'an actor with a future' and, quite suddenly, offered the role of 'Second Lieutenant Hibbert', a small but important part in *Journey's End* at the Arts Theatre Club before the production transferred to Broadway. 'Master Hawkins' had, in fact, been offered the leading role, but when producer Gilbert Miller discovered he was just eighteen years old, he was relegated to second-lead.

2

Making Whoopee

The voyage to New York on the *Aquitania*, a vessel justifiably called the 'wonder ship of the Atlantic', turned into a monumental drinking binge from the moment it left Southampton on the Saturday to arriving in New York at midday the following Friday. During a violent headwind, the cast boozed from one deck to another in anticipation that the 'Big Apple' would be 'dry' given prohibition. Even at this age, Jack was extremely fond of champagne, as he was of gin of all kinds. And, as a journalist from the *Graphic* noted, it was certainly the most luxurious setting for a party, as the ship could not be compared to anything on land: 'She has most of the attributes of a town. She has her own hospital, police, bank, daily newspaper, post office, shops, swimming bath, gymnasium, concert hall and ballroom'.[1]

Although the weather was bleak, and Manhattan blanketed with a thick grey fog, the American welcome was bright. After passing the Statue of Liberty, the *Aquitania* slowly pulled into Cunard's West Twelfth Street pier, where a gaggle of journalists, photographers, and a newsreel crew stood in wait. 'Imagine being in New York at eighteen with two hundred dollars a week and no Miss East,' Jack said. 'This was the start of my first love affair with that marvellous city and a journey of self-discovery.' After lugging his case to a waiting taxi, he was delivered to the Wentworth, a residential hotel on Forty-Sixth Street, two blocks from Radio City Music Hall. Catering to the theatrical trade, the hotel's elegance—and parts of it were very plush—was enhanced by a granite façade.

New York—the greatest city in the world, as Jack later called it—thrilled him. In those first days, he crisscrossed every inch of the metropolis, travelling on trolleybuses along Fifth Avenue through Greenwich Village, along Broadway and through Harlem in lower Manhattan. He strolled up and down the grubby pavements of slum areas in the city's East End, viewed the panorama from the observation deck of the Woolworth building, and often took lunch in the German district near Times Square. The work situation proved equally exciting, and he was surprised at the roaring triumph *Journey's End* proved to be. Directed by James Whale—who later found fame producing *Frankenstein* and *The Invisible Man*—the production, a drama set in the trenches towards the end of the First World War, opened to a tremendous reception at Henry Miller's Theatre on Forty-Third Street on 22 March 1929. 'No play in recent years has instantaneously made so profound an impression here as *Journey's End,*' Brooks Atkinson, the star critic at *The New York Times*, noted:

> Having recently heard (from London) uneasy tidings about the merits of the company many of us were prepared for a disappointment.... Not having seen the London production, I have no viable standards of comparison. But I can imagine nothing more hauntingly beautiful or affecting than the performance disclosed by our visiting troupe.

In another widely circulated New York paper, Julius Cohen noted that ticket speculators had bought most of the house for the following two months. 'They are now sorry they did not buy all the tickets for the next year,' he remarked. 'They would have easily disposed of them. *Journey's End* is the best drama on the New York stage. You cannot afford to miss it. Even those from Hoboken will make pilgrimages to Henry Miller's Theatre'. Publicity photos show Jack dressed in uniform—padded shoulders, brilliantine greased hair parted in the middle—and a virile smile.

Money granted him freedom and New York provided many distractions. By his own admission, having lost his virginity within weeks of setting foot on American soil, sex became a constant pursuit. He unleashed himself and just short of his nineteenth birthday, ran headlong into a discreet but 'convenient' fling with an American divorcee while pursuing other girlfriends, mostly English actresses. He also fell into a familiar routine of drinking at the El Fey Club, a speakeasy liquor parlour patronised by theatrical types, where, one night, he witnessed federal prohibition agents searching for illicit booze, which had been cleverly tucked away behind concealed trap doors and in potted plants and plaster-Roman columns. Drinking in such places came with risks—the previous year, speakeasy patrons were served undiluted poisonous wood alcohol resulting in thirty-two deaths, cementing New York's position as America's centre for organised crime. However, giddy with his new adventure, Jack mischievously set about brewing his own gin using a bathtub distillery. 'Hawkins Gin,' he boasted, tasted delicious and 'never killed anybody'.

For the most part, he found distraction at more respectable establishments like the Silver Grill on Times Square; Rudley's, the theatrical eatery; or Delmonico's on Beaver Street with its fine art and gooseberry wallpaper. 'I am a rather a gregarious character,' he later told *Desert Island Discs*, a radio programme where guests talk about their plans if stranded on a deserted island. 'I should hate the loneliness. I'd probably be a very bad-tempered, moody violent castaway, hating every minute of it.' Thankfully, the British star Evelyn Laye, who was starring in *Bitter Sweet* at the Ziegfeld Theatre, offered amiable companionship as did Jill Esmond, a young English actress starring in a *Bird in the Hand*. According to Esmond's son, Tarquin Olivier, when Jack met her at the New York piers on 26 April 1929, he impressed upon her the 'business-like' nature of New York theatres—Esmond later complained that she had never known 'anything so slack' and her Broadway dressing room resembled a 'bad theatre in the Midlands'.

Jack had no such grumbles as the year was turning out to be a personal triumph. Flush with earnings of $250 a week, he took up permanent residence at a furnished bachelor pad above the Hudson Theatre 'which featured a gramophone and a collection of records'.[2] He started to see music in a new light, he discovered George Gershwin and Cole Porter but shunned emerging jazz releases as trite and 'not good value' for money. 'Music means a lot to me,' he explained. 'I'm passionately fond of it in almost any form but my music is chosen for what it can give me in the way of beauty and solace.' Classically, he adored Handel and Stravinsky, but the Finnish composer Sibelius was his absolute favourite, especially *The Swan of Tuonela*: 'It's not what one would call a very bright piece. But it has wonderful colour and mystery. It's story-book music'.

He was in New York on Black Thursday when the market imploded as nearly 13 million shares were traded at a loss of $6 billion. As throngs of people gathered in front of the sub-Treasury building across from the New York Stock Exchange, Jack's energy was entirely devoted to wooing a British actress touring in another production. However, no Broadway producer was immune to the events of Black Thursday and when her play slumped, the company broke up and she was called back to Britain. Remarkably, the attraction was strong enough for Jack to pack up and follow her home, something he saw as an acceptable sacrifice for love. However, his return was not the great homecoming he had imagined. For reason or reasons unknown, the 'little actress' offered him an austere welcome and the 'affair fizzled out as quickly as it had started'. Years later, reflecting on this time, he could not bring himself to identify the actress by name (but it has been speculated that the woman—a former a student

at Italia Conti's school—could have been the fabled beauty Gertrude
Lawrence). After surviving the vicissitudes of love, Jack used his American
earnings to secure his parents (their fortunes were on the decline) a home
in Winchmore Hill, a middle-class suburb in north London. Kneecapped
by the financial crisis, his father struggled to keep his business running but
it finally collapsed, leaving both his father and brother, Tom, unemployed.

3

Coming of Age

The decade that followed was especially fertile for Jack Hawkins. On stage, he would appear in more than fifty plays—running the gamut from farce to Shakespeare. His first notable performance was as 'Patrick', a mouthy teenager in Somerset Maugham's comedy *The Breadwinner*, alongside Peggy Ashcroft and Marie Lohr, the celebrated Australian actress. The play, which ran from 30 September 1930 to 14 February 1931, told the story of a stockbroker who was fed up with his life and family and abandoned his home to spend the rest of his days blissfully doing nothing. After reasonable out-of-town try-outs, it settled at the Vaudeville Theatre. 'Marie was wonderfully dignified,' recalled William Fox, a young actor billeted with Jack in a backstage dressing room. 'Statuesque. A perfect lady on stage. But after the show she liked nothing better than sitting back on an easy chair in her dressing room, kicking off her shoes and getting me and Jack Hawkins to tickle her toes until she squealed with delight.'[1] As it turned out, the whole production was a giggle and became notable when Ashcroft uttered the hugely publicised passage, 'Don't you know that since the war the amateurs have entirely driven the professionals out of business? No girl can make a decent living now by prostitution.' The brouhaha that followed left several dozen critics suitably outraged. 'It is hard, bitter, occasionally over-brutal satire on youth, and some of the lines are unnecessarily coarse,' was the verdict of the *Illustrated London News*, which grudgingly conceded the play was 'provocative and interesting'.

In the early years of the Depression, as the financial crisis settled in for a lengthy stay, Jack began entertaining hopes of a cinematic career and agreed to representation from Sidney Jay, a mild-mannered man regarded as the principal film agent in the country.[2] He is said to have been over the moon when his first assignment came playing 'Alfred' in Basil Dean's/Associated Radio Pictures two-reeler *Birds of Prey*, an adaptation of A. A. Milne's stage play *The Fourth Wall*. The story tells of two young lovers unravelling a murder mystery when Scotland Yard fails. Technically, it was notable for becoming the first English talking picture to use a 'dolly' to create smooth horizontal camera movements. However, as the late film critic Barry Norman once observed, the movie was of such 'modest accomplishment that most reference books fail to mention it, as indeed did Hawkins himself in his autobiography'.

Shooting of *Birds of Prey* was in full swing when Dean also cast Jack in Dodie Smith's *Autumn Crocus* at The Lyric, a story about a shy schoolteacher falling in love with a Tyrolean innkeeper. *Picturegoer* described him as: 'Lanky, stooping, solemn, he wore shorts and glasses throughout the action and never for one moment left off sucking a heavy pipe'. The play—a decidedly odd production—led to his first encounter with Jessica Tandy, a tiny, mousy hair-haired actress with pale blue eyes and dark lashes who exemplified the perfect theatrical all-rounder. In the production, she played Jack's partner, 'indulging in a companionate marriage experiment'. Off the stage, the two were smitten. 'She was beautiful,' Jack recounted. 'I was instantly captivated by her.' Born near Stoke Newington in 1909, Jessie was the youngest of three children of Harry Tandy, a traveling salesman for a rope-manufacturing company, and Jessie Helen Tandy, headmistress of a school for intellectually disabled children. After her father died of cancer in 1921, her mother took secretarial jobs and taught evening classes for adults to support the family. From then, they lived in a terraced house in Hackney and Jessie attended Dame Alice Owen's Girls' School. Mrs Tandy instilled in her children an interest in books, art, and theatre, and money was put aside for trips to drama recitals. Her anxiety for the children's education resulted in her two sons winning scholarships to Oxford. As for Jess, after several bouts with tuberculosis, she attended the venerable Ben Greet drama school and made her professional debut at 'Playroom Six', a small theatre in Soho at the age of eighteen. 'My mother endorsed the stage as a dignified way for me out of our bleak existence,' Jess later said. 'It sounds terribly snobbish, but she raised us to be intellectually above our neighbours. She read to us, took us to plays, the pantomime and museums.'[3] By 1929, Jess was working with the Birmingham Repertory Company, and a year later, she sailed for New York to appear in *The Matriarch*.

Jessica had, in fact, seen Jack perform in *Saint Joan* years earlier. 'I went away from that production in a trance,' she later recounted. 'It was so marvellous. And I also remember feeling very jealous of that small boy, who was no older than I was, acting in a play in St Martins' Lane. I really envied him a lot.'[4] The two became romantically involved and Jess remembered Jack as a whirlwind of energy: 'He was great fun to be with and a very fascinating young man too. All the girls were mad about him, and I was very much in love with him. Well, when you're in love at that age of course you think it's going to be forever and ever—the fairy-tale come true'.[5]

As noted earlier, Jack's other passion was fishing and during the run of *Autumn Crocus* he became friendly with forty-three-year-old actor Arthur Hambling, who played the part of a fidgety old parson. Every night after the show, the pair drove down to a tent perched on the riverbank at Egham Weir, where they spent the summer fishing with long home-cut rods—despite appalling weather. Living an extraordinarily carefree existence, they bought a slice of land on the riverbank and the tent was later succeeded by a caravan. However, the expeditions ended with *Autumn Crocus*, which—despite shouts of 'rubbish' from the gallery on the first night—clocked up 379 performances and led Jack to the part of a naval officer in *While Parents Sleep* at the Royalty Theatre, an ensemble effort featuring Hugh Williams, Mary Hinton, and Diana Beaumont in a frothy yarn about two brothers causing immense disruption to the lives of their parents.

Given the previous twelve productions at the Royalty had been failures, the play's success came as a surprise to everyone, including Leo Genn, then working as a stage assistant (Genn was later nominated for an Oscar for his portrayal as Petronius in *Quo Vadis*). However, scarcely a week after opening on 19 January 1932, newspapers expressed shock at Jack's bursts of course language on stage—including his 'use of an unmentionable monosyllable for the part of the body on which one sits'. A great service came from critic Philip Page who complained the dialogue 'filled with expressions of extreme coarseness' was not only 'embarrassing but unnecessary'.

Years later, Jack—'the young man with the vocabulary'—conceded the play was indeed saucy but would be 'considered very tame nowadays'. When the play took off, a host of friendly reviews followed. 'Hawkins gives a brilliant performance as the breezy young naval officer,' one noted, while *Play Pictorial* featured him on the cover with Diana Beaumont. 'Mr. Jack Hawkins brings any amount of *joie de ruse* into the acting of the part and scores a great personal triumph in the process,' was the verdict of the *Civil & Military Gazette*. The show ran for 492 performances during its initial London run but Jack left in April for a one-off performance of 'Red Triangle' at the Savoy and to play Laertes in John Gielgud's hotly anticipated production of *Hamlet* on BBC radio, his first major national broadcast. By his own admission, he was fascinated by radio and jumped at the chance to work at the newly built Broadcasting House which had just sprung up at Portland Place. After hearing the transmission, Laurence Olivier confided to Jack that he might one day play Hamlet.

'Our production of *Hamlet* was a great success,' Jack recounted, 'thanks principally to Johnny's performance, and I remember going to visit Larry and him telling me that he'd like to give old Hamlet a try, to see if he couldn't do it better than Gielgud. It was a bizarre idea, really, since one didn't think of Larry in Shakespearian terms—he just didn't have the voice.'[6]

During this period, Jack kept careful track of his earnings and took any film work offered—his spendthrift lifestyle was a consuming motivation. So far as is known, a chance meeting with director Maurice Elvey (who had seen him in *Autumn Crocus*) led to his next cinematic outing opposite Ivor Novello in *The Lodger*, a talkie recycling of Hitchcock's silent film. Though the part of a mouthy journalist was not much—Elvey pitched a sorry tale paralleling the 'Jack the Ripper' killings about a boarding-house landlord and his daughter getting involved in a murder mystery following the arrival of a shadowy lodger. From the get-go, production limped along but on a salary of £8 a day, a hefty sum at the time, and a daily taxi to Twickenham studios, Jack found no cause for complaint. However, on the first day, he was left bewildered by Novello's itchy performance as the lodger, played with an implausibly thick Slavic accent. A one-time poster-boy of British cinema, Novello had been panned by critics in the 1920s for his attempt to become the new Rudolph Valentino. Left mystified by the poor press, he quit London and resurfaced in Hollywood writing scripts, before returning to Britain for a second shot at movie stardom.

At some point, the gruelling schedule caused Jack to twitch during shooting; the affliction, he said, caused 'fearful grimaces' and was only cured by aspirin. Like many theatre actors, he needed time to adjust to the different demands of motion picture technique: the need to moderate his voice, to modify gestures, and work out of sequence. Not only this, but there was also considerable on-set tension brought about by the fact that Twickenham studios had not been completely soundproofed and every time a train rattled past; the player's voices were drowned out. So, a man was posted outside the studio to press a buzzer every time a train came along, when the warning came, the shooting stopped.[7]

Although it performed reasonably well, *The Lodger* was not a critical success and Jack lamented his performance as 'something I prefer to draw a veil over'.[8] Decades later, he told journalist John K. Newman that 'it was too sloppy', and the disjointedness worried him.[9] Reviews were not all bad. 'You must look out for this young Hawkins,' one critic noted. 'He is as live and virile and pugnacious as James Cagney without being so hard to look at!'[10]

Towards the end of shooting, newspaper hacks were the first to learn of the chime of wedding bells, confirming the Jack/Jess relationship had more depth and strength than initially suspected. After accepting Jack's proposal, Jessica made plans for an autumn wedding fixed for 22 October, but it was not the happy experience they had hoped for. She had not contended that her employers at the Duchess Theater—where she was starring in *Children in Uniform*—would argue her marriage would undermine the play. 'How will they believe in you as a child if they hear you are an old married woman?' But Jess was adamant and let slip wedding details to a reporter from the *Weekly Dispatch* who was tickled to report that 'Miss Tandy has made arrangements for her wedding' after 'Mr. Hawkins had taken out a licence'. When it finally happened, the service at Winchmore Hill church was a curious affair. Afterwards, Jack's jaw dropped to the ground when during a champagne breakfast in the Tudor Room at Kettner's in Soho, Jessica's mother expressed displeasure after revealing she spotted a hole in the sole of his shoes when he knelt at the altar—and as if that was not bad enough, she also urged Jess to refrain from 'carnal relations' with her new husband. Though peace was maintained, Jack was chastened by the experience and thought his new mother-in-law 'a highly-strung, very odd' woman. In fact, he once remarked she was one of the most unbearable women it had been his displeasure to meet.

Setting a precedent for the future, Jessica vowed to still be her own woman, to continue working and enjoying her hectic social life. In fact, a few hours after tying the knot, she took to the stage in a matinee performance of *Children in Uniform* where she received an engraved silver serving dish from the cast as a wedding gift—the gesture left her in floods of tears.[11] Having fixed her differences with the Duchess Theatre, the production went on to run for 265 performances and, as Jess later confessed, provided the 'big chance for which every hopeful young actress prays'.[12]

Jack, meanwhile, made a bevy of undistinguished films, including: *The Lost Chord, I Lived with You, The Jewel*, and *A Shot in the Dark*. The Quota Act—which decreed exhibitors ensure that at least 5 per cent of films screened were British—gave a boost to local movie production in quantity if not in quality. In fact, Twickenham studios worked under such high pressure that a double shift was put into operation with one picture on the floor during the day and another during the night (*Shot in the Dark* was made during the nightshifts). 'I began commuting to the studios and found myself in a ghastly series of what we called quota quickies made for a pound per foot, as we used to say,' Jack recounted.[13] A rare meaty part came playing 'Albert' in J. B. Priestley's *The Good Companions*, a Michael Balcon comedy about a troupe of entertainers and of their ups and downs, featuring Edmund Gwenn and John Gielgud. 'Seldom has a great novel been translated to the screen with such meticulous regard for atmosphere,' the *Mid Sussex Times* enthused. It was about this time that he went for a screen test with another young actor at the prestigious Gaumont British Studios, the nation's leading film company. 'And,' Jack remembered, 'we were both turned down flat! The other actor was Robert Donat!'[14]

Before long, earnings from the quickies enabled the newlyweds to buy a little house in Winchmore Hill, barely half-an-hour's run from the stage of any West End theatre and close to Jack's parents. They enjoyed a well-upholstered, comparatively relaxed lifestyle. Free time was spent socialising with a growing cadre of good friends at the 'Motley Costume Shop', a meeting spot for some of the best young theatre artists. Anthony Quayle remembered it as the most haphazard coffee house in London where the people who dropped in from time-to-time included Peggy Ashcroft, Edith Evans, Gwen Ffrangcon-Davies, Robert Donat, the Redgraves, the Byam Shaws, Michel St Denis, and younger actors like Alec and Merula Guinness.[15] Jack thrived on interaction with fellow actors and creatives—the more, the merrier. Conversations ranged from religion, philosophy, nature, life after death, theatre, film, politics, and a sizable amount of gossip oiled the gears of creativity. Another favourite gathering point was at the home of publisher Rupert Hart-Davis at 213 Piccadilly, where his living room became a beacon for the theatrical and social elite. Hart-Davis always found plenty to talk about, but that year (1933) Adolf Hitler dominated conversation after becoming chancellor of Germany; soon after, the Reichstag burned down in mysterious circumstances, paving the way for the Enabling Act which unfolded the nightmare of Hitler's dictatorship.

Throughout this period, as Europe ignited with hate and violence, the scene in London remained positively tranquil. At Winchmore Hill, Jess encouraged Jack's outdoor life—he dabbled in football, and she occasionally accompanied him fishing or to the racecourse. After a year of marriage, she presented him with a daughter, Susan. Proud as punch, Jack told and retold the stories of the birth to anyone who would listen. He managed to spend more time at home, but in the evenings remained busy and reunited with Basil Dean for *Sometimes Even Now*, opposite Celia Johnson, though the project never quite jelled. A stint playing Orlando in *As You Like It* followed at the Regents Park Open Air Theatre. 'It was unforgettable,' he laughed. 'There were thunderstorms throughout the whole period we were rehearsing.'

Around this time, the *Evening News* drama critic forecast that John Gielgud and Ralph Richardson, a man admired for his calm and sanguine nature, were destined for stardom, but could be outstripped by Jack, who at just twenty-three years old, 'looked like training to be the irresistibly breezy, infectious, gay young hero—like the most indubitable matinee idols'.

Like so many others, when working with Gielgud, Jack occasionally felt the brunt of his acerbic temperament and tactlessness. On one occasion, after a year of *Richard of Bordeaux*, Gielgud addressed an audience jam-packed with regulars. In a statement exuding an air of worldly grace, he said: 'I know that many of you have been to see us thirty or forty times'. Then after a brief pause, he glanced at Jack, who had replaced Francis Lister, and continued, 'in spite of changes to the cast'.

Despite Gielgud's sour temperament, the good times marched on. In November 1933, Jack and Jess landed plum parts in *Iron Flowers*, a single Sunday performance by the Repertory Players at the Shaftesbury Theatre. The play, written for Tandy by Cecil Lewis, was one of the earliest produced to depict a sympathetic character who chose to have an abortion, and although Jess gave one of her most compelling performances, the critic from *The Stage* could barely disguise his disgust:

> Mr. Lewis's subject was none other than the long-tabooed question of abortion, now thinly veiled under the less disagreeable names of birth control or contraception, as discussed in a sort of lecture delivered by a very daring doctor, who ventures to risk his professional reputation and even his liberty, as well as the life of a girl, who has got into trouble with a married man by performing an illegal operation upon her. The fact that the operation was completely successful, and that the patient recovered, with the chance of trying her luck again, cannot explain away the innate distastefulness of the subject.

Shortly thereafter, Jack was coaxed into a supporting role in Ivor Novello's *Sunshine Sisters*, a musical comedy following three chorus girls stranded in Paris, rescued by a duke's brother, and dumped into a country house where everyone took them for prostitutes. The *Daily Herald* critic was not impressed by the 'energetic performances which distracted attention from most of the stupidity'.[16] After just three weeks at the Queen's Theatre, the play came to a sudden end on 29 November 1933, as bookings dried up. Novello was devastated and slipped almost unnoticed out of the limelight. By stark contrast, Jack's old chum Laurence Olivier, then in the early stages of a lengthy film career, was riding on the crest of a wave. 'Larry became a celebrity in London in a way he never had been before,' Jack recounted:

> But it was not something he took any pleasure in. In fact, I think he felt guilty and annoyed by it, because he came to believe what he was doing in the Swanson film was worthless, a charade.[17] I remember having him and Jill round for drinks one night, and his arguing with Jill (Esmond), 'If

this is motion-picture celebrity, I don't want any part of it. Why should people look up to you for being a film actor? It's all a sham.'[18]

No sooner had *Sunshine Sisters* wrapped than Jack was rushed into rehearsing the part of Orsino, Duke of Illyria, alongside Anna Neagle in *Twelfth Night* at the 'Open Air' Theatre where he received the most laurels for his 'clear-cut, sometimes passionate, performance', according to R. B. M., a critic with *The Era*. Soon after, in July 1934, he joined the cast of Ronald Mackenzie's play *The Maitlands* at Wyndham's featuring John Gielgud as a schoolteacher who had lost his wife to another man and hid himself away in a remote seaside village. 'It was a modern play,' Gielgud recalled, saying Jack was versatile. 'He could play modern stuff awfully well and he was a very good comedian.' During the run, Basil Dean rescued Ivor Novello from the doldrums for a film version of *Autumn Crocus*. Jack—wearing lederhosen trousers and a cappello alpino—delivered a hilariously aloof stagey performance but was outshone by a band of Tyrolean singers adding a touch of authentic tunefulness (Dean thought it would be a fine—and economical—idea to film his stage plays during their runs, with the same cast). The film was a success, and Jack was quickly rewarded with a part as a BBC producer in Val Gielgud's whodunnit *Death at Broadcasting House*, the first feature for Phoenix Films, which was soundly praised. He gave another finely shaded performance alongside John Gielgud and Jess in the much-discussed production of *Hamlet*, which opened in November 1934 at the New Theatre. However, while critics rhapsodised over Jack, Jess's performance left most critics unmoved and unexcited. One of the most vocal dissenters, Leslie Rees, groused that her Ophelia was the only mistake: 'she is, if I may say so without offence, an actress whose range is over-rated and has no real place here'. Understandably downcast, Tandy later claimed that her husband's sensitivity had saved her from the harshness of the reviews: 'I believe it's Jack's consideration that always gets me. When he played Horatio in John Gielgud's *Hamlet*, and I was Ophelia— severely slated by some of the critics—he kept all the notices from me, knowing I could not take it'.[19] Despite the critical scoffing, the production chalked-up 155 performances, a record for Shakespeare in the West End and led to a tour of the provinces where Jess continued to play Ophelia in Manchester, Edinburgh, Glasgow, and Leeds, while Jack stayed in London, and was replaced by Ellis Irving. Gielgud's love for Jess was evident in his decision to keep her on tour. 'During the run of *Hamlet*,' he remarked, 'she became one of my greatly valued friends. She is an actress of rare sensitiveness and perception.'[20]

In the intervening period, Jack secured a small role in Basil Dean's *Lorna Doone* with fellow Italia Conti graduate Margaret Lockwood, making her screen debut. The film 'pleased the King and Queen and is gratifying a few thousand fans a day as it continues its West End run,' the *Sunday Post* noted.[21] Lockwood, like Jack, had no forebears even remotely connected with the stage, but the picture secured her a three-year contract with British Lion for £500 a year but failed to ignite Jack's star. 'I had the wrong shape of face as a younger man, and although I believed in myself as an actor and worked like hell, I knew I should never become a matinee idol,' he confessed. 'But things went well enough, and I managed to make a bit of a name for myself.'[22] In fact, he understood the importance of physical appearance and became a publicist of immense skill, cultivating the press by associating himself with virile activity. His purpose in this was obvious: he wanted to promote his image and establish himself as a key cinema player, with a man's-man reputation. To this end, a chum at *The Kensington News* wrote a puff-piece noting he had a 'particular liking' for cricket and horse-riding: 'A friend of his keep's stables near Potters Bar and Jack likes nothing better than careering over the countryside. He is typical of the new generation of hefty athletic men who are breaking into British films'.[23] As it happened, the horse-riding became a skill that equipped him well for later film projects. Along the way, other papers zeroed in on how 'brave Jack' was accidentally 'pinked' in the hand during a furious duel with Anna Neagle when filming his first major feature *Peg of Old Drury*, a biopic of eighteenth-century Irish Actress Peg Woffington, shot at Vauxhall Gardens. Lavishly costumed, Jack recalled it was his 'first taste of largescale film-making and nothing like the pictures I had done before'.[24] He trained with Neagle for eight hours a day under 'Bertrand', a famous fencing master. 'It was rather nerve racking,' he remembered. 'I wasn't worried about the possibility of her stabbing me, but knew I wouldn't get any thanks if I put Anna Neagle out of action.'[25] In fact, he took an intense interest in fencing and trained diligently. Very occasionally, reporters—including the *Daily Mirror*'s gossip columnist—homed in on Jack's feminine side:

> Some friends visiting the country cottage of Jack and his young wife, Jessica Tandy—admired the elaborate flower design of a half-finished cushion cover and naturally attributed the work to Jessica's nimble little fingers. But when, after exploring the house and meeting the baby in the nursery, they came downstairs again, they were amazed to find Jack busily and skilfully rounding off a rose petal.[26]

Around this time, to capitalise on his growing reputation, he signed several lucrative commercial contracts, including one hawking De Reszke Minor—'the Aristocrat of Cigarettes'—in which he posed 'in the wings' for a series of advertisements declaring: 'Ten minutes to wait before I'm wanted ... so mine's a *Minor*!' Surprisingly, perhaps, in June 1935, Jack joined the cast of *Accidentally Yours*, a French farce with a wicked twist. One of his heroes, George Robey—possibly the greatest music hall performer of the age—played the part of Leon Lambert, a banker passing off his mistress to his wife as his hitherto unacknowledged daughter. Although until 1932 Robey had never played in legitimate theatre, Jack credited him with teaching him more about comedy than anyone else but admitted to being thrown off kilter by his ad-libbing and innuendo. However, the *Illustrated London News* praised Jack's performance as a novelist batting the 'slings and arrows of outrageous fortune'.[27] More radio followed, including an appearance with Robert Atkins and his Bankside Players in excerpts from *Much Ado About Nothing* on the BBC, alongside his old friend John Laurie. When *Accidentally Yours* wrapped, he marched into Byers Robertson's *Coincidence* from 5–9 November 1935, at St Martin's, a new play starring Ena Burrill.

A much bigger, more exciting project followed when he turned his hand to *The Frog*, a production at the Princes Theatre stuffed with shoot-ups, spectacular pyrotechnics, raids, and mysterious disappearances. Written by Ian Hay and based on the novel *The Fellowship of the Frog* by Edgar Wallace, the play featured Gordon Harker playing the shrewish Sergeant Elk of Scotland Yard, Jack took the role of Captain Gordon, his sidekick. While he had no history in such madcap productions, the idea of his playing with the veteran Harker was appealing. Famed for his slim expressive face and genial cockney delivery, Harker had enjoyed a long career in vaudeville and light comedy. As a young man, he had played Shakespeare and toured Australia with Oscar Asche but by the 1930s, he specialised in 'hoarse, pint-of-bitter Cockney' roles which made him universally famous. As Jack discovered, in real life, Harker was a cultured 'blazer and cravat' type. He was a keen reader of biographies, travel and history and a great lover of dogs. On balmy days, when the sun was shining, he could be found painting watercolours in the garden of his thatched cottage at Monxton in Hampshire, tucked away behind a hedge.

Given the excitement of the production, there was a chance of gaining some 'virile' publicity during rehearsals when producers stage-managed an explosion to occur too soon, resulting in falling debris. Supposedly, Jack was 'knocked out'. Remarkably, a photographer from the *Daily Mirror* was on hand to catch the drama unfold and the story (with photo) was 'splashed' on to the pages of the morning edition. There is little doubt the repartee between Harker and Hawkins was an essential part of the whole spectacle helping the play to achieve terrific success. 'You'll see nearly three and a half hours of hair-raising, squeal-provoking sensation,' one reviewer gushed. 'Is surely money's worth at a time when other theatres are going twice nightly!' The frenzied activity ended after 481 performances in June 1937, by which point Jack and Harker had already made a popular movie version at Pinewood between January and February 1937, though Graham Greene—then eking out a living as a film critic—gave it a less-than-charitable review describing it as 'badly directed and badly acted'. However, it gave Jack a level of public exposure that he had not enjoyed before and he enthusiastically signed up for another Gordon Harker vehicle, *Beauty and the Barge*. Filming coincided roughly with the beginning of his part as the lover in *Autumn* at St Martin's, which ran from 15 October 1937 to 5 March 1938. Produced by Basil Dean, critics opined that though the play lost most of its merit in reupholstering the plot from a Russian to an English environment, it was an excellent production. 'It would be foolish to scrutinize too closely the plot of *Autumn*,' the syndicated *London Letter* column noted. 'It would also perhaps be ungenerous to do so because it certainly gives Miss Flora Robson a magnificently emotional part, and she plays it so appealingly and with such shattering sincerity that one can forgive the play its faults.' Indeed, the play had more than a reasonable share of faults. Its plot, which told how the wife of an eminent K. C. pretended her own lover was really her stepdaughter's and was then upset when the two really did fall in love, was highly improbable in its beginnings, and even more so in its happy ending. Though the *London Letter* lamented the 'quite ridiculously stiff' dialogue, it praised the cast, noting, 'Jack Hawkins sketches an excellent portrait of the man in the case, but I cannot feel that a rising barrister would ever have worn such heavily waisted suits'.

4

Strained Relations

As Jack played the lover in *Autumn*, his own marriage to Jess was disintegrating, though not due to infidelity; they were simply too busy to find time for each other. 'There was a rift,' Jess later disclosed, 'which widened over the years. One of us probably disappointed the other in some way or there were sins of omission or sins of commission. We were obviously both too young,' she said, adding that they were not mature enough to understand what marriage meant: 'We expected it to be a matter of living happily ever after, which of course, even in the best marriages is not true'. She continued: 'What I remember about that marriage were the constant pep talks that Jack gave me and the constant arguments about money'. They had wildly different conceptions of finances, Jack felt that money was to be spent, and—to make matters worse—she did not appreciate his habit of unexpectedly bringing over visitors, or his complaints about her housekeeping. In an interview with Jess for his masterly work *Follies of God: Tennessee Williams and the Women of the Fog*, author James Grissom suggests that, over time, Jack found distractions and affection elsewhere, which Tandy 'accepted with little surprise'.[1]

As the marital cracks widened, Jessica's stage career kicked into high gear. She demonstrated her gift for romantic comedy in *Anthony and Anna* and, in February 1937, joined the Old Vic Company playing Catherine to Olivier's *Henry V*. It is interesting to note that though Jack and Jess's marriage was much more brittle than thought, the couple's problems escaped the attention of gossipmongers. In fact, several features appeared extolling their picture-perfect romance. For instance, in June 1937, one columnist noted, 'they have a daughter who is fast growing up, and who represents her mother and father's greatest offstage interest. Back in the West End, the couple are always in demand. They have a mutual enthusiasm for the parts they play. From Old Vic Shakespeare to sophisticated modern comedy, thrillers to farce, Jack Hawkins, and Jessica Tandy skip with brilliant versatility. Is their marriage the secret?'[2]

Considering the situation, the following passage stands out:

> I wonder what the cynics who still tell you that marriage is a mistake where actors and actresses are concerned would make of the romance of Jack Hawkins and Jessica Tandy? Here are two young people who have been on the stage from early schooldays. They found their feet in *Autumn Crocus* and decided on the threshold of their careers to marry.

Although Jess did not relish the role of absentee mother, during 1937 everything was subservient to work. She made her film debut in the Fox-British production *Murder in the Family*, and she had meatier fare at the Old Vic under Tyrone Guthrie's direction, playing Viola in *Twelfth Night*, a role included among her finest achievements. Worse still, for the marriage at least, she travelled to New York over Christmas to star in J. B. Priestley's play *Time and the Conways* with Sybil Thorndike. Over time, whispers about her troubled, loveless marriage became loud enough to be heard in the West End, where there was surprise, though not amazement. John Gielgud thought the emotional strain hindered Jess's performances: 'She should be one of the outstanding stars of the London stage, but at present her strict integrity prevents her from making those "showy" effects which have often carried other lesser artists to sensational success'.

During this time, Jack became consumed with a different project. Maybe it was the wish to leave London that he accepted an invitation from Michael Benthall to produce *The Taming of the Shrew* for the Oxford University Dramatic Society (OUDS) in the summer of 1938. Benthall, a student and keen actor, was in a romantic relationship with Robert Helpmann and volunteered to work as Jack's right-hand man. Founded in 1885, OUDS was the principal funding body to the many independent productions put on by students in Oxford (John Gielgud made his directing debut there in 1932). There was not much money involved, except a token stipend, guesthouse accommodation, and two meals daily. But what should have been a relaxing break turned out to be a frustrating experience. He rolled his eyes impatiently as rehearsals were hampered by the traditional university campus locking-up times, causing his actors to be spirited away in the middle of work. However, instead of bowing to ancient custom, Jack audaciously stuck out his chin and protested and, according to journalist Steven Watts, 'it took some time for the university to recover from the shock of being told by a chap in his twenties that they were treating men like babies'.[3] Adding to his headache, it was originally

planned as an outdoor production, but unsettled weather forced it into
the Old Playhouse. But despite the setbacks, critic Lionel Hale thought it a
charming and ingenious setting for the small stage: 'The whole evening is
better than any the Society has given us for years. Mr. Hawkins has a cast
not inspired but sound and teachable'.[4]

From Oxford, Jack chalked up another success with *Who Goes Next?*,
a film made at Wembley Studios by 20th Century Fox. Cleanly edited
and vividly told, the story was inspired by the real-life escape of British
officers through a tunnel from a German POW camp in 1918. Cameraman
Ronald Neame remembered it was a better than average quickie, because
it followed a successful formula:

> People in jeopardy, overcoming impossible odds to save themselves from
> disaster—in this case World War I prisoners digging an escape tunnel.
> Tension is created when characters are trapped in any enclosed space, an
> aircraft about to crash, a submarine on the bottom of the sea or an ocean
> liner turning over.[5]

At times, Jack must have felt like the busiest actor in London. After *Who
Goes Next?* wrapped, he joined Robert Gore Browne's play *Can We Tell?*,
presented before sold-out houses at the New Theatre from 7 September,
with Edna Best and Mervyn Johns. In the play, he portrays a village
grocer's son, Tom Hollick, a somewhat morose figure who rises to be a
car magnate and future peer. In eight scenes, the production showed the
course of his life over sixty years and required Jack to make several rapid
costume and make-up changes. 'This role is the best thing Jack Hawkins
has done,' the *Daily Herald* noted. 'And Edna Best shares the acting
honours with him. Both grow old credibly and artistically.'[6] One stinking
notice, however, came from the *Daily News* critic, who somewhat cattily
complained the 'play's general effect on me was of a lot of unutterably
pretentious and windy nonsense'.[7]

As *Can We Tell?* played to full houses, Jack was shaken by the unstable
European situation as the Nazis annexed Austria and carried out
pogroms against Jews in Germany (a precursor of the events that would
soon transform Europe into a battlefield). With the fragile state of the
world, the time was ripe, according to actor Leslie French, for a meaty
political drama. Along with twenty-two-year-old producer Alan Hay,
French joined the new breed of young theatrical entrepreneurs when he
announced Jack would star in *Traitor's Gate*, a story sourced from the
legend of Sir Thomas More and the struggle to get him to take the secret
oath accepting the divorce of Henry VIII and his marriage to Anne Boleyn.
After appearing in several lightweight dramas, Jack hoped to restore

some solemnity to his public image and, to this end, embarked on a short provincial tour before *Traitor's Gate* arrived at the Duke of York's in November 1938. His performance as More was perhaps his most mature thus far, prompting the critic of the *West London Observer* to describe it as 'cynical humorous, but a somewhat fearful figure at first, and ending almost a saint'.[8] However, such praise was not enough to prevent the play wrapping in January 1939. After taking his usual curtain call during one of the final performances, Jack's crestfallen co-star Basil Sydney was called on by the audience to make a speech and had a few plain words to say:

> We cannot understand why a play of this class has to come off after so short a run, but the business of the theatre decrees that this must be so. You are a wonderful audience—but why didn't you come before, in the early weeks? Now your support is too late to save us.[9]

Afterwards, Sydney told a reporter: 'It was ironic that we did not have packed houses until it was announced that the play was closing. Saturday's performance was more like a first night—a macabre feeling'. No sooner had the project finished than Jack dived straight into *Dear Octopus* on Broadway at the Broadhurst Theatre, alongside Lillian Gish, the actress later lauded as 'The First Lady of American Cinema'. Though brilliantly performed, her talent could not save the play from an early closing on 25 February 1939 after just fifty-three performances. But the trip was not a dead loss. While in New York, Jack secured the rights to a play that had been packing them into the Morosco Theatre. *Family Portrait* by Lenore and William Joyce Cowen was a study of Jesus of Nazareth as His family knew Him. Riding a wave of optimism, Jack explained the entire project to a reporter from *The Sunday Dispatch*:

> Jesus Himself does not appear on the stage but His personality is felt throughout. In one scene Jesus' nephew, Daniel, recalls Him as the kind uncle who built him a toy boat with a red sail. There is a dramatic scene in which Mary, Jesus' Mother, explains her Son's mission to a man who has never heard of Him. She tells this man that Jesus taught you to love your enemies, never to condemn or judge anyone, to be forgiving, and to make life as easy as you can for other people.[10]

In another scene, a young disciple of Jesus who gives an enthusiastic description of his master later reveals that he is Judas Iscariot, future betrayer of Christ. 'I saw the play in New York, where the leading part of Mary is played by Judith Anderson about six weeks ago and I was so impressed that I determined to bring it to London,' Jack explained. 'Far from shocking religious people I feel that it will give a new reality and beauty to the personality of Christ to many people.'[11]

Jack threw himself into action with characteristic gusto by seeking a second collaboration with Alan Hay, though the project foundered over staging issues and fears of a backlash from the conservative media. The real culprit, however, was the possibility of war. It seemed an anticlimactic conclusion to what could have been Jack's first venture into producing a West End show. In the meantime, Jess had a new audience to satisfy and needed little coaxing to cross the Atlantic to join the cast of *White Steed* in New York beginning April 1939, which kept her abroad for most of the summer (136 performances) meaning she missed Jack and John Gielgud perform *Hamlet* at Kronborg Castle in Elsinore—in a production specifically designed for open-air performances. 'He was jolly good,' Gielgud said of Jack. 'He was so alive—full of variety and tone and great virility and an awfully easy man to get along with.' Danish newspapers were also unanimous in praise of 'the world's best Hamlet', 'the biggest occasion in the theatre for years', and 'a great poetic creation'. *The Stage* correspondent reported Fay Compton 'charmed the audience as Ophelia', while 'Jack Hawkins again impressed in his two portrayals of the Ghost; and Claudius; and George Howe again won appreciation as Polonius'.

Meanwhile, with war imminent, London in the summer months of 1939 was a cheerless place. The mood of the nation underwent a dramatic shift towards war as the military rearmed and introduced conscription. There was an insatiable hunger for information and scraps of intelligence when London and Paris gave guarantees to Poland, against which Hitler was making sinister threats. Though it remained unclear what practical military measures Britain would adopt, London's best-known theatrical manager decided to push ahead with his autumn plans, undeterred by tension. H. M. Tennent offered the public a wide choice of what he hoped would prove to be first-class plays and hired Jack to join his first production, a revival of *The Importance of Being Earnest*, opening at the Globe on 16 August, featuring John Gielgud, Edith Evans, Peggy Ashcroft, Margaret Rutherford, and George Howe. When it opened during the last days of peace, the gentlemen of Fleet Street were tickled by Gielgud's 'crisp' portrayal of 'John Worthing' which they thought was robustly foiled by Jack as Algy, the superb dandy of the '90s. For her part, Edith Evans, as the lavishly upholstered Lady Bracknell, was a felicitous bit of casting. Left purple with laughter, the *Bystander*'s critic raved: 'It is a preposterous piece of brilliance'; while another writer, thought it a 'real holiday from the war of nerves and it is a theatrical experience that we shall still remember when we are very senior playgoers'.

After just two weeks of delighting audiences, the grim political climate worsened when Hitler sent his troops goose-stepping into Poland on 1 September. Two days later, across Britain and continental Europe, the public listened with dread as Prime Minister Neville Chamberlain broadcast an announcement to the nation: Britain was at war with Germany. The government's plans, which extended well beyond the mechanics of mobilisation, decreed theatres be shuttered. The following directive, issued on 6 September, ordered:

> All cinemas, theatres, and other places of entertainment are to be closed immediately until further notice. Sports gatherings—indoor or outdoor which involve large numbers congregating are prohibited until further notice. Churches and other places of public worship will not be closed.

However, when the overheated atmosphere calmed, theatres resumed business on 15 September with *Me and My Girl*, featuring the ever-popular 'Doing the Lambeth Walk', being one of the first shows to reopen, along with the *Crazy Gang*—led by Bud Flanagan and Chesney Allen. Outside the West End, *The Importance of Being Earnest* returned to the Golders Green Hippodrome where the cast arrived in gas masks before the matinee. 'It has been a gloomy time for everyone since the theatres closed,' John Gielgud told crowds queued along the pavement. 'We are all delighted to be back. It won't last long for some of us. Jack Hawkins and I are waiting to be called up' (Gielgud never was wrenched from civilian life). Such was the excitement that *The Daily Herald*'s P. L. Mannock found every seat filled at the opening matinee:

> Enthusiasm for John Gielgud, Edith Evans and Jack Hawkins reminded me of a first night. Maybe this theatre will become London's leading dramatic centre for a while. Even without the gallery (closed for safety) it seats 2,000 more than any in the West End. Ivor Novello, whom I spotted in the stalls, is writing a new comedy, which opens there on October 30, with Dorothy Dickson as leading lady. Emlyn Williams was there, too.[12]

Demand for tickets was overwhelming despite a 6 p.m. curtain-up, designed to allow people to get home before the blackout. There was a happy ensemble spirit as *Ernest* started a nationwide tour, stopping at Oxford, Blackpool, Brighton, Cardiff, Manchester, Newcastle, Liverpool, Edinburgh, and Glasgow. 'If the past theatrical decade had to be represented by a single production,' *The Times* asserted, 'this is the one many good judges would choose.' Everywhere it played, the tour received outstanding notices—in the south-west, for example, it was dubbed 'Bristol's biggest theatrical event for years', and by Christmas, *Ernest* was back at the Globe on Shaftesbury Avenue. Throughout the run, Jack threw himself into the role with passion and gained the reputation of being the greatest eater on the contemporary stage. In the first act, he had to nibble five cucumber sandwiches, and in the second, four raisin muffins. 'All this eating,' a columnist observed, 'made it very difficult for Jack to arrange his off-stage eating. And there were also good manners to be considered. Even actors must not speak with their mouths full, and he had to rehearse (with muffins) for hours in order to fit in his dialogue between bites of muffin and cucumber.'

During the run of *Ernest*, Jess had received a surprise phone call from the British Council inviting her to join a tour of Canada to perform *Charles the King*, *Geneva*, and *Tobias and the Angel*. She did not hesitate to accept the job and left by sea on 11 October, despite the threat from German submarines stalking the Atlantic.

With the onset of war, the coldest winter for forty-five years descended on Britain as troops from the British Expeditionary Force landed in France to shore up its defences. While many thespians seemed loath to touch the issue of war work, some quickly offered themselves to the Entertainment National Service Association (ENSA), a new unit producing 'all-star concert parties' and troop shows. Enlistment with ENSA—which meant donning khaki—was considered 'war service'. Among the London theatres that remained open was the Windmill with its exotic 'non-stop revue' of scantily dressed girls and its boast 'We Never Close'—a promise it kept, even throughout the Blitz. However, there would be problems throughout the war with audiences hesitant to travel into London during raids.

5

Hawkins on Parade

Jess's North American tour ended in New York on 28 February 1940 (she had briefly performed in Shaw's short-lived *Geneva* on Broadway after appearing in Canada). Though, after six months abroad, Jack was not at Liverpool docks to meet her, the couple took a wholesome dose of Bournemouth air (there was no rekindling of their romance) before appearing onstage together in *King Lear* on 15 April with John Gielgud in the name part.[1] The play opened just a few days after Hitler invaded Denmark and Norway and was described by *The Times* as 'the first genuine theatrical occasion of the war'. According to those in attendance (many in uniform), the first night was a tense affair. One audience member recounted: 'People crowded every seat, stood all down the aisles, hardly dared breathe, and certainly dared not cough'. 'It has great merits, especially in the rarefied atmosphere of the closing scenes,' *The Tatler* noted, 'and Gielgud is supported by a magnificent cast ... Hawkins is outstanding.'[2]

Soon after, in the second wartime production at the Old Vic, Jack was praised for his 'magnificent Caliban' in *The Tempest,* while Alec Guinness, portraying Ferdinand, lauded it as 'one of the best ever'.[3] Typically, Herbert Farjean, the notoriously opinionated *Bystander* critic, complained the acting was 'not too good'. The play, written in 1610–1611 and thought to be one of the last that Shakespeare penned, sees Prospero use magic to conjure a storm and torment the survivors of a shipwreck, including the king of Naples and Prospero's treacherous brother, Antonio. Prospero's slave, Caliban, plots to rid himself of his master, but is thwarted by Prospero's spirit-servant Ariel. 'Mr. Gielgud seems too young, and not impressive or harsh or commanding enough,' Farjean grumbled. 'Miss Jessica Tandy's Miranda looks delicious, but her voice is not harmonious charmingly and the music of this play must not be marred.' Farjean thought Guinness was preferable to the 'pudding-Ferdinands we so often see,' while he acknowledged Jack had some grand moments as Caliban. 'If he lacks the embryo-human quality that makes Caliban such a marvellous character, his get-a-new-master frenzy is tremendous.'[4]

As the war began to dominate daily life, Jack remained one of the busiest actors in London, but was never too tired to accept a film part. Thus, he relished playing a slippery crook in *The Flying Squad*, another of the myriad of crime stories from the pen of Edgar Wallace, where smuggling was the game that engaged Scotland Yard's attention. Sebastian Shaw played the part of Detective Inspector Bradley, intent on running down a dope-smuggling gang; Jack made his character Mark McGill a loathsome, Brylcreemed individual and Kathleen Harrison played the dithering Mrs Schifan. However, progress slowed when Harrison learned that her son, Guy, had refused the draft while studying in Aberystwyth. Panicked by the news, she travelled to a conscientious objectors' tribunal in Wales where, before a judge, Guy held fast to a set of righteous beliefs and insisted that by serving in the war he would 'merely be a pawn to blundering or conniving politicians', and 'committing a crime against the world community'. Thankfully for Kathleen, there was no stiff sentence as Guy was put in 'Class B' to do forestry work. Perhaps understandably, as Churchill's propaganda machine invoked a spirit of struggle, Jack deplored being a remote investor in the national effort. He was pressured to remain on stage since male actors—having been lost to the forces—were getting thin on the ground. Worse still, theatrical empresarios H. M. Tennent vehemently opposed the conscription of actors and pushed for 'important' people to be reserved. After mulling the request, the Ministry of Labour agreed that certain actors could finish the runs of their productions to prevent 'hasty closures'. With varying degrees of reluctance, Jack, Hugh Beaumont, Rex Harrison, Roger Livesey, Emlyn Williams, and Alec Guinness were deemed as being worthy of 'temporary deferment'.[5] (The actor Robert Morley was astonished by the decision and later quipped: 'They thought actors were less dangerous to our side in the theatre than on the battlefield'.)

Eventually, after some procrastination, Jack did a bit of 'idling around the back door of the War Office', before his colleague, Andrew Cruickshank—who was also playing at the Old Vic—volunteered to join the Royal Welch Fusiliers. 'At the theatre that night I told Jack Hawkins and Andre Morell what I'd done,' Cruickshank recounted. 'They cursed me—and volunteered soon after.'[6] Speaking to the author, Cruickshank's daughter, Harriet, remembered her father joined the Fusiliers 'because my mother, Curigwen Lewis, was Welsh and he always told us children that Jack Hawkins joined the same regiment although as you can see, they didn't join up at the same time. They did remain friends of course.'[7]

After wangling his way into the army, Jack joined many thespian brothers in arms spread out across the forces. Not long after, Alec Guinness received a commission in the Navy, Ralph Richardson joined the Fleet Air Arm, and David Niven abandoned Hollywood to march with the Rifle Brigade.

Jack quickly discovered that basic training as an unpaid lance-corporal was hard work, made worse by extended absences from Jess and Susan. Those first months, he traipsed around the parade ground until his new boots produced blisters on the heels. He became *au fait* with the weapons of war, polished boots, made his own bed, swept, and scrubbed. Periods away from home grew longer when, after five months in the ranks, he was 'picked out as officer material' and sent to the Officers' Training Corps at Pwllheli.

This, however, turned out to be an even more miserable experience. Confronted with abysmal conditions, he learnt to use ammunition, dig trenches, fill sandbags, shoot wildly at cardboard targets, and endure physical training. 'This was the way things were done,' he gloomily appraised, 'this was the world whose strict rules of discipline I adopted. But I began to regret not remaining a private soldier.'

After months of spit and polish, he came through unscathed and was issued a second lieutenant's uniform, complete with prince of Wales plumes, coronet, and circlet insignia of the Royal Welch. However, after such long separations, there was no big family celebration as the seams that bound Jack and Jess together continued unravelling. The turning point came when Jess engineered an engagement in the play, *Jupiter Laughs* at the Biltmore Theatre in New York, after leaving her role in *The Tempest* (she was replaced by Peggy Ashcroft). 'I had a young daughter,' she later explained. 'I needed to go where I could survive.'[8] In later life, she reflected that Jack was a 'fine actor, but a poor husband—it was not a good marriage'.

At the end of a radiant summer's day, Jess and Susan boarded an American liner on 25 June 1940. The vessel was packed with child evacuees and £2.2 million in government gold bullion, and after five days of pitching through mountainous seas, she landed safely in New York on 1 July.[9] On hearing of her arrival, John Gielgud made a special announcement to the audience at the Old Vic: 'Ladies and gentlemen, I know you will rejoice with all of us in relief at the news just received— Jessica Tandy is safely in America!'[10]

From here on, Jack's life irrevocably changed. His army duties were interspersed by enduring long journeys for leave breaks in London, whiled away at the Marlborough Arms, the 400 Club, and the Savoy. La Popote, a favourite haunt of the society set hidden in the basement of the Ritz, became a much-loved spot for supper during the buzz-bomb raids and blackouts. It was there during the Blitz in the autumn of 1940 that Alec Guinness remembered gossiping merrily with Jack when sirens began blaring. Hermione Gingold, an actress known for her eccentric persona, was also at dinner, draped in a tightly beaded gown. Within seconds the lights were out, and the screaming of a German bomb sent everyone diving for cover. However, there was no explosion, but from somewhere under the maze of tables, the thin dazed voice of Gingold announced: 'Now I look at my best'. As everyone counted their blessings, Guinness vividly recalled trebles were ordered and 'Jack, I imagine, was paying'—a reference to his unfailing generosity.[11] During this period, Jack was a regular visitor to the West End where American musicals like Cole Porter's *Something for the Boys* and comedies such as Noël Coward's *Blithe Spirit* and Terence Rattigan's *While the Sun Shines* proved a hit with audiences seeking a brief escape from the horrors of war.

During the summer of 1941, as the Germans wound down their bombing of London, Jack's mood perked when he was given leave to appear in the War Office production of *Next of Kin*, a film set against the backdrop of the Nazi occupation of France warning audiences of 'careless talk' and loose lips. Financed by £30,000 of public money, it was written, acted, and edited in conditions of great secrecy at Ealing Studios. The cast was headlined by Mervyn Johns, Ronald Adam, and Reginald Tate. Even though Jack's part was small (billed as '2nd Lt. Jack Hawkins') he was full of energy and authority playing a British officer and giving an early display of the solid-sturdy temperament for which he later became famous.

Strangely enough, the film scored a major coup after being banned from public exhibition on the orders of Winston Churchill who thought it told the enemy how the British could inflict damage on them. In response, the press asserted it was made to 'frighten the masses into keeping their mouths shut'.[12] The *Daily Herald* led the outrage by screaming that 'Whitehall did not remember it is officials and high ups who do the most talking and it is their relatives who blab at the hairdressers and in dress shops'. When 10,000 members of the forces were shown the film, the Ministry of Information—under pressure from the press—allowed public exhibition in April 1942. Critics singled out Mervyn Johns, that 'unspectacular yet fine actor' for his performance as 'Mr Davis', a Nazi spy.[13] Naturally, the war itself did nothing to improve the film-making process as frequent air-raid warnings, ack-ack fire, and distant explosions sent everyone scampering for shelter. Jack's experience was also coloured by financial problems. After checking-in to the Savage Club, where £1 a day covered breakfast and board, he found his budget strained (he received only his army pay of 13 shillings a day for his part—which ranked as his lowest priced film job). When producer Michael Balcon refused him an extra allowance, it was Gordon Harker that rode to the rescue with the occasional 'donation'. But because Jack made such a fuss about it, Hannen Swaffer at the *Daily Herald*, caustically enquired (in print): 'Why were Jack Hawkins and other actors loaned by the Army to act in the film paid nothing when actors released to play the parts in films made by private firms are allowed to earn £300 to £400 a week?'[14]

In the period after *Next of Kin*, life in the military fell into place. As the German's approached Moscow, and the fighting in the north African desert raged on, Jack's days were spent overseeing the transfer of the Auxiliary Territorial Service (ATS) Western Command Training Centre to the former Welch Regiment barracks at Wrexham, where women recruits learned everything from repairing tanks to operating shortwave radios. After that, a more permanent posting followed at a new garrison spread over Prestbury Park and the Cheltenham racetrack, where—as there were almost no buildings—his office was in a wooden horse box.

It was here that any prospect of his relationship with Jess having a second act finally ended when a one-page letter arrived from New York. 'Darling,' Jess wrote, 'I don't want to shock you, but I want a divorce.' Feeling a touch of *Weltschmerz*, Jack drowned his sorrows into the wee hours before hitting the sack to nurse and almighty hangover.

In the letter, Jess admitted to having spent her sunniest days in the company of Hume Blake Cronyn, a dashing young actor from Ontario. They had first met in 1940 when he went backstage at *Jupiter Laughs* and it was love at first sight—for him. 'I kept saying no to him for two or three years,' Jess recounted. 'But he wouldn't give up. Night after night he would be at the stage door with flowers.'[15] She admitted that eventually their friendship became more than platonic.

Many years later, Jessica's close friend, Susan Cooper, remembered her as one of the most private people on this planet, but 'always got the impression that her first marriage suffered from the fact that career came first for both of them, and that the chance to play a particular part was always more important than their being together—witness, of course, to the fact of her coming to the US in the first place'.

In the years ahead, Jessica's career flourished, and she won the New York Drama League award for the best performance of 1942. The divorce, granted that same year, was a relatively amicable process with no ugly accusations, or squabbles. Jess married Cronyn in Beverley Hills, California, on 27 September 1942. 'I only marry good actors,' she later quipped. 'But Jack was not such a good husband. I don't know what the secret is between Hume and I, but we like and respect each other and are good together.... If I knew the secret, I would bottle it.'[16] Regarding

Jack, she later remarked, 'I think we both learnt a great deal from our disappointments in that relationship.'[17] As for Hume, he later recounted how at about the age of twelve, Susan came to him and said that she'd like to change her surname to Cronyn. 'I felt proud and rewarded,' he wrote. 'To all my children I have always been "Father," because for Susan "Daddy" belonged to Jack Hawkins—and of course the two younger ones followed the lead of their older sister.'

6

Under Asian Skies

Forced to reflect and reconsider his future, Jack regained his solitary composure. In fact, there were no moments of self-pity as he prepared for his next big wartime adventure. After being instructed to collect his full fighting kit, the thirty-three-year-old lieutenant received inoculations for yellow fever, cholera, smallpox, and typhoid before joining the British 2nd Division on a long journey to India. After the Japanese bombed Pearl Harbor in December 1941, dragging America into the war, the conflict had widened across Burma, Thailand, the Dutch East Indies, Malaya, Singapore, and the Pacific. Hong Kong was the first British possession to fall in December 1941, after eighteen days of fighting. Japan went on to chalk-up an extraordinary series of victories. On 2 January 1942, they took Manila, followed by an attack on the Dutch East Indies on 11 January. The next day, Kuala Lumpur fell, and seventy-two hours later, Burma was subjected to the might of the Japanese onslaught. Then, Malaya was gradually occupied at the cost of 50,000 Allied prisoners of war. The capture of Singapore in February 1942 was one of the great blows to Allied morale and the largest surrender of British-led military personnel in history, as 80,000 British, Indian, and Australian troops were marched into captivity.

On arrival in this lively theatre of war, Jack received instructions to lead a Bren gun platoon. He was posted deep inside the Indian jungle—a shadowy terrain, bursting with venomous snakes, spiders, and mosquitoes. The most dreaded snake was the Russell viper. When it struck, there was only one thing to do. Get a sharp razor blade and hack out the flesh round the bite. Just as awful were leeches with the thirst of vampires which fell through the lace holes of boots and sucked blood until they were the size of a matchbox. They also dropped from trees and snuck under men's eyelids. At times, the humidity was so great that it sapped thinking power, and covered life with a blanket of boredom. Clutching a gun, Jack took charge of a 'battle school', teaching jungle warfare and survival. Long marches on cotton soil, clashing personalities, the loss of autonomy, butchering goats for rations, and the fear of getting hurt or killed, all conspired to create a miserable existence. From an army camp bed, he penned long letters home detailing his despair and received many in return. 'It was pure hell,' Jack reminisced. Far from suggesting grace under pressure, he failed to take it all in good humour and could often be heard loudly cursing and grousing, as his enthusiasm for army life boiled away. He also noisily declared his heartfelt ambition to 'stay alive'.

Tired of his constant grousing, the army plucked Jack from the jungle and installed him at the Poona Divisional Battle School, an oasis of calm where his job was to narrate demonstrations of combat techniques over a loudhailer for visiting top brass. The garrison, situated in the western Indian state of Maharashtra, was run like a holiday encampment, with an officers' mess, social club, and lively canteen. Among the pastimes were archery, horseback riding, swimming, and athletics.

Unsurprisingly, this new life was highly agreeable, until one day, while minding his own business, he was summoned by General John Grover, a beefy warhorse known for his straight-talking. 'He had found out I was an actor, and I was ordered to organize a concert party,' imitating variety shows seen in British theatres. Within weeks, the 'Cross Keys' concert party, named after the division's insignia, was in business, staffed by an assortment of gifted actors, musicians, and playwrights—all plucked from the ranks. Jack ran a tight ship, and the theatre of war on the India–Burma front affected him only in terms of where his next show would be.

'Somehow, I kept it going for eighteen months, with a complete change of programme every three weeks,' he remembered. 'I was comedian, sceneshifter, baritone, and female impersonator—the lot!'[1] Looking back, he recounted how helpful General Grover was: 'I have never known anyone give greater encouragement and yet interfere less than he did'. One of Jack's first signings was tenor singer, Ted Cooper, a gunner who never forgot entertaining fighting lads on all fronts amid the sound of gunfire and while 'the enemy stalked just around the corner'. Within a few weeks of operation, they had presented 'six snappy revues' before frontline audiences and staged *The Amazing Dr. Clitterhouse*, the thriller by Barré Lyndon. Ted recalled the unit had the finest mobile stage in India and Burma. They made their own props, and the female impersonator designed costumes and altered outfits.[2] Ted Webb, a trombonist from the Dorsetshire Regiment, was often shaken by the disquieting sounds of enemy chatter radiating from the jungle. On one occasion, Japanese artillerymen near Mandalay dropped a shell too close for comfort: 'Footlights on our stage were switched off and for half-an-hour, the players and the audience lay in the dark … then we carried on with the show!'[3]

Major Donald Neville-Willing, a hotshot impresario who usually kept a sunny disposition, thought Jack sparkled when caked in filthy greasepaint and warbled numbers like 'Sing a Song of Sunbeams' and 'My Melancholy Baby'. He also could not fault his wild sense of the ridiculous:

> One night in Bombay, I looked in at a soldiers' show I had not seen before. One turn was listed as a Spanish dance and song act. On to the stage came prancing a magnificent figure of a woman clacking castanets and casting amorous looks at the boys in the audience. I don't know if anybody fell for this apparition. There was certainly no excuse when the 'senorita' opened her mouth to sing. Out came the manly baritone of Jack Hawkins.

That year was full of happy days and nights. A Kodak snap shows Jack wearing a khaki tunic with a cigarette dangling from his lips, jauntily holding what looks like a script. He found India magical, faded, and beautiful. It was also surprising. He never forgot during a stop-off at Lahore finding *Beauty and the Barge* playing at the Globe cinema, 'they were actually showing my old films in India … and people paid to watch them!' But bigger surprises were to come. During early 1944, his job with the Cross Keys led to a meeting with Eric Dunstan, a broadcaster of great charm who happened to be in Bombay leading a small ENSA troupe. ENSA was the British equivalent of the USO and fell directly under the control of Jack's old mentor and tormentor Basil Dean, who—working from London—oversaw a vast portfolio of actors, comics, musicians, and administrators.

Thanks to Dunstan, Jack was quickly seconded from the Royal Welch to ENSA in July 1944 and assumed the position of 'Principal Liaison Officer between ENSA and the Forces in India'. Basil Dean recounted that Dunstan's 'pull' at GHQ made 'the transfer of this accomplished actor an easy matter'.[4] Before long, Jack was promoted to colonel and the burden of responsibility for the whole of ENSA in India rested on his shoulders, as he took charge of all the groups who came to entertain the troops. In fact, working out of Bombay, he proved a superb planner and organiser. One journalist, intrigued by his enthusiasm and endless supply of ideas, noted how Jack pioneered the concept that soldiers would like 'something other than a line of high-kicking girls and red nosed comics and his most successful shows were straight plays'. Indeed, after being instructed to 'put himself in the picture', he embarked on arranging everything from drama productions to concert party trips in far-off places. 'We were quite star struck in Jack's company, but he was very charming to us,' Celia Nicholls, a young ENSA singer remembered. 'We were stationed first of all in the Apollo Bunder Hotel in Bombay and I'm afraid we began to put on weight as we enjoyed all the fabulous meals on the menu, such a luxury after war rationed Britain.'

Over time, Jack expanded ENSA and moved its headquarters to Calcutta, where he took over the Garrison Theatre. Though often on the move, he considered Bombay different to the rest of India. It was more cultured and the population more cosmopolitan. He drank up the lazy atmosphere, the weathered surroundings, the blood red sunsets, and lunches at the sumptuous Taj Mahal Palace Hotel, with its polished foyer, enormous chandeliers, and oak-panelled library. It was a city filled with artists, writers, and musicians, as well as military top brass. At night, the company would adjourn to the Strand Hotel, a favourite haunt given the manager, E. A. Newman, an Englishman, kept a stash of good malt whisky for 'special ENSA customers'. On balmy evenings, he barbecued steaks and sausages for everyone on an open-air grill.

'Jack looked exactly the same,' recalled actor Ronald Waters, who met him in Bombay during the blistering summer of 1944, where temperatures topped 41 degrees. 'He was in the throes of arranging the tours of Elsie and Doris Waters and Stainless Stephen. This is no easy matter as the distances to be covered are vast, air transport is not always available, and trains are bad.'[5] (In India, because of the long distances between the places, ENSA even had a special rail coach with sleeping compartments and a kitchen to make tea and cook.)

Shortly afterwards, Basil Dean arrived for an inspection tour and clocked Jack sporting the insignia of a high-ranking officer, complete with a burgundy-banded peak cap: 'He wore the red tabs of his colonelcy with becoming solidity'. Dean's main worry, however, was that Jack felt frustrated and dissatisfied about the 'temperamental reluctance' of some leading artists, as well as lesser lights, to journey and work in uncomfortable circumstances. Since taking the reins of ENSA, Col. Hawkins had waded through endless complaints about threadbare living conditions, the discomforts of heat, cold, fleabag hotels, inoculations, rats, parasites, bedbugs, and other pests. Even Dean found himself detained in hospital in Calcutta with dengue fever. Malaria was another tricky problem. It came in waves and could be debilitating, leaving those infected bedridden for weeks. The singer Vera Lynn was one of the few big names to visit the Burma front without complaint. She described the heat as 'terrific', and once gave a show to two injured men at a frontline casualty station, 6 miles from a Japanese patrol:

It's no picnic. Soon after I arrived, the monsoon burst. That brought out the insects. Enormous cockroaches, looking like huge beetles, flew in my face throughout my act at one performance. They came at me so quickly, I was waving and fighting them off the whole time. Added to that, my clothes were going black from perspiration and the boys were having a good laugh. We could never use a spotlight because it attracted the insects. Each time you sang you were liable to get a mouthful. We lived mostly in bamboo huts, with a pail of suspect, tepid water and on a diet of corned beef and soya beans and rice pudding without milk or sugar. Bush rats and bull frogs were around us day and night. The boys enjoyed the shows, and I enjoyed their enjoyment.[6]

Likewise, Celia Nicholls still shivers when reminiscing about her billet in a jungle camp, where rats ran over the corrugated roofs at night. 'We had to make sure that we put something into the big leather boots that we used in the jungle to stop perhaps a snake crawling into them at night,' she said. 'We didn't want to put our feet into our boots in the morning to a nasty bite!'

Meanwhile, after recovering from dengue, Jack arranged for Dean to accompany the American music-hall trio, Forsyth, Seaman, and Farrel, and singer Lyle Evans on a whistle stop tour of the Fourteenth Army camps in Burma. Sergeant G. Agnew remembered the 'admirable little performance' receiving a great ovation. 'They had just arrived from Blighty, and at the end of the evening's show we had a bigger surprise when Basil Dean came on to the stage,' Agnew wrote to the *Liverpool Echo*. 'He is out here to organise ENSA for us. He gave an excellent speech, assuring us were now going to get the best ENSA had to offer, and was most emphatic and sincere about it. This has bucked the boys up no end.'

A Fine Romance

Back in Bombay, Neville-Willing, the hotshot impresario, who by this point was acting as Jack's wingman, never forgot when another troupe of entertainers arrived. 'The leading lady was a blonde called Doreen Lawrence,' he said. 'We entertained the visiting company. And Jack did most of the entertaining of Doreen.'[1]

Typically, Jack always painted a more comical version of that encounter: 'One day there was a knock on my door and a curiously assorted group entered. There was a man with a cork leg, a lady in a bright tartan skirt, another man … and a very pretty blonde! Naturally enough, my eyes came to rest on the blonde … and she looked back at me'.[2] He remembered they fell in love rather like people in the movies often did, with pounding hearts: 'We maintain now that when our eyes met across that office—as the romantic writers will have it—"we knew". We've always been quite sure of that fact'. Dee remembered it differently. She said it was only when Jack lifted her onto a truck (she was wearing a tight skirt and unable to jump), that she felt a dramatic sensation 'like being hit by a bolt of lightning'. Photographs of Dee taken in India show a radiant young woman. It was, as she would say many years later, 'the most unforgettable time of my youth'. She also revealed this was not her first encounter with the man on whose life she would make an indelible imprint. She had, in fact, seen Jack perform in *Autumn* with Flora Robson in 1937 and knew of his position in the English theatre. Dee quickly discovered that under his stiff khaki uniform there was a dry sense of humour, and a highly defined sense of the ridiculous. 'This,' she said, 'was further enhanced by his talent as a quite unconsciously gifted mimic.'

For a woman of twenty-five, Dee had acquired a wealth of theatrical experience. Born Doreen Mary Beadle in Southampton in 1919, she started her theatrical career as a child playing small parts at the city's Grand Theatre. More ambitious than most, she was touring with a troupe by the age of fifteen, followed by the grind of repertory before joining ENSA sometime during the spring of 1942, which took her to Africa and Cairo.

At eighteen, she was briefly engaged to Peter Cushing, the actor who later gained fame for his roles in the Hammer horror films. However, the relationship was doomed when he began bringing his parents on dates (he was also easily moved to tears). 'But,' Dee added, 'Peter was the most wonderful, kind man.' With Jack, though, the chemistry was obvious, according to Neville-Willing, who 'could almost feel' the passion. 'The first time Doreen and I actually acknowledged our love was at a famous party given by the Aly Khan (the son of the Aga Khan) when we danced under the stars together,' Jack recounted. The weather was beautiful and clear, and 'this romantic ending brought us closer, and Doreen and I found we had so much in common.' Despite industrious carousing, an impediment to their future happiness lay in the fact that Dee was still married to a heavy-drinking, irrationally jealous, intelligence corps officer named Patrick, a man known for his physical aggressiveness. They had married in 1940 when he was a stage manager at the Sheffield Lyceum. As a result of the torment she suffered, Dee vowed to seek a divorce. In the meantime, another crisis arose as Jack explored the possibility of keeping Dee in Bombay but 'unfortunately', he explained, 'we could not see each other very often because her party were always on the move. Of course, I felt rather sad about this. Then came the dreadful day when I just could not find a play suitable for such a small cast and the powers-that-be decided that they must all return to England. I thought my romance was finished.'

But this did not deter Dee, who flopped into a chair, pulled out a notebook and scribbled down every play she could think of, until she remembered the prophetically titled *Love in a Mist*, a bedroom farce by Kenneth Horne about two couples stranded for a few days in thick fog in a desolate stretch of countryside. What happened to them when they found a lonely farmhouse to sleep in made unusually good theatre. It was a simple story with a handful of characters and a single setting and, as Jack noted, a perfect distraction for 'sex-starved' servicemen. The play proved such a hit that it received strong ovations from troops across India and Ceylon. So much so, that when Jack ordered a small break for the cast to recuperate, the formidable General William Joseph Slim—commander of the Fourteenth Army (known as the so-called 'Forgotten Army' because its operations in Burma were overlooked by the press)—telegraphed ENSA to insist on the shows immediate return. After meeting General Slim, a man Jack described as charming 'but blunt', the cast were permitted a short break before resuming the tour. 'There was no way Jack could refuse such an order,' Doreen remembered (Slim even attended a performance of

Love in a Mist). Stuart Gelder, a correspondent from the *Daily News*, saw the show in Burma and felt troops owed Doreen and her sprightly young colleague, Pamela Roberts, some gratitude following a wave of hoity-toity criticism of ENSA. 'The individual efforts of girls like these are beyond praise,' Gelder chirped. 'For nearly two years they have travelled nearly 30,000 miles in Africa, Egypt, India and now here, cheering the lives of men in some of the most remote war zones.' In a quarter-page feature, 'Two Girls at War', Gelder had explicit opinions on the lack of recognition and appreciation for entertainers on the frontline. In summary, he wrote:

When you think of criticizing think also of Pamela Roberts, of Hertford, and Doreen Lawrence, of London, who are here now, where I don't think you would like to be, living as hard as soldiers, facing the same dangers from illness which can send a man down. Not very long ago, Pamela Roberts was stricken with cerebral malaria in West Africa. When you've got that in these parts they say, 'You've had it,' and begin to say nice things about you whatever they have thought while you were alive.

Nine out of ten people would not have recovered. Nine out of ten people, if they had, would have gone home. Amoebic dysentery and other forms of malaria were a few other minor inconveniences she suffered. But she stood on her dainty feet and gave Death the smile which is now charming thousands of men hungry for the company of women and the refinements of home. And she is still standing and smiling.

Such women lend grace to courage. Doreen Lawrence could tell much the same story if she would. And whenever you feel like grumbling about little things at home it might help you to remember it and think of two girls giving their best in a play called *Love in a Mist* in a temperature of 90 in the shade in the cool of the evening and no ice in the drinks with which they wash their dusty, aching throats.[3]

On the road, Doreen bumped into the likes of Joyce Grenfell, Edith Evans, and the northern crooner Gracie Fields, 'who sang her heart out with that powerful voice and no microphone'. She recalled Noël Coward 'only needed a piano and would go anywhere to entertain the troops and improve morale'. But rather less popular was George Formby's thunder-faced wife Beryl, who demanded top hotels and star treatment. Amid her extraordinary adventures, Dee corresponded with Jack from the frontline by letter and telegram, but remembered, his responses were hardly amorous nor lengthy or reflective: 'Jack is taciturn, he does not write romantically'.[4]

When Pamela Roberts returned to Britain, Dee found good company with a new roommate, Angela Dowding, who later married the younger son of the princess royal, Gerald Lascelles. They served together in Rangoon and, as Sergeant Charles Annand, an assistant stage manager recounted, she played the part of Lady Elizabeth Randall in *While the Sun Shines*: 'We were just one big happy family, and Miss Dowding, especially, was a grand trouper'.

After enjoying an amazing run in ENSA, Doreen was handed her last pay packet, with no bonus, in January 1945. Jack eventually proposed in Calcutta in a little Chinese restaurant as they 'enjoyed a meal of sweet and sour prawns and bamboo shoots'.

Then a few weeks later, on a clear blue day in Bombay, Dee dissolved into tears as she waved goodbye to Jack at the 'Gateway to India' before embarking on a journey steaming through Suez, across the Mediterranean, and up to Liverpool. In London, she set up lodgings on Bedford Street, in a tiny flat tucked away in one of the backstreets, a block from the Adelphi Theatre. 'This tiny bedsitter would be our home when Jack was eventually demobbed,' she recounted. 'We didn't grow despondent at being separated … we knew our time would come.'

With the war in Europe and Asia winding down, Jack confessed he did not feel right about saying 'Thanks boys, and goodbye'—especially with so many troops still spread across Asia—so he decided to remain at his post.[5] There was, though, a brief visit to London where he was astounded to see large swathes of the capital in ruins. As well as being briefly reunited with Dee, he also met Alec Clunes from the small independent Arts Theatre Group who promised him a job on his return to civilian life (Doreen remembered during this trip, Jack needed constant reassurance, fearful he might never get another job). After meeting Basil Dean to discuss ENSA events in India, *The Stage* reported Jack looked 'extremely well and vigorous' and had 'happy memories and hopeful plans'. Dean, though, was distracted following a slew of high-profile departures from the ranks of ENSA. Even though he was described as one of British theatre's greatest champions, his wartime creation faced a barrage of criticism concerning accounting irregularities, dubious contracts, lewd comics, poor performances, and exorbitant expense claims.

The vice-president, Sir Herbert Dunnico, described working with Dean as being like 'an absolute dictatorship' and accused him of wasting public funds. The allegation left staff reeling and led to Dean's personal private secretary resigning in sympathy with Sir Herbert saying: 'Nothing would give me greater pleasure than to resume my work for the troops in a new regime'. Matters worsened when Colonel Eric Dunstan—the man who had recruited Jack in India—also threw in the towel, saying he could not agree with the way Dean ran the organisation: 'There were serious differences of opinion, and I found the situation growing intolerable'. Despite calls for an inquiry into ENSA, Herbert Morrison, the then president of the council, refused to take action. In a letter to his son Martin toward the end of the war, Dean appeared bitter, and suggested that his recompense from ENSA was minimal, especially as he had given up the whole of his time to organising national service entertainments.

Meanwhile, back in Bombay, Jack listened to the BBC with astonishment on 12 April 1945 when the long reign of President Roosevelt ended with his death by cerebral haemorrhage. Then, less than a month later, impromptu ENSA-sponsored singsongs erupted when European hostilities ended with the surrender of Nazi forces. As most ENSA old hands headed home, Jack was charging at full blast, and between June and the end of August 1945, he oversaw 250 artists, made up of twenty-six parties. Two months later, in October, John Gielgud arrived with *Hamlet* and *Blithe Spirit*. 'Gielgud was sweeping the Far East,' Jack wrote to his superiors in London. 'Frills, legs, and variety, so necessary an antidote to battle strain, have given place to a wish for good theatre. A new taste for the theatre has been awakened in the men, and I believe it will live on when they come home.' On arriving in India, Gielgud observed Jack in uniform clutching his treasured brown leather swagger stick and looking, 'very much the sort of head boy. I think he rather enjoyed the authority'. However, the demands of ENSA left Jack with little social life, but he found solace travelling through India, Burma, Malaya, and at the picturesque hill station of Darjeeling some 7,000 feet up commanding stunning views of the Himalayan Mountains, where he glimpsed through the haze to marvel at Mount Everest. Throughout this period, ENSA companies continued playing to leave camps for British, American, and Canadian troops enjoying rest and recuperation. Jack helped inaugurate a new series of ENSA broadcasts on All-India Radio, and although he never saw the show, one of the young 'turns' playing for ENSA caught the eye of a reporter from the *Bombay Sunday Standard*. 'The "baby" of the show is Peter Sellers, aged 19, the boy-drummer and impressionist,' the paper noted. 'A big future lies before him.'

In his final months of duty, Jack faced a new challenge as natives called for independence. In Bombay, the streets were dotted with posters showing Ghandhi, and reports of angry mobs stopping traffic, tossing Molotov cocktails through windows and ransacking shops poured in from all over the country. On one occasion, Jack and the actor Stafford Byrne were both spat at by demonstrators after they accidentally stumbled upon a political gathering and a mêlée ensued.

India was an exhausting but wholly unique experience, but he was glad to leave. In the end, ENSA's final act was left to the gangly comedian Tommy Trinder—a standard bearer for the organisation—who changed his catchphrase in August 1946, just for once, saying: 'You unlucky people!' to an audience somewhere in Burma before ENSA's curtain rang down forever. One of the players in that last performance later said:

> Whatever they might say about Basil Dean, ENSA looked after the song-and-dance people very well. The pay was very good, and I was even able to save money because meals and accommodation were free. Mind you, it was terribly hard work. Dancing is the last thing you wanted to do on an open-air stage in the airless oven heat surrounded by flies.[6]

8

A New World

In 1946, Jack's life entered new era, when, at the age of thirty-six, he was demobbed with the honorary rank of full colonel and, as if a switch had been thrown, every aspect of his life changed. Under Asian skies, he had gained weight, became less cocksure, and developed a marvellously modulated voice, deepened by his two-pack-a-day Senior Service habit. 'As was the case with many thousands of young men, Jack Hawkins emerged from the war a different man,' *Picturegoer* later noted. 'He took on a different personality. Maturity had caught up with him. He had broadened mentally and physically. His shoulders were wider, his whole build heavier. His face had gained character lines.' Indeed, there was even a suggestion of grey in his hair and a warmth and humanity about him which had never been developed. The war had given him experience of the world at large, which he had never had before. As journalist John K. Newnham observed, Jack had lived an oddly sheltered life:

> He had never had any stretches of unemployment. He had never known highlife and had always lived very well within his income. His world had always been entirely the world of entertainment. True, it had geographical breadth in that he had travelled a bit and had been to America, but he had never been outside the world of theatre and films and that world is a small one.

Back in London, Jack was acting again within three weeks, playing in Shaw's *The Apple Cart* at the Arts Theatre Club. During the day, he joined Alec Clunes, Anthony Quayle, and Fay Compton to rehearse *Hamlet*, *Othello*, *Candida,* and *The Apple Cart* before embarking on a tour of war-ravaged Europe on one of the many projects sponsored by the British Council (he reflected that his only 'flaw' in this production of *Othello* was his passion for the character which led to floods of tears. He never had any difficulty producing tears on cue). Beginning in Prague on 30 September, the curtain rose on a five-month, 6,000-mile tour, crisscrossing through Belgium, Austria, Holland, and France, playing to over 100,000 people. 'In most cases stools have been placed in the gangways transforming the auditorium into a block of humanity,' Jack recounted. During the tour, the company never saw an empty seat.[1] Nor, he noted, were audiences composed of the intelligentsia or a snob section of the public: 'So far, the proudest moment of our tour occurred in Austria at Graz, where we were presented with an illuminated scroll signed by 375 Styrian schoolchildren and their teachers'. Strangely enough, theatregoers in Europe, he said, were 'genuinely anxious' to appreciate the drama and imaginativeness of other countries: 'Playgoers are amazed to discover so high a standard of acting in artists from a country which possesses no national theatre. They enjoy our work; every country is expressing the hope that there will be a regular exchange of companies between Britain and the Continent'.

Though drawing favourable reaction, detractors at home suggested government money could be better spent. 'Critics who accused the British Council of wasting time and money would be inclined to revise their ideas if they could spend a week with us in any of the seven countries we are visiting in our present tour of Europe,' Jack wrote in a syndicated article. 'Such contact between actors and audiences of two different countries is bound to promote better understanding between nations, and it leads us to hope that we actors are helping in a small way to foster the preservation of world peace.' When published, his words had precisely the desired effect and won the broader support for which the British Council had been seeking (the letter was, as far as is known, Jack's first foray into publishing).

Meanwhile, as the dreary aftermath of the war was receding, Dee embarked on a divorce from Patrick. Hugh Latimer introduced her to London's best lawyers, setting in motion a long drawn-out, costly, and tiring process. However, her emotional state was perked up when Jack's Europe tour ended in February 1947, allowing them a few weeks together before he set out on a provincial tour, followed by a season at the Piccadilly Theatre performing *Othello* and *The Apple Cart,* both triumphs. In the latter, more than one close associate observed that he gave a masterful portrayal of King Magnus. 'No more telling anti-republican argument has ever been staged and no country ever had a more attractive monarch than that presented by Mr. Hawkins,' an anonymous critic of *The Stage* wrote.[2] Elizabeth Frank from the *Daily News* thought 'Jack Hawkins has voice, diction, presence and personality; all that he says carries complete conviction.'[3] That review was spotted by Bill O'Bryen, an associate of Hungarian-born film producer Alexander Korda, who saw the merit in Jack's performance. Surviving files from London Films show that after making two tests, Jack was signed to a three-year contract at the princely sum of £50 a week—a deal sealed with a handshake at 143 Piccadilly. Korda—who lived at Claridge's in great style—was an engaging, intense man who devoured books in his leisure time and frequented the movie houses on weekends. 'The marvellous thing about Korda,' actor David Tomlinson once mused, 'was he could do it all, couldn't he? He could probably act the parts as well. He wasn't just a promoter like so many of them are—he was responsible.'[4] Since arriving from Budapest in 1931, the Hungarian placed British productions on the map after building a studio at Denham, north of London. Known for his generous budgets and lavish showmanship, he won international acclaim producing *Henry VIII,* a triumph for the portly actor Charles Laughton.

Jack's first Korda script dropped onto the doormat at Bedford Street during a delayed celebration for Dee's twenty-eighth birthday. They sipped Perrier-Jouët Brut, reading his part of Lord George Murray in the much-publicised, but ill-fated, *Bonnie Prince Charlie*, a supporting role alongside Hollywood star David Niven, who was to play a rosy-cheeked 'Charlie'. A studio memo notes the film—a convoluted costume drama—officially began production on 6 July; however, after long delays, location shooting in Scotland commenced in late August 1947. Director Anthony Kimmins, who took part in Operation Claymore, the successful commando raid in Norway, was not joking when he once remarked that 'making *Charlie* was a much tougher operation'. When things finally started moving, supporting player Will Fyffe was killed after falling from a hotel room window, meaning £100,000 worth of film had to be re-shot. Then, 2,000 extras stood around valiantly for days in the cold to enact a spectacular battle scene—but in the end it had to be 'fought' on a sound stage at Shepperton studios. According to Niven, kitted out in knee-high socks and a braided coat, no one was happy when, more than once, the misty Scottish weather began playing havoc with the new colour cameras, sparking endless hold-ups. During these long breaks, Jack could often be found propping up the bar of the Rusacks Hotel in St Andrews, exchanging philosophies with Niven, who joined in enthusiastically. 'They had the same boyish sense of humour, and both were great raconteurs,' Doreen remembered. 'If you got them at a table together nobody else got a word in!' She reminisced how Niven—whose humour could be as salty as seawater—sidled over to Jack one morning, costumed in a capacious kilt, paste-on stage whiskers, and ill-adjusted wig:

> 'Just tell me one thing; do I look like an utter prick?' he asked.
>
> Jack thought about that for a moment and then said, 'Yes,' and they were friends forever afterwards.[5]

After the divorce from Patrick came through in September, Jack and Doreen tied the knot at a Registry Office in Chelsea on 31 October 1947. After much back and forth, the couple arranged the reception at The Moore Arms, a cosy pub on Cadogan Street, a deal secured as the landlord promised a crate of champagne. 'That was the real beginning of a life of great happiness together,' Doreen recounted.

A few days later, Jack was back on the set of *Bonnie Prince Charlie*. By this point, Niven was lamenting that the film was a huge, 'florid extravaganza that reeked of disaster from the start'.[6] There was never a completed screenplay, and during the eight months of shooting, writers were never more than two days ahead of the actors: 'In confusion we suffered three changes of directors, with Korda himself desperately taking over.… I felt sorry for him, but sorrier for myself as the Bonnie Prince who would assuredly bear the blame for the impending debacle'.[7]

The virtue—or curse—of *Bonnie Prince Charlie* was that one day, between takes, Jack glimpsed Hjördis Tersmeden, a twenty-eight-year-old divorced Swedish-born model, visiting Anthony Kimmins. He alerted Niven, a serial seducer of women, who was immediately enchanted. 'I had never seen anything so beautiful in my life—tall, slim, auburn hair, uptilted nose, lovely mouth and the most enormous grey eyes I had ever seen,' he recounted. 'I goggled. I had difficulty swallowing and I had champagne in my knees.' The sheer force of Niven's charm convinced Tersmeden to tie the knot six weeks later at South Kensington registry office. It was a decision he would later regret.

At the time of the wedding, Jack was embarking on his second Korda feature, *Lost Illusion* (re-titled *The Fallen Idol*), a stylish Graham Greene melodrama of domestic tragedy seen through the eyes of a little boy, the son of a foreign ambassador, left home with the butler and his wife, during his father's absence. The butler is his hero, with his godlike authority and gentle manner, and magnificent yarns of his adventurous life on foreign shores. The child believes these stories unreservedly and is never happier than when he can trot along beside the big man like a devoted puppy. In this way, he becomes an innocent witness of the butler's unhappy love affair with an embassy secretary, whom he secretly meets at a local teashop and at London Zoo. Ever suspicious, the wife pumps the kid about these secret meetings and the child lies for his hero's sake and when the wife, in a fit of jealous passion, accidentally falls down the stairs and breaks her neck, the boy fancies the butler has killed her, and lies manfully and very badly to the police.

For the project, director Carol Reed, a soft-spoken man of exquisite sensitivity, gathered a first-rate cast, including Ralph Richardson to play Baines, the butler, while Bobby Henrey, was much praised as Philippe, the little boy. When the cameras began turning, Jack delivered a nimble performance as a sharp-nosed police officer, Detective Ames. 'Carol and I had been crossing paths for nearly twenty years,' Jack recalled, saying they enjoyed an artistic and temperamental rapport. Speaking to the author, Bobby Henrey recounted a slow-going production but one in which Jack stamped his own mark. 'He was a nostalgic figure for me. The heavy coat, big shoes—he cut a big figure on the set, world-weary, very heavy set … he commanded attention in every scene.' Like everyone else, Henrey was astonished by the 'magnificent set' designed by Korda's brother Vincent which included a glorious staircase, sweeping from the lobby to the first floor. It was here where the jealous wife would break her neck in the most dramatic scene. 'Art directors have been satisfied to build a plaster staircase,' *The People* intoned snidely. 'But not Vincent Korda. His artistic conscience rebelled at the thought of a plaster staircase. He must have a real one—made of wood. And seeing that the script described the staircase as being a mahogany one, Vincent went the whole artistic hog and fixed himself up with a genuine mahogany staircase.'[8] In the finished picture, as well as beautiful sets, *The Fallen Idol* benefits from the stylish black-and-white photography of Georges Périnal, his city scenes had a special beauty, especially the shots of London at night, punctuated by William Alwyn's score. After being rushed through editing and promotion, *The Fallen Idol* opened in January 1948, earning Korda a small fortune, rave reviews, and the International Prize for the Best Screenplay at the Venice Festival. *The Sketch* critic thought *The Fallen Idol* was one of the most human pictures he had ever seen, 'a film about perplexed people who mean to be honest but are forced by circumstances into deception'. The *Herald-Tribune* called it 'a beautiful and engrossing screenplay which ranks with the finest of screen importations'.

By this point, Jack was certainly seen as popular enough by the BBC to be booked for appearances on *Worker's Playtime*, *Calling All Forces*, *Garrison Theatre*, and *Variety Bandbox*. When there was free time, life continued more or less cheerfully. The Hawkinses found a new home on Sloane Square, secured with Doreen's earnings from a small part in Laurence Olivier's film *Hamlet*. 'They live in a spacious flat on the Chelsea embankment,' *Photoplay* noted, and 'consider their view of Chelsea and Albert Bridges to be one of the finest in the whole of London.' During the summer, their social circle widened. Neighbour and long-term friend Patrick McNee remembered Jack became 'part of the furniture' at The Moore Arms, the same pub where he had held his wedding reception.[9] His taste for fine food and wine also made him a regular patron at every colourful locale, including the Pelham Court bistro and the Magic Cornet Inn on the King's Road, where steaks were served by the light of candelabra.

At weekends, he was often seen watching the cricket from the Lord's Tavern pub on St John's Wood Road, close by Lord's Cricket Ground. It was from here, a few years later, that he joined John Mills, Trevor Howard, Nigel Patrick, Roger Livesey, Denholm Elliott, Naunton Wayne, Basil Radford, John Snagge, Roy Plomley, and Brian Johnston, to establish the Lord's Taverners, a charity to raise money for the National Playing Fields Association, even now, in 2024, the charity donates over £3 million annually to help young people participate in sporting activities.

Not long after *The Fallen Idol* had ended, Korda set Jack to work portraying R. B. Waring, a 'gorgeously large and bonhomous' civil service careerist who uses his job with a wartime scientific section to further his own ends in Nigel Balchin's *The Small Back Room*, a Powell and Pressburger production.[10] The narrative concerns a wartime scientist trying to crack the mechanism of a new German booby-trapped bomb, and featured David Farrar, Kathleen Byron, Michael Gough, Leslie Banks, Cyril Cusack, and a baby-faced Bryan Forbes, making his debut as a wounded soldier. '*The Small Back Room* is the best-acted British picture I can remember,' averred Bruce Lockhart from the *Tatler*. 'It is rich in fine character performances.' When production was complete, Jack gained his first meaty part as 'Prinny', the prince of Wales, in *Elusive Pimpernel*, another Korda costume melodrama with David Niven, who again expressed doubts about the project. The film chronicles the adventures of the cretinous Sir Percy Blakeney (Niven), who turns out to be the charming 'Scarlet Pimpernel', rescuing nobility from bloodthirsty revolutionists.

While the staging was glorious, directors Michael Powell and Emeric Pressburger failed to make up their minds whether to treat its plot seriously, leading to unnecessary gags in what was essentially a drama. And despite his handsome salary, Niven was not enthusiastic but remained good-humoured on location in Brittany and Bath. More remarkable was that the picture took so long to make—almost three years from conception to release—that Doreen gave birth to her first son, Nicholas, when filming commenced, and a second child, Andrew, was born just as editing wrapped.

In the end, *Elusive Pimpernel* seemed a lost cause. Reviews were dour. Niven 'makes his first embarrassed entrance like the dame in some nightmare pantomime,' said *The Times*, and for that matter, even Sam Goldwyn told Alexander Korda, 'It's the worst picture I have ever seen in my life.'

As Dee relaxed into motherhood, Jack joined the cast of Thomas Costain's *The Black Rose*, a 20th Century Fox medieval spectacle filmed in the flinty wilderness of Morocco, and directed by Henry Hathaway, a cigar-chomper, famed for cutting his teeth on Gary Cooper and John Wayne westerns. Backed by money from London and Hollywood, *The Black Rose* required the biggest location unit ever sent from Britain, comprising seventy-five people, £200,000 worth of equipment, and a large quantity of props.

Though dreadfully miscast, Jack took the part of a high testosteroned archer as the project offered him the chance to work with Hollywood A-listers Tyrone Power, Orson Welles, and newcomer Cecile Aubrey. But like the *Elusive Pimpernel*, the film was long in the making. The story tells how Power, playing an embittered young Oxford scholar, along with his friend (Jack) leave England and set out for the East to discover its mysteries. On their journey, they meet a lovely girl known as the Black Rose (Aubrey) who appeals to them to get her to England. Welles, hidden under layers of make-up, played a sinister Mongolian warrior taking an army to conquer China.

For the most part, shooting took place miles away from civilisation, with the crew billeted in tents pitched on an ancient caravan route in the rolling foothills of the Atlas Mountains. About 5:45 p.m. every afternoon—as the sun set in the west—the cast arrived back at the encampment for a meal roasted on a spit. Water proved a big problem and was rationed one mug full a day, and with that the crew had to complete their full toilet. 'It was hard work recording the daily progress of the film, with the sun at its hottest and the only shade a thin umbrella,' recalled Peggy Warrington, who was assigned to the production team. Part of her work was to marshal 407 horses, 712 camels, and five jumping horses, together with their retinue of trainers, grooms, and attendants in temperatures of 100 plus in the shade. Warrington witnessed Richard Galloway, an expert on period weapons, teaching Jack archery—a talent requiring practice and a steady hand. 'Jack is a skilled archer and was letting the arrows fly through the air to record lengths,' a journalist noted during a location visit.[11] From their very first meeting, Jack struck up a close friendship with Power—known as 'Ty' to friends—who he thought a 'joy to work with'. Affable, and soft-spoken, Power had a reputation of causing female fans to swoon. During the shoot, Jack helped him memorise lines from the play *Mister Roberts* in which Ty was to star at London's Coliseum Theatre the following year. Casting a cloud over the final weeks of filming—literally—was a series of flash floods, resulting in the temporary disappearance of Aubrey, who had driven into the desert just before the storm broke. To make matters worse, Power and Welles were travelling from Meknes, 250 miles away, to join a film unit but were unable to cross the raging flood water. Characteristically, studio publicists ensured this dramatic episode was relayed to journalists in Casablanca for distribution to the wider press:

The French actress and her retinue were trapped by three days of torrential rain in Southern Morocco. During the time they enjoyed native hospitality in a Moroccan village. Tyrone Power and his wife Linda Christian were also stranded. They were found at Toufliat, where they passed the time in a native inn teaching the innkeeper to play bridge.[12]

To keep on schedule, Hathaway put on a rush and filming was extended from 6:30 a.m. to 8 p.m. Not surprisingly, the combination of long hours and bad weather created a miserable experience for Hathaway. In a bout of temper, he had sour words for Aubrey who, he thought, had no qualities nor a 'lick of sense', while he snapped that Jack was too old and the part 'should have been played by someone like Van Johnson'. Moreover, he was especially sickened with Welles who refused to follow direction and was determined to add his own thoughts: 'It pleased him to outwit people. That was the trouble with him throughout his career'.

Though the reception to *The Black Rose* proved dispiriting, by the time he returned to London, Jack was fully focused on a new assignment. That spring, newspapers were filled with articles about new eastern European dictatorships, an idea which gave birth to Sidney Gilliat's thriller *State Secret*, a drama portraying life on 'the other side' of the Iron Curtain.

As the story's pivotal figure, Douglas Fairbanks Jr played a soft-spoken American surgeon who operates on the dictator of a Central European state and was forced to flee for his life after his patient dies. Dressed in a grey Nazi-looking tunic and cap, Jack played his pursuer, the swarthy Colonel Galcon. Such a role suited him—the toughest officer in the country, intimidating his underlings. According to Geoff Brown, biographer of Launder and Gilliat, his intention was to 'condemn totalitarianism in general rather than Communism specifically'.[13] Yet, by making the film intentionally topical, it was interpreted by most as a powerful indictment of the USSR and the system of politics behind the Iron Curtain, where surveillance, intimidation, poverty, and endemic corruption were rife. Filled with ideological dialogue, distrust, and paranoia, the two chief protagonists argue the relative qualities of freedom, progress, and duty. For location shooting, Gilliat transported the entire crew to the Trento and the Dolomites, while indoors were filmed at Isleworth Studios. Gilliat went to great lengths to make Vosnia authentic.

Before filming started in October, Jack was instructed to study the fictitious Vosnian language, specially created by Georgina Shield, a linguist from London University. Drawing on the six real languages she spoke, Shield built up a grammar and a basic vocabulary of 2,000 words. Her masterpiece was the Vosnian national anthem: *Tunisti paesti Vosnia nayt skalve* (Oh happy land where Vosians shall never be slaves). Jack took considerable pride in his ability to learn the language and joked, 'My wife thinks it terrifying. My son speaks a language of his own which I shrewdly suspect is Vosnian, too!'[14]

After filming wrapped in December, the lights went out on the 1940s, a decade which had brought the world to its knees but had seen Jack serve his country, return to the West End, and inch closer to screen stardom. In fact, Bill O'Bryen, from the Korda organisation, which still had Jack under contract, said he was the most useful actor on his books and what he would later describe as a commodity: 'Almost every film that comes up has something for him. I don't mean "types", he is so adaptable and versatile. And he is constantly in demand by other companies for loan-outs. I wish we had more like him'. However, speaking to *Picturegoer*, Jack said he would be terrified at having to 'carry a picture', preferring to stay in supporting roles.

Christmas was celebrated in Chelsea with Dee, Andrew, and Nicholas before Jack embarked on a brief stint playing 'Jacques Breval' at the Piccadilly Theatre in the *Purple Fig Tree*, a new play by George Ralli. Beginning in the spring of 1950, he joined the cast of *The Adventurers* at Pinewood in which he portrayed a man who stumbles upon a fortune in diamonds in the African outback. Dennis Price, playing his famed caddish Englishman, and Gregoire Aslan, a local landlord, completed the ill-assorted quartet setting-off on a dangerous trek to retrieve the diamonds. By November 1950, Korda nudged Jack into a small role in *No Highway in the Sky*, based on Nevil Shute's best-seller, telling the gripping story of an absent-minded scientist convinced that a new plane would crash after it had travelled a certain distance. Though there was not much dialogue, the part offered Jack an opportunity to perform with Hollywood 'A-listers' James Stewart and Marlene Dietrich, as well as British players Glynis Johns, Pete Murray, and Kenneth More, a young actor on the cusp of celebrity.

As it happened, real-life drama spiced up the entire shoot, as Dietrich set everyone's teeth on edge. Fresh out of hospital after an emergency appendectomy, Stewart despised the German's antics of trying to hog the best shots from the other female players, as she struggled to find a footing. 'She was depressed about the part,' director Henry Koster remembered, saying that by this point, Dietrich's fortunes were on a downward slope. 'She didn't feel she had enough exciting or impressive scenes.' Koster, a thoughtful director who had worked with Dietrich in the 1930s, was convinced she only made the film for money. 'Dietrich's problem,' said Stewart's wife, Gloria Hatrick McLean, 'was that she was so much the ageing movie star that she didn't even get the character Jim played to fall in love with her—he fell for the stewardess, who was much younger and prettier.' Jack's attitude toward the script, despite his limited dialogue, was positive and he enjoyed his first movie part without appearing in a wig, period costume, or body armour. During the brief time he spent on location, he became fond enough of Dietrich to describe her work on *No Highway* as a magnificent performance and lauded her knowledge of lighting and camera techniques. He also praised Stewart's portrayal of the scientist as one of 'great brilliance'. The film proved to be a credible thriller, but it remains underrated. 'I thought it was a marvellous story and I had a marvellous script by very fine writers,' Koster said, calling it one of his finest pictures. Indeed, even the notoriously pernickety *Daily Herald* praised, 'a beautifully contrived film.'

A Good Life

At the beginning of 1951, Jack's career was riding high. After finishing the final shots for *No Highway*, he received an invite from theatrical producer Peter Glenville to play Mercutio alongside Olivia de Havilland in *Romeo and Juliet*, a production billed as one of the major events of the Broadway season. Though he had reason to feel apprehensive about the ability of thirty-five-year-old de Havilland given her modicum of stage experience (and her casting as the teenage Juliet), the temptation of New York proved too enticing. On top of that, solid support was promised from reliable veterans, among them Malcolm Keen, James Hayter, and Evelyn Varden, known for his light touch onstage.

For this job, Jack took Dee for her first visit to America and decided to fly rather than take the weeklong ocean voyage. Back then, the air journey took fourteen to seventeen hours but was slowed by refuelling stops at either Shannon in Ireland, Goose Bay, the Azores, or Gander. Dee treasured her memories of that trip—and the Big Apple's glittering sparkle as she embarked on a round of concerts, plays, museums, and fabulous shopping opportunities—a world away from austerity-ridden London. Meanwhile, as he had feared, Jack was gravely frustrated from the moment rehearsals commenced. Writing decades later, de Havilland's biographer Charles Higham asserted the danger signs were apparent from the offset: 'She had become used to the protection of the film studio, where lights could be constantly reorganized to compliment her face now that she was no longer very young; and where her odd shifts of mood, latenesses, procrastinations, and difficulties with lines could be hidden from the press'. Higham believed she also lacked the vibrancy, warmth, and sheer lovingness necessary for the part of Juliet.[1] A further problem was that the popular producer Dwight Deere Wiman died suddenly at the age of fifty-seven during rehearsals, casting a cloud over the production. After tepid out-of-town try-outs in Cleveland, Boston, and Detroit, the play limped into the Broadhurst Theatre on Broadway on 11 March 1951, where reviews were solemn. One, though, did single out Jack for his powerful and deeply poignant performance. 'He is romantic, cynical and bawdy,' wrote William Hawkins in the *New York Telegram and Sun*. 'He dies cursing both the warring houses in a performance which is satisfactory with flashes of distinction.'[2] However, the production was still rife with challenges and the cast began to resent de Havilland's prissy husband, Marcus Goodrich, resorting to any stunt to shield her from press attention, resulting in a dearth of publicity. De Havilland herself even confided to friends that Goodrich had an irritating tendency to appear at rehearsals and either critiqued her or went to the extreme absurdity of asking certain actors to turn their backs to the audience during her big scenes.[3] This professional psychodrama became so severe that on several occasions she claimed to have food poisoning, leading to matinees being cancelled. Perhaps the kindest review came from the *Theatre Arts* magazine: 'Olivia de Havilland is pretty, strives adolescently demure, and reads her lines exceedingly well for one with so little stage experience. Douglas Watson's Romeo is appealing and masculine, while Mercutio, here played by Jack Hawkins, as usual gives the play its most mercurial moments'.[4]

In the upshot, *Romeo and Juliet* folded after forty-nine performances. For de Havilland, failure was a bitter pill to swallow, and she suffered months of illness and depression.

The trip was not a complete dead loss, though, as Dee kept Jack bucked up and engaged in a whirl of activity and took time to renew friendships. The couple enjoyed dinner with Jessica Tandy and daughter Susan at the Algonquin, a popular bolthole for British actors. Despite not having seen each other for nearly a decade, the gathering turned out to be a joyous occasion. By this point, Jess was considered 'Broadway royalty' after appearing as Blanche, alongside a young Marlon Brando in Tennessee Williams's *A Streetcar Named Desire*, one of the most critically acclaimed plays of the twentieth century.

Despite his film-star status and all the trappings that came with it, Jack's life took on an almost suburban routine of being up with the larks for breakfast, followed by a glance at the papers, a hectic drive to drop the boys at school (a duty shared with Doreen), writing letters, reading scripts, occasionally shooting, and retiring early to bed. A well-tailored Savile Row wardrobe and gleaming new Jaguar were just a few of the acquisitions by which he celebrated his success. He also joined the exclusive Garrick Club in the heart of London's West End and became a frequent sight at art sales. He was knowledgeable about antiques and, over time, ploughed some of his growing wealth into purchasing paintings by Delacroix, Cezanne, and

Corot. And, although he looked like a star, he confessed to still having the 'true actors feeling that this present job is the last one. I have the feeling I'm going to be found out, that that man is looking over my shoulder.'[5]

But the work kept coming. Director Edward George More O'Ferrall thought that Jack would be perfect for the role of Group Captain 'Tiger' Small in *Angel's One Five*, a Battle of Britain flick being adapted from Pelham Groom's bestselling book *What Are Your Angels Now?* Well-known for the authenticity of his details, Groom had been sector controller at the famous fighter aerodrome at Biggin Hill during the Battle of Britain and wrote the book when demobbed. Prior to the war, he penned *Whistling Wires*, a thrilling account of an airman's life, chronicling his RAF career back to 1927 when he was granted a short-service commission. After a crash, he was invalided out in 1933, but re-joined three years later.

After meeting producers John W. Gossage and Derek Twist, both RAF veterans, Jack devoured Groom's 112-page draft script in a single afternoon and 'jumped at the chance to return to films in such a story'. 'It was a good part and a good script' portraying the dark summer of 1940 told through the eyes of airmen at an RAF station in Kent. The cryptic title is based on RAF lingo: 'Angels' is a code word used to report aircraft height in thousands of feet, so that 'Angels One Five' means a height of 1,500 feet.

Armed with a £150,000 budget and a two-month shooting schedule, O'Ferrall kicked-off production on 13 April 1951. Jack fell into the role of Small—a tough but fair station commander—alongside Michael Denison as Squadron Leader Peter Moon, Cyril Raymond as an affable flight controller, and a young John Gregson playing Pilot Officer 'Septic' Baird, a loveable but nervous 'rookie'. For added authenticity, Ronald Adam—an elder statesman in the profession—took the role of the group controller. Adam had been a flyer during the First World War, later serving as fighter controller during the Battle of Britain, dispatching fighters to intercept Nazi planes. An RAF Spitfire pilot later remarked that Adam's voice had a 'quality of calm and unhesitating certainty. The contribution of such men to the outcome of the Battle of Britain was incalculable'.[6] When shooting was underway, a visiting journalist observed other cast and crew members were made up of old RAF types and the air was filled with the clipped cries of former pilots talking 'RAF lingo'. Perhaps the best-known attribute of the picture was the use of dramatic expanses of sky and landscapes around Kenley aerodrome in Surrey, one of the busiest wartime fighter stations. Jack could not have been but affected by the enthusiasm of Groom, who turned up on location every morning as a 'special advisor' and even managed to persuade the Portuguese Air Force to provide five aircraft when it was discovered that only two British Hurricanes were flyable.

What emerged was a thrilling and beautiful film, worthy of the great deeds of a great service. However, turbulence struck just before release when a minor flap prompted Jack and Gregson to kick up a fuss after the title of the film was changed to *Hawks in the Sun* on the grounds that *Angels One Five* was not a 'sufficiently commercial title'. Joined by the RAF and other cast members, Jack charged the new name was suggestive of a cheap American Western. After a mini hoo-ha, the title reverted to *Angels One Five* and peace reigned again.

The publicity around the film was extensive and it opened to a standing ovation during 'Battle of Britain Week' in March 1952. Some of the guests at the premiere were in uniform, including RAF hero Douglas Bader, the pilot famed for flying with two artificial legs and shooting down twenty-two Germans; and Urwin Mann, who shot down eight. Former Prime Minister Clement Atlee and his deputy, Herbert Morrison, were there too. A raft of generally enthusiastic reviews gave both Jack and Gregson a well-deserved pat-on-the-back. 'Jack Hawkins, as Group-Captain "Tiger" Small, gives a superb performance in the part of a strict disciplinarian, who is yet a man who understands other men, and has both an abounding sense of justice and an unfailing sense of humour,' was the verdict of the *Truth*'s film critic.[7]

After the British publicity grind, Jack embarked on a brief foray back to theatreland in Christopher Fry's plays, *Thor, with Angels,* written for the Canterbury Festival in 1948, and *A Phoenix Too Frequent* at the Lyric in Hammersmith, alongside Dorothy Tutin, George Cole, Jessie Evans, and Winston Churchill's daughter, Diana, a larger-than-life figure enduring a battle against depression. She played the mournful Ephesian widow, who planned to join her husband despite housing difficulties with the town council, while Jack took the part of Cymer, overlord, and father of a warlike household. After watching a performance in arctic silence, John Gielgud shot off a caustic letter to poet and playwright, Christopher Fry: 'Went to the Hammersmith today—loved *Thor*. Hawkins splendid, Jessie Evans too. But oh dear, Miss Churchill—and Martina (Dorothy Tutin) was a disappointment'.[8]

Despite the odd crease during rehearsals, George Cole—later famed for playing Arthur Daley in *Minder*—remembered a happy production: 'The Lyric was right above Hammersmith tube station and every few minutes the theatre would vibrate a little and you would hear the sound of a train passing underneath. I would hear him (Jack) saying under his breath, "There goes the 9.57". It was hard to keep a straight face. Jack was enormous fun'.[9] The run of *Thor, with Angels,* coincided with production of Korda's *Home at Seven*, an adaptation of a stage thriller, popular at the time. And again, like in *The Fallen Idol*, Jack faced Ralph Richardson as a police officer, but this time in the tale of a man returning home to discover he had suffered a memory lapse and may have committed murder. Leaving his old lavishness behind, the film was notable for intensive pre-production, which, as Jack noted, saw Korda convert West End plays into films 'virtually as they stood', excluding expensive locations and sets—this enabled the picture to be shot in just thirteen days.

The following week, the Hawkinses stole a weekend in Paris before Jack immersed himself in a 'remarkable and moving experience' in the role of Dick Searle, the harassed head teacher at a school for the deaf in Sidney Gilliat's tearjerker *Mandy*, featuring Phyllis Calvert, and seven-year-old Mandy Miller, the girl famed for singing 'Nellie the Elephant'. It was a fateful decision: the film made Jack a major movie star despite being created on a small budget and dealing with the grim plight of disabled children at a time when the subject was hardly discussed. Of all his films, Jack was proudest of *Mandy*, which he called a 'human story', unveiling the fears besetting two young parents when they realised that their only child would never hear—and may never speak. Added tension was caused when the mother and the teacher became attracted to each other. Oddly enough, there was not even a script available when Jack accepted the part. Director Alexander Mackendrick, producer Leslie Norman, and casting director Margaret Harper Nelson were discussing the film with him, and they outlined the whole story. As *Picturegoer* noted, 'and thus he had the advantage of the script's being written when it was already known he would be playing the master.'

'Sidney Gilliat carried the idea in his head for a long time,' Jack explained. 'Then he wrote it, directed it, and did a good job. From the actor's viewpoint, well, you read a script, you either like it or you don't.' As Dick Searle—a passionate, angry man, prone to upsetting his superiors in his quest to secure the best treatment for his pupils—Jack exhibited a warmth which endeared him to audiences for years to come and helped *Mandy* become a critical and box-office success, while also shining a light on a hitherto 'taboo' subject. Even behind the Iron Curtain, the film was praised in the *Berliner Zeitung* which singled out Miller, noting 'it remains almost incomprehensible where this little girl gets her magnetic power.'[10] Jack never forgot being greeted with a standing ovation at the premiere, prompting *Picture Show* and *Film Pictorial*, an influential movie magazine, to take note of his growing fame:

> Six feet one and a half inches tall, Jack has brown hair and eyes. His approach to work is very serious, and he gives a great deal of attention to every fresh role. Underlying Jack's seriousness, where his work is concerned, is a strong sense of humour.

Meanwhile, Jack eased himself back to work by replacing Michael Redgrave in *The Planter's Wife*, an action thriller featuring raven-haired beauty Claudette Colbert, telling the tale of rubber planters fighting native communist bandits during the Malayan Emergency. It was a timely feature given the news was filled with articles about the menace of communism. In America, Julius and Ethel Rosenberg had been convicted of conspiracy to commit espionage and sentenced to death; while, at the same time, the United Nations declared China an aggressor in the ongoing Korean War. Describing his motivation for the project, Jack said: 'We all know very well, and without any disparagement to them, the Americans believe there is only one war at the moment—that in Korea. This picture will show the American public that we are holding our own in a very large territory and carrying on the normal daily life under very great difficulties'.[11] The film, he added, would be widely released in the United States to show Americans what the British were doing in Malaya. As the start date for *The Planter's Wife* approached, he was fitted in khaki and high socks for his role as Jim Frazer, Colbert's husband, a hard-bitten, burly British planter resisting terrorists, and protecting his home with guns and barricades. 'Roles don't get much more satisfying than this,' he told a visiting columnist. 'This kind of epic, with a good story and strong cast is where I belong.' There was agreement among the crew that Colbert—who had mostly retired from movies in favour of television—was inspired casting. She was bagged after the head of Pinewood Studios, Earl St John, despatched director Ken Annakin to Los Angeles to select an American for the female lead. After interviewing Colbert, Joan Crawford, Loretta Young, and Olivia de Havilland, only Colbert was happy to leave the USA for a long shoot and snatch the chance to earn £20,000 in a British film. The rough-and-ready subject suited her perfectly, says Colbert's biographer, Bernard F. Dick: 'Claudette looked very much at home driving along a jungle road, firing a machine gun, and picking off a guerrilla before he got her'.

Jack, too, was thrilled with his leading lady, who he thought a knockout: 'She has such a marvellous sense of humour,' he remembered. 'She also saw the funny side of the tradition in which film love scenes seem invariably to be shot as early as possible in the day! She is a most consummate actress and an intelligent personality—a complete professional who knows every side of the job.'[12] He often told the story of a scene with Colbert at Pinewood when the pair—comfortably seated in bamboo chairs— was having drinks on their veranda, supposedly in the tropical heat of the jungle (surrounded by tamed jungle foliage). However, pretending to be toasty in a bitterly cold studio was not easy. Only when the director noticed they had goosebumps was Jack padded with hot water bottles under his shirt while Claudette climbed into two woollen vests!

Firm support came from Anthony Steel—a good-looking, wavy-haired contract player—as a police inspector and child actor Peter Asher—later, half of 1960s pop duo Peter and Gordon—playing Jack's son, Mike. 'Of course, I remember the scene where a cobra and mongoose fight to the death which created quite a sensation,' Asher laughs, 'and kissing Claudette Colbert who was playing my mother, she was extraordinarily beautiful! But Jack was my dad. He had a kind of moral strength, and his natural expression was one of the most likable things about him as a performer.'

'We all enjoyed it,' says Asher. 'The whole shoot was freezing as we made it in the middle of winter. As a child actor the one thing you really don't like is when people treat you like a child. Jack and Ken Annakin weren't like that. Jack played the scenes with me as he would with any other actor. Ken—who I got on very well with—was the same. He would speak to me about scenes in a very clear way.'

When shooting wrapped, Jack made a valiant effort to promote *The Planter's Wife*, which emerged as a picture of epic proportions. He had lived the role of Jim Frazer, into which he put all the pain of his predicament. Within a week, the film shot to the top of box office programmes, and eventually became the sixth most popular movie in Britain that year. 'Hawkins has a role tailor made for his brand of sturdy craftsmanship, his mature, satisfying style,' the *Londonderry Sentinel* wrote ecstatically. 'It is the role of his life, and as the film will have a general release in America, the producers are confident that it will make him a star on both sides of the Atlantic.' However, not everyone thought the picture praiseworthy. A critic from the *Daily Worker*, a paper sympathetic to the communist cause, was sniffy about 'the most viciously dishonest war propaganda picture yet made in Britain.' That fulmination, apparently, pleased Jack enormously.

10

The Call of the Sea

This is a story of the Battle of the Atlantic, the story of an ocean, two ships, and a handful of men. The men are the heroes; the heroines are the ships. The only villain is the sea, the cruel sea, that man has made more cruel...

After *Mandy* and *The Planter's Wife*, Jack had an unbroken skein of successful films, and his value increased progressively. With his popularity at its peak, he was even asked to model for Madame Tussauds. The *Picture Show* feature was published as interesting things were happening in British cinema. With so many ex-servicemen sharing tales of wartime glories to their young families, the film industry found its own way to respond, aided by a new cycle of post-war novels, including *The Wooden Horse*, *The Colditz Story*, and *Albert R.N.*, all snapped up for cinematic treatment. Likewise, Nicholas Monserrat's book *The Cruel Sea* became an immediate bestseller, moving more than 30,000 copies in a week during 1951. His brutal examination of the wartime horrors faced by sailors touched on powerful themes such as death, fidelity, and friendship and would become the vehicle for Jack's finest cinematic performance. It was not a mere fluke that Charles Frend, a producer known for *Scott of the Antarctic* and the wartime documentary *San Demetrio London*, persuaded Ealing to buy the rights. Frend had already envisioned Jack as Lieutenant Commander George Ericson, a sailor haunted by the loss of his past vessel at the cost of many hands. 'From the outset I had the feeling it would either be a complete flop or a very great success,' Jack reminisced. 'But either way it would never be mediocre.' In looks, he was perfect for Ericson—haggard, burly, but still in shape. Professionally, good fortune also struck Donald Sinden, an unknown actor cast as the second lead, who approached the project with characteristic zeal. 'It was remarkable for me, really,' Sinden recalled. 'I was just 30, I think, and literally plucked from obscurity and cast as Lockhart alongside Jack Hawkins. I remember my wife thought I was pulling her leg when I told her the role was mine!'[1] Sinden, making only his third film, bonded instantly with Jack. 'I was completely thrown by him. Very distinguished, an absolute rock, no pretension, no front … just a bloody nice bloke.' Solid support came from Denholm Elliott, Stanley Baker, Liam Redmond, and twenty-one-year-old Virginia McKenna, adding sophistication and sensuality in her film debut. 'For me, acting in *The Cruel Sea* was an amazing and unexpected piece of good fortune,' McKenna told the author. 'The part of Julie Hallam was small but important—most of my scenes were with Donald Sinden. I met Jack in the studio, he was the nicest, kindest, and most "unstarry" of people, and as courageous in real life as in the characters he played. The subtle way in which he expressed emotions, such understatement.' That understatement was crafted by Eric Ambler who managed to compact Nicholas Monsarrat's 500-page novel into a script crystallising the book's significant action and words (but omitted some of the novel's grimmest moments).

Studio archives reveal that complications arose when *The Cruel Sea* and *The Titfield Thunderbolt,* a comic yarn, began location shooting at Devonport and Bath respectively, leaving studio boss Michael Balcon juggling two productions simultaneously. While the *Thunderbolt* unit prayed for sunshine, *The Cruel Sea* team sought stormy weather. Balcon spent much time on the set and on location and managed to secure co-operation from the Admiralty on the condition that shooting did not interfere with the navy's work. There was nothing simplistic about producing *The Cruel Sea*, which opens in 1939, when HMS *Compass Rose*, a corvette escort ship, set out to the Atlantic to protect Allied convoys against Nazi U-boat attacks. Of her officers, her captain, Lieutenant-Commander Ericson (Jack), was the only professional sailor. The others were civilians turned wartime sailors—men like Sub-Lt Morell (Elliott), a lawyer, and Lt Bennett (Baker), a former car salesman, whose harsh and accusatory bullying made him universally unpopular. 'I was in America. And when I read the book, I was determined that I wanted to play that part,' Baker recounted. 'It wasn't the star part in the film, but to me it was the best part. It was the flashiest part; it was the easiest.'[2] As the action moves on, the *Compass Rose* is torpedoed, men are lost, but a few survive. Interwoven with this were close-ups, used frequently, showing corpses bobbing in the ocean, the chaos when the ship began to list and the harrowing ordeal of sailors clinging to a raft. Later in the story, a poignant scene shows Jack ordering depth charges to be dropped, although it meant slaughtering British survivors of another ship swimming towards him, seeking salvation. The compelling sequence invokes one of his own men to scream: 'Bloody murderer!' It was galvanising cinema showing Ericson living in turmoil, trapped in reflection and regret. At one point, as the camera frames him against a backdrop of the dark ocean, he shed a tear. Remarkably, this wonder was nearly spoiled by Balcon, who, reckoning men did not cry, wanted it cut. This is a tale that grew in the telling, but it seems that a few months after putting the kibosh on the teary moment, Martin Rackin, head of Paramount production demanded, 'The shot with Jack Hawkins crying stays in the picture … it has balls!' The point was well made, the tears represented emotional vulnerability as an integral element of George Ericson's identity. Grudgingly, Balcon agreed. *The Cruel Sea* would be a film of stunning, yet primitive, visual effects. Donald Sinden—who was perpetually astonished by the movie's success—remembered the frigate scenes set during arctic blizzards were created by caking the corvette in white plaster. They used snow and ice made out of bandages, and rock salt 'and it looked very effective'. Sinden also suffered from negative buoyancy, meaning he could not float or swim, a condition, he recalled, that led to a close call in the open-air water tank at Denham studios: 'The night was cold, and the cast and crew shivered as we waited for the "sea" to become rough enough'. Then, with the call of 'action', Sinden jumped from the side of the tank expecting to land in a puddle of water, but it was much deeper: 'Down I went … all the others arrived safely at the bank and thank God, Jack heard someone ask, "Where's Donald?" Jack Hawkins—bless his heart—dived in, came over and rescued me and took me to the bank. But for him, I wouldn't be here today'.

Realising that Ericson was perhaps his most enduring movie role, Jack was willing to do whatever it took to make *The Cruel Sea* look as credible as possible. 'All the rescue scenes,' he explained, 'we did at night, and they chose October for them.'[3] 'When I look back at the long hours we spent at sea, it seems that for a time I was no longer an actor, but a sailor,' he told the *New York World Telegram and Sun*. 'The actor who goes into films must expect to put up with just as many hardships as the character he portrays.' He explained how endless days were spent on the ship at Portland in Dorset retaking shots spoiled by pleasure boats sailing past. Brian Halliday, who played a member of the ship's crew, remembered, 'one of the fringe benefits was that we all got fresh fish' when depth charges were set just below the surface of the water, bringing blasted but edible fish up with them.[4]

Never one to miss an opportunity, Jack turned his attention to more familiar pursuits during breaks in shooting. Mainly by trial and error, he had taught himself angling and amassed plenty of gear, including waders, nets, tackle boxes, rods, hooks, and reels. 'Like most anglers, I started my fishing with a hand-line on the pier,' he recounted. 'It takes a lot of skill to guide your line away from the razor-sharp barnacles on the pier supports.' By this point, though, he had graduated into all four branches of sea angling—shore fishing from the beach, shore fishing from piers and jetties, fishing from small inshore boats, and deep fishing from large powerboats. 'Beach fishing is a tough sport,' he explained:

At weekends on the east coast when the cod are running, parties fish regardless of the weather. When the tide is late at night, you sometime see them casting their lines in falling snow. The beach fisher looks forward to rough weather because it brings the fish close inshore to feed. To me, deep sea fishing is best of all. You see the dirty inshore waters give way to the clear blue of the open sea. You stagger the rising swell with the taste of salt on your lips and watch the spray breaking back from the bows of a stout boat. If you're lucky, you hear the flopping tales of fish beating the deck or feel the sudden snatch of a large Pollock curve the rod into a dancing arc. This is angling's big thrill.[5]

Jack was quick to introduce Nicholas to the joys of fishing and at the age of six, he caught his first 3-lb Pollack before the lens of Russell Westwood, a photographer for *Illustrated* magazine. The caption reads: 'Nicholas strains on the rod as the Pollack snatches the bait just below the surface. Jack lends a hand. What a catch! Nicholas grasps the Pollack's tail. It is the proudest moment of his six months angling'.

When *The Cruel Sea* wrapped, Nicholas Montsarrat thought Jack's performance came closer to Ericson's character than the original conception of him: the underplaying, the dependability, the emotionally stable exterior.[6] Ericson's last line in the film, spoken as he winds down operations on the *Compass Rose*, became a warmly remembered cinematic moment. 'Finished with main engines!' he proclaims after the vessel docks for the last time. Alan Rawsthorne's score swells above a naval whistle to a final, stirring crescendo as the camera pans across the sea. A poignant moment beautifully realised on film.

The New York Times thought 'Mr Hawkins' projected with conviction and polish, 'the picture of a man ready to accept the staggering burden of command. He is, to the credit of the script and direction, a man with human frailties who almost cracks under the strain but is made of stern enough stuff to finish the job.'[7]

Michael Balcon considered it his greatest Ealing achievement 'because when we saw that for the first time, we realised that we really had brought it off. It seemed to just gel and be absolutely right. Sometimes you don't get that feeling, but with that one we all did.' Desmond Carrington remembered Ealing got more advance publicity on *The Cruel Sea* than on any prior feature. Then hosting a film review show on Radio Luxembourg, Carrington never forgot the 'tremendous anticipation, from former servicemen. And they weren't left disappointed.'[8] Interestingly, even before it appeared in cinemas, *The Cruel Sea* became a sort of passport to future assignments for the people that appeared in it. Donald Sinden was offered a rank contract, Virginia McKenna found a role on the London stage, Stanley Baker joined the cast of *The Red Beret* (with Alan Ladd), and Denholm Elliott filmed *Heart of the Matter*. 'Even our small part players seem to be more in demand since their *Cruel Sea* work,' said the assistant director.[9]

Though the Leicester Square premiere was dampened by Queen Mary's death, causing the duke of Edinburgh to skip the event, Carrington thought it resembled a 'Hollywood gala' and opened the floodgates to a string of gushing reviews. 'It is one of the finest films ever to grace the screen,' the anonymous critic of the *Dundee Courier* reported. 'I was prepared to view just another synthetic naval story, but none of the scenes gives the impression of artificiality. It will live in my memory. Special praise must go to Jack Hawkins in a role which suits him admirably.'[10]

Another critic called it harrowing, terrifying, yet inspiring: 'It is a brilliant, starkly factual British war film and does the nation proud and will impress the world. It is the finest film ever to come from Ealing Studios'.[11] In fact, as Carrington correctly recalled, it pleased virtually everyone and became the most successful picture at the British box office that year: 'We weren't surprised about that at all, it was, I think, as close to perfection as you could get. And don't forget the contribution of Stanley Baker as the sour officer and a dashing Denholm Elliott'. In his memoirs, Montserrat related 'one other curious tailpiece to this comet-ride across the film world' when the The Nag's Head pub in Hampstead was renamed The Cruel Sea, 'and Jack Hawkins and I went up to open it'. This was one of many boozy encounters. Montserrat remembered if Jack was talking business, he always sipped a cheerful gin and tonic, if out with friends, he had a taste for 'black velvet' (half-and-half champagne and stout). *The Cruel Sea* effectively ushered in the age of the big-budget naval spectacular, resulting in *Above Us the Waves*, *The Caine Mutiny*, *Run Silent, Run Deep*, *The Battle of the River Plate*, and *The Silent Enemy*.

'*The Cruel Sea* was tremendously important to Jack,' says Barry MacGregor who featured in a radio adaptation of the story. 'Prestigious war dramas emerged as his forte. Like the film, Jack put a great deal of effort into *The Cruel Sea* broadcast, and it went very well, without a hitch ... he was a sharing actor, which means a lot.' Expanding, MacGregor added:

There are some actors who work with you who are total shits—they just work on their own and you happen to be there in the scene with them.

And then you get the actor that listens to you. I would put Jack on the same level as Paul Schofield. I remember the first reading of Lear which Peter Brook was directing in the RSC which I was in with Schofield. Every time he asked a question as King Lear in the play to a character, he would put the script down and look very hard at the reply which was a wonderful sharing thing because it made you realize he wanted to know about you, and to me Jack Hawkins was that kind of actor. When we were working together in rehearsals, Jack was listening to you. He was part of it, and it was a joy to work with someone like that.

As MacGregor intimated, Jack often opined that some thespians made the mistake of thinking only of their own parts. 'I have found from experience that it's best to read a script as a whole rather than think of any part in it,' he once explained. 'One particular character may seem to be outstanding, but one good part doesn't make a good film. The story itself is the most important thing.'[12]

With *The Cruel Sea* in the past, Jack and Dee threw themselves into preparations for a month-long vacation with David and Hjördis Niven in Switzerland at an Alpine retreat for what they anticipated would be a joyful holiday. However, while they continued to enjoy Niven's playfulness and war chest of anecdotes, they were dismayed how much Hjördis had changed since Jack spotted her on the set of *Bonnie Prince Charlie* six years earlier. The cooing lovebirds had wearied of married life, and she developed a reputation as a disagreeable drunk that frequently belittled her husband, creating a strained, uncomfortable atmosphere. Typically, Niven was conciliatory to her moods and whims, his genial nature hid any emotional strain. 'I don't know why David puts up with it,' Jack confided in a dispirited tone to Dee. 'She's insufferable.' How, they wondered, did it come to this? The long dark Swiss evenings took on a familiar patten: dinner was served, and then as everyone proceeded to get tipsy, Hjördis got smashed. Unsurprisingly, accounts of her *louche* lifestyle and behaviour—fuelled by long pulls from bottles of Fernet Branca, bourbon, and vodka—were invariably unflattering. In the legend that grew up around Hjördis, Roger Moore once described his disgust at seeing liquor dribbling down her chin and listening to her endless yammering: 'She never sobered up'. Another friend remembered her car rolling up to Niven's funeral in 1983 and she came tumbling out 'wig askew and pissed'. And although time did not make her any drier or endearing, Jack's love for David ensured he remained a frequent visitor to the Swiss Alps.

Several long summers were also spent in Fregenae, north of Rome's historic centre. 'As far as I'm concerned the Romans are the luckiest people on earth,' Jack explained. 'I can't describe Fregene [*sic*]. There is, I suppose, only one word for it—beautiful. You never have to worry about the children. All the days are fine, and they can play outdoors from dawn till dusk.' From the mid-1950s, family vacation weeks in late July and August were sacrosanct.

He was still in good spirits back in Britain where life was rendered still fuller by a large assortment of friends. There were evenings of laughter and song with Kenneth More, the curmudgeonish Rex Harrison, and old pals from ENSA and the West End. Such occasions could be riotous affairs. At one dinner, Carol Reed, a notorious hypochondriac, complained about his fear of having a kidney stone removed. In an attempt to ease his nerves, Kenneth More—who had undergone the same operation—assured the whole process was painless and proceeded to open his shirt. 'I was so used to this scar that I failed to realise the effect it would have on a man as sensitive to matters of health as Carol,' More recalled. 'For a second, Carol stared at this livid weal that looked like a grinning tiger—and then he damn near fainted in his chair!' Lauren Bacall remembered both Jack and More did a certain amount of drinking together and occasionally got carried away with the *joie de vivre* 'but in a good way.... The Mores and Jack and Doreen Hawkins became close chums.' Indeed, Dee remembered: 'After Bogey died, I saw more of Betty [Bacall] and we became closer. We recognized a personal affinity which is always there with a true friendship as in any close relationship'. Elizabeth Rees-Williams, one-time wife of both Rex Harrison and Richard Harris, was another close friend. She never forgot Dee's legendary hospitality. 'Not a lot of people like tripe but everyone liked Doreen's,' she laughs. 'Her cooking was sublime. We would be served tripe and talk tripe.' Rees-Williams reminisced how Doreen knew how to comport herself in any situation and put people at ease (Jack once described Dee as 'the perfect actor's wife'). 'Doreen was extremely charming,' says former politician Jonathan Aitken, also a friend in later life. 'I don't think I ever saw her without a smile. She had a how-do-you-do for everyone.' Not just that, Dee took control of the household finances and supported the National Women Citizens' Association's call for wives to have a wage. 'Of course, a wife should have wages, and the more the better,' she said. 'Men aren't to be trusted with money. They always think that prices remain the same. It is only when you send them shopping occasionally that they realise costs have gone up. Then they get all upset. I budget better than Jack—and that is saying very little. Of course, Jack pays the big bills.'

She even went as far as saying a wage for a wife gave her independence and saved her from the 'recurring indignity' of asking her husband for money:

> It is well for a wife to agree with her husband on a regular allowance, however small the amount. That saves her the indignity of having to ask for money in dribs and drabs and gives her the opportunity to save up for big occasions. Of course, if a wife has a fixed allowance, the husband will always borrow from her. Jack hardly ever borrows. I will say that for him. When he does, I often get it back. I will say that for me. I stand out for definite weekly allowance, and I think all other wives should do the same. Women are better at budgeting than men. Men are such fools about money. It is the niggling weekly accounts which need the feminine flair. Men Just don't know how things have gone up. They may be able to take care of the pounds, but the darlings just can't take care of the pence.[13]

As it happened, large chunks of Dee's housekeeping kitty were used to prepare her prized homemade dinners for journalists. At one such gathering, Jack told *Picturegoer* that 'luck' was the key to his sudden success:

> I have had very little competition in the particular roles for which I have been most suited. The truth of the matter is that this success or whatever you like to call it has been brought about largely by my walking into several pictures that have happened to possess good scripts. The films have been popular for that reason, and I have had the benefit of this popularity.[14]

One sure sign of his burgeoning celebrity came when he joined the ranks of illustrious castaways on radio's *Desert Island Discs*, where a well-known person is asked: 'If you were to be cast away alone on a desert island, which eight gramophone records would you choose to have with you?' At 12:30 p.m. on 25 April 1953, he breezed into studio B2 at the BBC's Broadcasting House to record his only appearance as the 185th guest. Back then, host Roy Plomley preferred highly scripted joshing as opposed to the semi-serious interview format used nowadays. Although no recording survives, a script does—complete with annotations pencilled in by Jack and Plomley—showing a seemingly congenial exercise. 'In a practical sense, I think I'd make out quite well,' Jack said, when asked what sort of castaway he would be. 'I'm fond of fishing and I'd be quite happy to live on fish.' He described himself as a 'moderate' cook, 'I'm not quite sure how I'd light the fire. There would be a lot of trial and error about it, and even more cursing.'

Jack explained how he thoroughly enjoyed music, but only if it had the quality of permanency. 'It's no good buying a record that you're going to take home and play only two or three times,' he mused:

One thing I am certain, though, this desirable quality of permanency is more frequently found in what is mistakenly called serious music, than it is in what is mistakenly called light music. Anyway, the fact that there is no jazz among my selection is not due to the fact that I don't like it—I do—but I suspect that it is not good value for money. Music means a lot to me—I am passionately fond of it in almost any form—but my music is chosen for what it can give me in the way of beauty and solace, rather than to act as background music to desert island musings about my past life.

Asked how he would survive the loneliness of a desert island, he remarked, 'I did toy with the idea of taking a sound-effects record of a babble of voices talking in a pub—then I rejected it as a probable waste of a record. I certainly would want a record of the most beautiful voice I know and that is Isobel Baillie. I'd be very happy with any record of hers. I think my favourite is "Hark! the echoing air" from *The Fairy Queen.*'

From here, Jack's activity was scaled back for the summer. After a brief holiday navigating French waterways, he returned to London for Queen Elizabeth's Coronation Ball at the Albert Hall, an event filled with picturesque pomp, before embarking on Ivan Foxwell's production of *The Intruder* at Shepperton. Based on the novel *Line on Ginger* by Robin Maugham, the intruder is a young armed thug who is caught burgling the home of Wolf Merton, a prosperous stockbroker who was once the colonel of a tank regiment. The ex-colonel (Jack) recognises the intruder as Ginger (Medwin) one of the most courageous troopers under his command in the Western Desert. Merton, trying to get the reason for Ginger's downfall is sympathetic with him but Ginger, believing that Merton has telephoned the police, makes his getaway. Appalled at how casually he has lost track of the men who served under him during the war, Merton takes it upon himself to find Ginger and put him back on the right road again.

The role helped firmly establish Jack as the embodiment of the British fighting man in uniform and spawned the joke: 'Wind up the Jack Hawkins doll and he will salute'. Indeed, in a restless world, his rugged on-screen persona made him appear as steady as a rock, the sort of man you know you could always rely on. Dee, too, revealed most people she met thought her husband tough, most at home in heroic roles. 'People sometimes ask me if cruelty and toughness are a pre-dominant part of his make up,' she explained. 'Of course, that isn't so. Jack is, above all, an actor. But in his private life I don't think he's like the stubborn, stiff upper-lip type at all. He's really a very gentle person.' Although he was rugged and strong, Dee said 'he was a tower of family strength ... and his devotion to the children was well expressed.'[15] There is little doubt Dee's attention was always focused on Jack: what he said, how he looked, how fans reacted to him. She was entirely dedicated to his support. Aware of the effect his military roles were having, he often lampooned himself during interviews. 'Every time a Navy, Army or Air Force part comes up, they throw it at me, there's nothing left now but the Woman's Services. But although I appear to have acquired the reputation of being able to make better love to a battleship than to a woman,' he joked, 'I've played fewer Service types than Trevor Howard.'[16] Reporter Alan Dick acknowledged that while Howard could knock-back five fingers of whiskey without gagging or watery eyes, Jack was handsome 'in the ugly way what women like and men forgive, hefty without looking too well fed, with laughter in his eyes and life in his hair, and a voice like a dinner gong.' Jack liked a chinwag at the local, Dick noted, but did not drink too much and 'doesn't bore you about the dear little woman and what the youngest said yesterday. His greatest delight is talking with his friends—he is a born mimic, but never uses the gift viciously.'[17]

Jack and Dee had the opportunity to take a brief holiday in France before work started on *Malta Story*, a war epic reflecting the bitter days of the island's siege and later triumph. Back in uniform, he was cast as Vice-Marshal Frank—an officer beset by all the headaches of a man trying to maintain Malta's defence against enemy attack.

Billeted at the Phoenicia Hotel in Valletta with Alec Guinness, who had the important role of an RAF reconnaissance pilot, the crew prepared for a seven-week shoot. Soon after, they were joined by Muriel Pavlow, the romantic interest, and Anthony Steel, playing a dashing Spitfire ace. Shortly after filming began, the problems started. A rapid rebuilding programme made it difficult to find locations typical of the battered Malta of 1942 and, on top of that, another snag was finding enough locals for crowd scenes who could be persuaded to wear their oldest clothes and look hungry, tense, and frightened. Like on *The Black Rose*, the shoot suffered from a lack of water. 'When we arrived, prayers were being offered for rain,' a cast member recounted. 'I intervened with prayers to a couple of Irish saints—and we've had good weather throughout!' The British Forces on Malta joined in the production with great gusto. Jobs for the army included the installation and firing of AA guns and the 'bombing' of Valetta, and the laying of charges for a spectacular 'attack' on the Siri airfield. For that sequence, art director John Howell scoured Malta for the remains of Spitfires destroyed in the German onslaught a decade earlier and had them carted to the airstrip to add to the scene of devastation.

However, just three weeks into shooting, events were further hampered by locals complaining that certain shots—for instance an old woman picking for food in a dustbin—were not true. The reaction perplexed Jack and annoyed Guinness. Filled with disquiet, Guinness even made a statement to the effect that the crew were trying to convey a faithful impression of the ordeal and heroism of Malta during the war, 'although we will probably end up by displeasing not only the Maltese, but the Navy and Army and everyone in Malta.' Guinness knew the island having served in the Royal Navy in 1941 after becoming commander of a vessel which was frequently in and out of Valetta. On one occasion, he was even brought to the island as a survivor after his ship had been wrecked by gales in the Adriatic.

As things turned out, Jack found the experience an ordeal. Wherever he went he was trailed by a horde of kids, regular citizens, and a photographer from *The Times of Malta*. Evenings at the Royal Navy's officers' mess perched over Valetta harbour afforded some respite. It was there, during an evening of excessive smoking and drinking, that Anthony Steel, a bulwark of virility, told reporters he was making a valiant effort to create a screen lover. 'In all my pictures so far, I've either been the other man, the solid reliable friend of the family, or already married when the story begins—this doesn't give a chap much chance to be romantic,' he enthused. 'In this picture—which is more than just a war story—I fall in love with an English girl during the siege. It is a passionate romance—and believe me, I intend to play it for all its worth.'

Instinctively, Jack knew he had turned in a good performance before he shook the dust off his shoes and returned to London to play John Grant, a rugged all-knowing news editor in *Front Page Story*, a weak yarn filled with staccato dialogue about eleven hours in the life of a London daily (that had lost its bite). 'It's quite a switch for me. In a way I feel like I'd just been demobbed,' Jack explained. 'Not that I didn't get a kick out of being in uniform film after film. It's just that everybody needs a change.'[18] However, real Fleet Street reporters disliked the scenario and viewed his portrayal of an editor as a bully, driving his staff for the sake of circulation. The *Daily Herald* had minimal regard for the work and even ran a feature under the headline: 'Fleet Street is never like this', in which Paul Holt observed the reaction of critics to Jack's performance:

They saw him choosing a young neurotic to report a murder trial at the Old Bailey and picking an old drunk to get the story of an atomic scientist slipping secrets to another Power. Such things a good news editor would never do. For his job depends on giving the right man the right job to do. This poor news editor loses his wife because he hasn't time to take her out to lunch and he breaks into tears because some slum orphans have lost their mother. And he delivers a homily to a whole room of reporters on the ethics of the newspaper business. The critics' faces, as they left the cinema, were grave and puzzled, for such things do not happen in Fleet Street.

Bad reviews notwithstanding, *Front Page Story* failed to sizzle at the box office.

Meanwhile, Jack's domestic life was set to undergo a transformation. After thoughts of putting down roots away from urban pressures filled his mind, a search for a suitable property ensued. As luck would have it, the hunt ended after Dee chanced upon a dream home on Dover Park Drive in suburban Roehampton, which, back then, twinkled with village charm— the local pub, store, butcher, and bank were all were picture postcard perfect.

Fronting on a 2.5-mile common—and just sixteen minutes by car from Piccadilly Circus—the property came cheaply after Jack complained the house was in depressingly bad repair: 'it was filthy, full of broken, glass and peeling plaster'. With the help of a £5,000 mortgage, the deal was sealed. Named 'Westmead Lodge', the property was placed well back from the lane, hidden behind trees and hedges, shielded from the public. 'It gives me the security I need,' Jack said after moving in. 'It is absolutely necessary to know where my roots are. And I tend to feel insecure about my work— all actors do— and I now think it is necessary to keep on one's toes.'[19] As they unpacked, Dee busied herself filling the wall spaces with family portraits painted by Hein Heckroth, the German-born designer famed for such pictures as *Red Shoes* and *Gilbert and Sullivan*. In the living room, Jack's display of porcelain would have done credit to any small museum. As an astute collector, he owned an extremely eclectic selection including the only genuine figurine of Queen Victoria as a young girl. 'It is my most valuable piece—the Victoria and Albert is always trying to get her away from me!' he boasted. Journalist Anne Leslie thought Westmead was the sort of home a retired general would plump for: 'It is near cozy and convenient Putney. It is rambling and English and full of chintz and fresh flowers and honey-coloured carpets. It is as comfortable, comforting and "square" as carpet slippers'. When his batteries were running down, Jack tended the garden—watched over by a fat black cat named Suzy. 'I get a lot of happiness from being possibly the worst gardener in the country,' he joked. 'I always hoe at the wrong time and in the wrong place. But I get a thrill when the few beans I have planted come up with that tremendous growth.'[20]

The Hawkinses, Leslie reflected, seemed constantly prepared for visitors and laid out nuts and biscuits in cut-glass bowls, 'whorls of cigarettes are propped into wine glasses, and a loaded and glittering drinks tray is waiting at the ready.'[21] Roehampton was a parish community, and it did not take long for the Hawkinses to settle, as Jack revealed to *Picturegoer*:

Where I live, I'm next door to a peer of the realm. The Home Office pathologist is on the other side of me, across the street, a pickle manufacturer. I don't suppose there's another actor living within miles of me. When I go out in my village, Roehampton, the locals say hallo and 'I liked your picture,' or 'I didn't like your picture,' but there's no asking for autographs or any of that rot. I'm just one of them.[22]

However, Dee ensured—without bragging—that Westmead received its fair share of press attention. It became the focus of a syndicated puff-piece titled, 'Home hunt for the Hawkins', illustrated with colour photos, including one of Jack leaning against a magnificent white stone fireplace. Over six-glossy pages, the report highlighted the dining room, described as 'severely beautiful with a bare parquet floor, lustrous mahogany furniture and gleaming silver candelabras'. Readers were whisked on a tour of the property, through a spacious lounge that swept right through the house from front to back.

A wide bay window at the front looks on to an old English rose garden. At the other end of the room, floor to ceiling windows take up the entire width and can be folded back to give access to the flagged terrace. The walls of the lounge are spruce green—a colour that seems to emphasise the gleaming richness of mahogany and gives full value to the warm crimson of the Knowle settee and matching armchair.

For the main bedroom, a pretty feminine room, Mrs. Hawkins chose pale walls and a pine green carpet. Mirror-faced doors and mahogany furniture are the perfect foil for pink posy-splashed bedcovers, curtains, and dressing-table petticoat. One of the friendliest rooms in the house is the nursery. It is cheerful, comfortable, and well-furnished. The boys are very proud of the tapestry rug with its colourful design of a clown. It is Jack's own handiwork, made a few years ago before he became the busiest star in British films. One eye-catching piece of furniture is a 'whispering sofa' which Mrs. Hawkins discovered in a dark corner of an old village shop and bought for the surprisingly small sum of £3.

In the midst of all this promotion, Dee's enthusiasm for showing off Westmead dampened when burglars targeted the property on two separate occasions. During the first break-in, crooks helped themselves to jewellery and a large silver cigarette box with the inscription: 'To Jack Hawkins from Basil Dean, 1928'. Then, for the second time in four months, a thief used a ladder to reach an upstairs window and ransack the front bedroom. Other than smashing up Jack's make-up kit, there was little damage. 'But there was nothing very valuable for them to take,' Jack's secretary told the press. 'They cleaned us out last time.' Unsurprisingly, the police thought it probable that the endless publicity mongering alerted burglars to the possibility of rich pickings. After that, Westmead never appeared in a glossy again.

It was at this time, when battling the stereotype of characters in uniform, that Jack undertook one of the most difficult acting parts of his career in *The Public Prosecutor*, staged as part of the BBC TV's *Sunday Night Theatre* series in October 1953. The BBC paid £800 for the broadcast rights, and Jack involved himself in the development process to a remarkable degree. 'It's a tremendously long role,' he explained, saying it was a meaty counterpoint to much of the 'light entertainment' seen on television.[23] 'And,' he added, 'it's almost the length of *Hamlet*.' Jack himself suggested the play, a dramatic thriller set in the time of 'The Terror' in France in 1794. A translated copy had been sent to him by its Swiss author, Fritz Hockwaelder, a couple of years earlier. Impressed, he earmarked it as a possible theatre production when he could find time to do it. 'I still hope to do it on the stage,' he told journalist Dai Pole.

While working on *The Public Prosecutor*, Jack's agent Albert Parker had been engineering his client's quiet separation from obligations to Alexander Korda with a move to the Rank Organisation—marking the beginning of an entirely new phase of his career and fame. The deal for six pictures over three years was helped along by his long-time friend Bill O'Bryen, a former Gainsborough publicist (and husband of Elizabeth Allan). He could have continued indefinitely with Korda, but if he stayed there would have been nothing for him except more of the same, namely loan outs to other producers and secondary roles. And though Korda was hit hard by his sudden departure, it was a graceful exit. 'Dear Jack, good luck,' he said. 'I am the man who had a golden sovereign in his pocket but did not know it.' As journalist John K. Newnham observed, the amicable parting was typical of Jack: 'It is uncommonly difficult to find anyone who will tell a single story against Hawkins. You come up against the same attitude everywhere. He's the one star I have ever come across who doesn't seem to have a single enemy in the whole show world'. Newnham claimed to have a strong suspicion that Jack's innate pleasantness might have accounted, to some extent, for the slowness of his screen career. 'The film business is a tough one,' he opined, 'Metaphorically speaking, you've often got to cut the other man's throat in order to make progress yourself. But all his life, Hawkins has been of the live-and-let-live school.'[24]

However, the Rank contract brought its own burdens and took almost a year of long, drawn-out negotiation. Parker, the husband of actress Margaret Johnson, successfully demanded his client should always have first star billing and 'top line' public relations. Like many London agents, Parker cultivated an image of sureness, and became recognized as one of the most influential people in showbusiness, even though he was virtually unknown to the public. He spent several days each month with Jack to discuss projects and engaged a part-time assistant at Roehampton to answer 'innumerable telephone calls and deal with his enormous fan mail'. When finally rubber-stamped, the contract came complete with a 'princely salary' reflecting Rank's position in the entertainment world. 'I get £20,000 a year from the Rank Organisation for two pictures,' Jack divulged, before sourly adding that taxation made it 'impossible to save … outside your family circle you're in a rat race and I'm quite aware of it.'[25] The tax narrative—delivered to every reporter he met—would continue for the rest of his life. From here on, Jack's base was at Pinewood in Iver Heath in Buckinghamshire, a survivor of the old Hollywood-style fully serviced studios. Based at the old Heatherden Hall estate, he found the idyllic country setting, carefully designed to remove all obstacles to creativity, the perfect workplace. The studios boasted four big stages and occupied a beautiful estate of 50 acres—large enough to provide outdoor settings.

However, unlike the relaxed atmosphere under Korda, he quickly discovered that life at Rank could be extremely tiring. The company PR machine—driven by Theo Cowan, a plummy-voiced former Royal Artillery colonel who was once described by *The Stage* as 'the greatest showbusiness publicist of his generation'—ensured Jack's name was kept in the media. Known as 'Beau Nosh' given his enormous appetite, Cowan generated the ballyhoo of positive headlines by sending stars out to promote films at dancehalls, cinemas, and holiday camps. Terence Morgan's widow, Georgina, related how on one such occasion after trotting up and down Britain cutting ribbons, Dirk Bogarde was introduced at a PR event as 'this up-and-coming young star' prompting him to spring onto the stage and announce, 'Well I'm up and I've come.' Though Jack's appearances were more measured affairs, Dee was often roped into Rank gala film premieres, usually in Leicester Square, which all spouses and contract players had to attend. Studio etiquette demanded she wore long white gloves and beamed as exploding flashbulbs lit the red carpet. Dee was a natural; she had rhythm, posture, and a glowing smile. She never missed the annual garden party at Rank to which absolutely everyone was invited to watch glamorous young stars waddle around in snazzy dresses for the newsreels. Reminiscing about what fun he had had at the Venice Film Festival, Donald Sinden remembered being with Jack, John Gregson, and James Robertson Justice where 'we really made the best showing of all the national contingents. We arrived in a turbo-prop Viscount airliner—and then a fleet of motor launches all flying the Union Jack took us, in perfect formation, across that fabulous lagoon. It was a beautiful piece of stage management. Everyone who saw it was impressed.'[26]

By this point, Jack was living a life he loved. Filmgoers even chose him as the leading actor of 1953, though the *Daily Mirror* sourly noted his success broke all the rules of star popularity: 'He is forty-three, portly, and has hardly had a screen kiss in twenty years of films'.[27] This image, however, appealed to a broader market and led him to a string of endorsements peddling everything from foodstuffs to stationary. Even Dee enthusiastically embraced the whirlwind and used her name in several advertising campaigns. In one, she was surrounded by the children cheerily pitching butter: 'I always have heaps of bread and butter ready—and I see that it's delicious New Zealand butter,' she gushed. 'I know how important it is that the children should have all the goodness and vitamins of New Zealand butter at this growing stage. As for Jack, he says it's the best butter he's ever tasted.' She also pushed Batchelor's Pea Soup, advising: 'This thick pea soup is a real heart-warmer—a meal in itself!' Andrew and Nicholas appeared together in a Start-Rite Shoes 'back to-school campaign', while Jack plugged instant coffee. 'Nescafe certainly makes good coffee,' he exclaimed, 'and another thing, it's so quick to make, I can be sure of enjoying it the minute I get that hankering for a good hearty cup of coffee.' For the cigarette manufacturer Capstan, he donned Royal Navy garb to declare: 'You know, after I've smoked this Capstan, I'll be ready to sink 50 U-boats. Shouldn't be surprised if I end up an Admiral'.

While Jack shot another commercial and tended to keeping the kitty replenished, Rank set about marketing him as a romantic lead, a strange move given he was beginning to look his age. Driven by Theo Cowan, his new image was poured on thick during the promotion for his first Rank feature, *The Seekers*, a £250,000 full-blooded adventure story, which the studio hoped would prove to be the biggest event to come out of Britain. Cowan boasted the picture would feature the most exciting battle scenes ever filmed with 'Hawkins in the thick of them all'.

Almost from the inception of the project, director Ken Annakin had been plainly bewildered by the casting of Jack saying, 'he was too old and too well fed for the part'. However, the star dutifully left Roehampton on New Year's Eve 1953 bound for New Zealand and the natural landscape of Whakatane, North Island.

Surrounded by a cast of seasoned Rank players, among them Glynis Johns, a frequent and electrifying presence in British cinema, *The Seekers* told the story about the clash between the first white settlers and 'savage' Māori tribes. 'Since the war I've made some interesting pictures and I've enjoyed making them,' Jack explained upon his arrival. 'But an actor needs change. There's ample scope in *The Seekers*, you know, the pioneer stuff with tons of character. The story is more history than Hollywood and there's also some strong romantic interest.'[28] As a kiss was all the sex you could show on screen, the 'romantic moment' was a graceful split-second embrace with Glynis Johns. 'Your very beautiful,' Jack whispered, as audiences witnessed him plant one squarely on her mouth.

As it happened, the kiss was the highpoint in a production endlessly beset by challenges. Annakin adored the unique semitropical locations but was unnerved by something he had never experienced—deep rumblings among the crew against the producer:

The unit was seething because George [George H. Brown, the producer] had cut the crew to the absolute minimum. For me, this was an important lesson. George was behaving like a general who had got himself into an almost impossible corner, and now had to use fair means or foul to win the battle—or, in this case finish the picture! However, British unionism caught up with us and punished us in a way I'd never experienced, then or since. We had come to this great showplace of Rotorua to shoot the big geyser, which only blows off once a day—regularly as clockwork at 11am. Here we were, having travelled halfway round the world with our camera all set up and Noel Purcell and Jack Hawkins costumed and ready to play a scene backgrounded by the geyser. Then, Nobby Clark, the shop steward, refused to allow us to shoot! Why? Because George was late with providing the morning tea-wagon![29]

Jack was not spared from suffering either as the non-stop action proved exhausting, leaving him uncharacteristically tired. 'I have been cut, bruised, scratched, trodden on, robbed, kicked, tripped and punched,' he complained. It was no exaggeration. As if fighting with bats in a burial cave and being headbutted in the stomach by an angry tribesman was not bad enough, he was also required to swim from a knife-wielding Māori in a raging torrent. He spent two nights in a muddy trench under continuous rain. With flaming spears and arrows flailing dangerously near, he fought off hordes of Māori warriors from the roof of a blazing hut and badly damaged his foot in single combat with a tribesman. And in a swordfight with Francis de Wolfe, his nose and cheekbone were slashed. Back at his hotel, short of breath, clogged up with sinus trouble, and racked with pain, he was administered morphia and penicillin. Soon after, Dee arrived to administer comfort, before winging homeward to the cloistered existence of Roehampton. As the final shots at Pinewood got underway, Kenneth Williams, a spindly unknown actor cast in a minor part as Peter Wishhart, marched onto the set.

Typically, the future *Carry On* star hated every minute, and described his character as a 'psycho neurotic coward' in a film jammed with 'stock situations and clichéd dialogue'. In a letter to a friend, Williams blew the experience into a brouhaha: he complained the shots were all taken in a torrent of rain, 'and I had about five hoses playing on me, and I was soaked to the skin. Of course, I promptly got influenza' (he was also convinced that both Jack and Annakin nurtured an intense dislike for him). 'No one has introduced me to Jack Hawkins,' Williams confided to his diary. 'And while he could easily speak to me, he avoids doing so, and I cannot very well go up and introduce myself. I'm so frightened of him, but I know I shouldn't be.'[30]

The Seekers went into distribution twelve weeks after shooting ended. After positive trade reviews, audiences were lured by an advertising crusade pushing an action-packed saga of adventure: 'They found the most exotic wilderness that man has ever known'. Mercifully, it proved an outstanding money-spinner—an extraordinary circumstance, given its listless pace. 'It had everything but a good script,' was the verdict of critic Dennis W. Clarke. 'But ninety minutes later I emerged a disappointed man, convinced that if this is the best the film industry can do for the Empire then the American colonists were right.'

After *The Seekers*, Rank hoped to shoot more adrenaline through moviegoer's veins by placing Jack in *Simba*, a bloated epic portraying the 'full tense and terrifying experience of people battling against the horrible Mau Mau threat'. Confident of securing Jack's services, producer Peter De Sarigny had already dispatched a crew to Kenya and taken the liberty of hiring a 'Jack double' for long shots designed to be spliced with studio takes. The bad news for De Sarigny, however, was that Jack—with unusual frankness—said he was not interested, and Dirk Bogarde was shoehorned into the lead. But, as Desmond Carrington remembered, the double footage had already arrived back at Pinewood and was used in the final cut, 'despite Bogarde being considerably shorter, gaunter, and slimmer than Hawkins. You don't need a sharp eye to see something was not right!'

Meanwhile, Cowan's publicity swirl kept selling Jack Hawkins as a romantic leading man, projecting physical passion and sex appeal. 'Month in month out,' Cowan claimed, 'Jack received more proposals of marriage by post than any other leading man in Britain.' Studio publicists pushed the same line *ad nauseam* throughout 1954. 'Here is a new Jack Hawkins,' screamed *Cineman*, a syndicated film column. 'Gone is the Service uniform and the hints of the girl he left behind. Here is Jack Hawkins the lover. The old, tough, courageous, inflexible character is still there—but now we have Hawkins the twinkling eyed romantic, too.' The showbiz reporter at the

Sunday Graphic, a trashy weekend tabloid, reckoned that women fell like a ton of bricks for Jack's strong, silent charm: 'They have made him the biggest romantic idol in British films since the heyday of James Mason'. Though it is probable that Jack was uncomfortable with being marketed as a screen hunk, rather than being eased into mature roles, he sighed to journalist Howard Thompson: 'Here I am now, a kind of idol of our bobby-soxers'. As usual, he played along when Theo Cowan arranged for him to provide some silver oratory as the host of Marlene Dietrich's first cabaret appearance in England at the Cafe de Paris. It was a perfect chance to place Rank's biggest star next to the German glamour-puss. Reporters were not disappointed when, garbed in plumes and furs, Dietrich blew a husky kiss to 'my lovely Jack'.[31] The positive press coverage was made even better when the *Motion Picture Herald*, the American film trade newspaper, voted him Britain's most popular film actor for 1954.[32]

A little while later, he was celebrating another joyous milestone when Dee gave birth to a daughter, whom they named Caroline. 'There wasn't a dry eye in our family when she arrived,' Dee recounted. 'Our little princess. She looked so tiny when Jack held her.' Caroline's birth became legendary in cricket circles, as Jack was faced with a difficult conflict of loyalties during his term as president of the Lord's Taverners. He was due to make his promised appearance at Mitcham Green for a keenly awaited match against the South Australian touring side. But Dee, heavily pregnant with Caroline, began to feel birth pangs just before he left home. A doctor arrived and the scene was set for a home birth, however, as promised, Jack attended the cricket and arranged for messages from home to be sent to the nearby pub. Journalist David Foot, in his history of the Lord's Taverners, explained how news of Caroline's birth came as Jack and Richard Attenborough were going round the boundary with their collecting boxes:

> Dennis Castle got onto the Tannoy and called him over—with the cryptically relayed information that it was a daughter after two sons. The president shed all customary inhibitions as he bounded across the square, waving his arms in parental triumph. Those South Australians didn't quite know what was happening. Licensing hours were miraculously extended as Jack ordered champagne and there was much celebrating round the bar. It seems almost superfluous to say that the Taverners lost that game.[33]

Back at Pinewood, Rank's efforts to push Jack as a romantic lead were paused when he set his sights on *The Prisoner*, a gritty, emotional story of a Roman Catholic cardinal arrested for treason and thrown into prison inside the Iron Curtain. He devoured and then read through the screenplay again before taking the part of a cultured, calculating ex-aristocrat turned mastermind of a crypto-communist police state. At the time, British writers had discovered the Cold War, with Bolsheviks and Communists replacing the Nazis. His role represented a dramatic change in his screen persona, uncovering (like in *State Secret*) his darker capabilities. Confined mainly to a bleak prison cell and a bare interrogation room, he triumphed in making the static consistently dramatic. Alec Guinness, playing the cardinal—with a shaven head, donned in traditional bishop's attire with rochet, chimere, and pleated cuffs—gave a masterly characterisation of the cardinal enduring a mental wrestling match. At first the interrogator makes no progress, leading to the state authorities growing impatient and trying to trick the cardinal with fake evidence. Eventually, Jack finds the prisoner's weak spot—his horror of his corrupted childhood and his hatred of his loose-living mother, a revelation which leaves the cardinal a shambling, bewildered, distraught man. Humiliated, he agrees to plead guilty to anything, believing that the only way that he can save his soul is to disgrace himself in public. However, as many critics recognised, the film was a barbed critique of authoritarian regimes in Eastern Europe. 'It is one of the most exacting parts I've ever played,' Jack told *Picturegoer*. 'Alec didn't help matters much. He's quite a contradiction you know. While making a comedy, he's very serious about the job when not in front of the camera but when making a drama, he's just the reverse.'[34]

Critic Doreen Turney-Dann, thought Jack was stern and forceful enough as the interrogator 'but he lacks the sinister chilling touch that this character needs.'[35] *The New York Times* was kinder, describing a grim and gripping drama 'that will make you shiver—and think.' Although it performed well, the film's legacy lay beyond pounds and pence. In the US, where communism was regarded with a combination of fear and loathing, the film was selected by the National Board of Review of Motion Pictures as the best foreign movie of the year. However, its underlying political comment proved sufficient to have it banned from Cannes and pulled from the Venice Film Festival after being dubbed 'so anti-Communist that it would be offensive to Communist countries'. Jack, however, noted it as one of his most rewarding acting experiences, despite a 'dreadfully low' fee.

After being briefly considered for a part in the thriller *Tiger in the Smoke*, Rank's CEO John Davis instead loaned Jack to Michael Balcon at Ealing to play the title role in *Touch and Go*, a silly story by William Rose, which gave him his first chance in years to play a comedy role. The film's other parts were filled by Margaret Johnston (the wife of Albert Parker), John Fraser, June Thorburn, and Roland Culver, the sterling veteran of stage and screen. Rose, an American, had also written the British comedy successes *Genevieve* and *The Maggie*. Jack said he sometimes wondered if Rose's great success at depicting the British for the export trade might not be due to a facility of making them correspond to 'the image American's have of Britons' (Cockney's in the pub, nosy but kind-hearted neighbours, etc.). In the film, Jack stuck closely to Rose's characterisation of Jim Fletcher, a world-weary father, and nominal head of the household planning to emigrate with his family to Australia. However, along the way, predictable mishaps see his daughter fall in love, the cat refuse to be rehomed, and the mother have second thoughts. 'This bloke is just the ordinary, average man who fancies he has complete control of his household,' Jack explained. 'But he discovers that he has no more control over it than any other ordinary, average man.' Tragedy struck when, with the film barely half-finished, Jack broke his arm after slipping on ice in Roehampton, holding up production for five weeks. 'In the case of Hawkins,' Balcon gaffed, 'we just wanted him and no one else, so the loss had to be laced.'[36] When the cast reassembled, Jack was put into a specially devised light plaster and rested his arm in a sling between takes. Despite the pain, he delivered a reliable performance, but it was a physically draining shoot—made worse by long periods of night work introduced to make up time. Worse still, there was near pandemonium when *Touch and Go* was forced to share floorspace with *The Ladykillers* (also written by Rose). 'Day and night the studio doors swung open,' an Ealing technician remembered. 'Sets were rolled in and out ... it was something like the shopfloor in a despatch office. Sometimes, it was a state of chaos'. However, even before it wrapped the film was considered one of Ealing's most forgettable comedies. While most reviewers remained divided on the choice of Jack in a comedic role, Alex Walker, a discerning critic, called the film 'anaemic' in a blistering review in which he argued Jack appeared ill-at-ease and out of place:

> Mr. Hawkins is among our 3 or 4 top actors—*but he is a straight actor*. In his role of comic—albeit his first—he seems to think all too often that a funny face is all that is needed. He tortures his features like a marksman squinting down a barrel and saying 'Attention please: I am about to deliver one of my famous cracks'. It makes me sad to think Ealing, who are closing next year, should choose to go out with such a faint-hearted swansong.[37]

These were the first inklings of a negative reaction to Jack to find their way into print. For sure, *Touch and Go* is not a high-water mark in his career, but neither is it an embarrassment. And while he cared little for the opinions of Walker, Jack did air misgivings about working ten-hour days, 'with unspecified hours of unpaid overtime in an emergency'. Though there was no enmity with Balcon, he grumbled that producers abused the term 'emergency' and without strong union action an actor could be made to work night and day to finish a film on time.[38]

In another interview, he was prissy about never being given star treatment 'as Hollywood understood it', meaning a story scripted from the start with him in mind. 'I'm always inheriting stories from other people,' he protested. 'I'm never in on the start of a script. Sometimes, I turn to the first page and see that they've forgotten to rub out the name of the person suggested to play the part. It's always the same old names ... Gregory Peck ... Errol Flynn and half a dozen others. Then someone thinks of me. Hawkins can play it—especially if it's one of those damned dependable characters.'[39]

Away from the studio, life ticked over peacefully. Many of the performers who had appeared in *Touch and Go* were invited to Caroline's lavish christening, an event society journalist, Michael Sherard, chronicled in swooning detail.[40] The Baptism robe, he noted, was stitched from Brussels lace and tulle:

> ... and there was fierce competition among the girls in the House for the pleasure of making it. They love to work on Mrs. Hawkins' clothes because she has a superlative figure, as well as beauty, and is, indeed, in my opinion, one of the best-dressed women in the country. Her clothes are always simple and soigné.[41]

Jack also found time for simple pleasures, like kicking-off a match between the North London and Hendon Sunday Football Leagues on behalf of the National Spastics Society. Comedian Eric Sykes often dined out on the story of how on one 'horrendous freezing night' under floodlights at Brentford, Jack turned up for a charity match and supplied the gin:

> After the match he came off looking as well-groomed as he had when he began, which is hardly surprising: when I come to think of it, he hadn't moved one inch in any direction, although he did a lot of pointing, like a French traffic policeman during the rush hour, indicating where others should be running into position; and if my memory serves me right, he walked off slowly waving to the crowd.[42]

While Sykes was establishing himself as one of Britain's first television stars for the pioneering Rediffusion, Jack openly fretted over the encroachment of TV on the film business. Along with many other film actors, he was alarmed by the enormous success of ITV, the new commercial service, showing an endless parade of dramas, old films, and American imports. However, unlike many actors that slinked back from the 'unblinking eye', his attitude was quite unequivocal: if TV engagements paid well, he was available. Throughout the year, offers came thick and fast and, at one point, ITV even petitioned him to consider anchoring news bulletins in the manner of Ludovic Kennedy, the well-known announcer. 'Not for me,' Jack replied, but he did express the desire to host general interest programmes. 'I get on quite well with people,' he explained, adding he might be suited to a chat show. 'My aim would not be to serve-up heavy stuff.'[43] And, in the usual way, he laid his displeasure of high taxes, saying he would gladly accept more television work at considerably less pay but the taxman compelled him to stay in the big-money earning class. 'I am not the only one,' he bemoaned. 'So many of my chums are in the same boat, especially since the war when taxes have become so enormous. It's so bad; you feel you're a good boy if you pay your taxes. To put something away for retirement is almost impossible.'

Male Britannia

Despite his interest in TV, Jack gravitated back to film and began work on a picture that was to become one of his most hated and derided when he accepted £30,000 to play Pharaoh Khufu in the monumentally ill-advised *Land of the Pharaohs*, a Cinemascope epic shot on location in Egypt about the building of the Great Pyramid. Director Howard Hawks, the man responsible for introducing Rita Hayworth to films, settled on Jack because he was not considered an international box-office name. 'Almost every one of our actors should be fairly good figures because the costumes make a fat man look pretty bad,' Hawks told Jack Warner, the head of Warner Brothers. Studio correspondence reveals that signing Jack, though, became something of a headache. 'Hawkins agent Al Park [*sic*] causing a great deal of trouble,' Hawks notified Warner in a telegram. 'As each situation cleared, Parker makes new and difficult demands.' Forced to tackle the problem, Jack Warner enlisted the help of J. Arthur Rank to iron out troubles.

When shooting finally got underway, the sixteen-week project proved hard going under the Egyptian sun, where temperatures topped 40 degrees. Worse still, there was no escape from the sand—the insidious, all-pervasive dust that crept ghostlike into costumes, seeping through cracks in the cameras, microphones, lights, and sets—covering everything in a mantle of mustard coloured powder. Strong gusts often darkened the sun for several days and buried the main road with 8 inches of drifting sand. On arrival in Luxor, as Jack leafed through the pencil-scrawled shooting script, he found flaws at every turn. His memoirs describe a 'perfectly ridiculous' plot littered with 'frightful lines'.

Hawks understood the level of effort his forty-five-year-old lead was putting into the role acting in gold Kaftans under the blazing sun but also had to contend with American model Ivy Nicholson who was playing Princess Nellifer, Khufu's love interest, and presenting more problems than the script. Alarm bells should have rung during her screentest with Jack, where instructions read: 'You're quarreling, and he slaps you. Just react naturally, as you would if you really got slapped'. But when the cameras rolled and Jack faked a slap, with sulky theatricality, Ivy let out a terrifying yell and bit deeply into Jack's hand, leaving him reeling in pain. Predictably, she only lasted a few days before being sacked. 'The ex-Nellifer was very difficult,' recalled Joan Collins, who stepped into the princess's sandals at a fee of £5,600 for eight weeks' work.[1] 'Apparently stardom had gone instantly to her head, and she started going round telling Howard Hawks and Jack Hawkins what to do.' A technician on the film remembered, 'Ivy was a flawless beauty but a royal pain in the arse ... absolute hell. Joan, however, was great; she perfected the evil schemer bit.'

After a few arid months in the desert, the cast were transported to Rome for interior shooting. Meanwhile, on the other side of the Atlantic, Warner Brothers were convinced they were putting a blockbuster in the can. 'This footage ... makes anything DeMille has done about Egypt look like a child at play,' studio representative Matt Blumenstock cabled Jack Warner. With the studio desperately in quest of a hit after passing on box office smashes *From Here to Eternity* and *The Caine Mutiny*, Warner began celebrating the 'greatest stuff he had seen in his life'. In this jubilant atmosphere, even Jack's faith was lifted after he viewed rushes showing hordes of soldiers and camels and teaming vistas of slaves hauling blocks over the sand at the pyramid of Baka—all moving to a background score by Dimitri Tiomkin. The shots were starkly beautiful, capturing the blinding blue sky, the red-hot sun and baked desert in stunning Technicolor. To create such magic, Hawks had engaged 9,787 extras, many Egyptian Army conscripts. Other scenes were shot at a quarry at Tourah, near Cairo, and at Aswan, a granite mine located 880 kilometres away.

Seen today, the film has the scope and flavour of a Hollywood spectacular, including thrilling crowd scenes, glorious sets, and strong acting. But whatever the cause, and no matter how much Warner Bros flogged *Land of the Pharaohs*, it was a commercial failure and made just $2.7 million, a loss of $200,000. Equally, most reviewers were lukewarm. 'Jack Hawkins looks pretty gloomy about the whole thing,' was the verdict of the *Times of Cyprus*, which called it a 'fanciful version of life on the Nile'.[2] For Hawks, though, the failure still had several acts left to run. Dumbfounded by the press reaction, he disowned the picture and as his bitterness deepened, he eventually requested its omission from the retrospective at the National Film Theatre. Remarkably, the project jangled his nerves so much, he even took a two-year break from work to recover from the ordeal. And as if that was not bad enough, the film was banned in Egypt on the grounds of 'distortion of historical facts'. Around this time, Jack severed his links with Rank and became a freelancer, working under his own company, Roehampton Productions, of which he was a director. The move gave him freedom and independence. 'I'm glad I left Rank,' he said, 'I was being tied down too much.'³ Though he had a gentleman's agreement to make some films for Michael Balcon and a similar gentleman's agreement with Mike Frankovitch of Columbia, he began to tap markets outside England and seized the opportunity to star as Rufio in a colour TV production of George Bernard Shaw's *Caesar and Cleopatra* for NBC in the United States which guaranteed a hefty fee and first-class passage on the *Queen Mary*. Though Jack and Dee sailed into one of the coldest winters in New York's history, Doreen remembered they were 'wonderfully happy' after decamping at Tyrone Power's penthouse apartment on 72nd Street. As always when they travelled, the Hawkinses mixed business and pleasure. Working on a tight itinerary, they crammed as much socialising and sightseeing as rehearsals allowed (and even caught the US premiere of *Touch and Go*). In the first week, they managed to spend a day with Susan, who had married a young engineering student, John Tettemer, and was planning a family and a move to Los Angeles. They also spent time with Anthony Quayle, who oversaw production, and they chummed around with cast members Sir Cedric Hardwicke, Judith Anderson, and leading lady Clare Bloom, a young stage actress discovered by Charlie Chaplin to co-star in his film *Limelight*.

As he wandered around NBC's Rockefeller Centre studio, marvelling at the magnificent sets, Jack was fascinated by the enthusiasm and experience of the staff, who, he thought, kept things running like a 'well-oiled clock'. Such excursions gave him everything he wanted: he could enjoy the company of friends and family while reaping the rewards of his fame without long-term commitments. Asked if he had ever considered moving to America, he said, 'British films have been good to me, and I'm not prepared to risk my career breaking up all the worthwhile things I've obtained in the way of a peaceful homelife ... well, as peaceful as it can be with three kids.'⁴

The widely publicised *Caesar and Cleopatra* telecast went well, and after three weeks in New York, Jack returned home to begin a gruelling location shoot in London and Snowdonia for *The Long Arm*, a Michael Balcon noir crime flick which went on to win the Silver Bear at the 6th Berlin International Film Festival.

Meanwhile, in May 1956, Al Parker concluded negotiations with producer Sam Spiegel for Jack to play Major Warden in *Bridge on the River Kwai*, a war drama slated to be filmed in Ceylon. A stroker of egos, Spiegel had a hard-charging disposition, an acute savviness, and a reputation for silver oratory. Typical was the old joke which told how if he were dropped naked without a penny into any capital city, by the next morning he would be garbed in a Savile Row suit and eating caviar.

Budgeted at $2.5 million, the film was written—lengthily— by Pierre Boulle set in a Second World War Japanese prison camp where British prisoners were forced to build a bridge as a morale-building exercise. Before filming commenced, Jack found time to work with Arlene Dahl on her second British film, *Fortune is a Woman*, a Launder-Gilliat production for Columbia tightly scheduled for a three-week shoot at Shepperton during September 1956. Though entirely forgotten today, the picture was based on a bestseller by Winston Graham and saw Jack play an insurance assessor who becomes involved with a client. The film is notable in that Arlene gave Jack his first real screen kiss. 'The director made us do the big kiss scene twenty-four times,' Dahl said. 'But oh my … Jack Hawkins, he kisses like a real expert.' Furthermore, *Fortune is a Woman* helped Jack come second to Kenneth More as 'top film star in Britain' in a poll for the *Motion Picture Herald*, the American cinema trade journal. It was the only bright spot during a period of thumb-twiddling as work on *Kwai* was delayed. A glance through the production notes reveals Jack was slated to go before the cameras in late September but as Christmas approached, he was clearly annoyed by the setbacks, as a letter to theatrical lawyer Arnold Weissberger reveals: 'We are off to Switzerland tomorrow for a couple of weeks. A couple of weeks is a little tentative for me as I am due in Ceylon at any sort of moment and can't really get any sort of sense out of the Sam Spiegel office as to the exact date'.[5]

The hold-ups, it later transpired, came after Spiegel requested the assistance of the Royal Air Force, but as the script was passed around Whitehall for official approval, objections arrived from all directions. In a lengthy series of letters to Spiegel, members of the Far East Prisoners of War Association insisted POW officers were obliged to focus on escape and sabotage, rather than assisting their Japanese captors. 'I do not think much of this story,' wrote Major A. G. Close, a War Office public relations official. 'In the first instance it is quite untrue and only very occasionally resembles the facts as they were at the time,' he tartly noted. 'I am perhaps biased as I worked for three and a half years on this particular railway.' Close then went further, informing that having sent the script to others, 'they agree with me that it would not go down well with the British public.' This level of respect for accuracy is difficult to understand from a modern perspective, but with the events still raw, the War Office was eager to avoid controversy. However, after considerable rigmarole, they grudgingly agreed to RAF cooperation but were 'not entirely happy about this film story'. And so, after several false starts, shooting finally got underway in January 1957. The real construction of wartime bridges was probably nothing like the breath-taking extravaganza conceived by David Lean. His bridge, specially built for the film, was an impressive structure, standing higher than a six-story building and was one-third longer than London's Westminster Bridge. Built at a cost of £80,000, it was touted to be the largest single movie set ever constructed on location. Forty-eight elephants and several hundred labourers worked for over eight months in the Ceylon jungle to construct it. Over 1,500 trees were felled from the surrounding forests to provide the timber. Adding to the expense, Spiegel bought a fifty-two-year-old locomotive and six coaches from the Ceylon government and hired several thousand extras. Most of the Japanese soldiers were played by Chinese; several of the British prisoners of war by Germans and Italians; and all the Indians by Sinhalese.

For the most part, *The Bridge on the River Kwai* was a tense, unhappy movie to make. Everything during production was difficult: relationships, living conditions, script—even Ceylon, where the story was filmed, proved inhospitable. Everyday provided little melodramas—Alec Guinness's nose was conked out of joint when he discovered director David Lean 'didn't particularly' want him for the role of Colonel Nicholson, a proud but dull-as-soap British officer. According to author Bob Thomas, Laurence Olivier was the first choice for the role, but declined, saying: 'I can't imagine anyone wanting to watch a stiff upper-class colonel for two and a half hours'.

Sessue Hayakawa, who played Colonel Saito, the Japanese commander, observed the 'coolness with which each man regarded the other was almost solid enough to be seen'.[6] As if that was not bad enough, Jack noticed considerable friction between Spiegel and Lean and they rarely spoke to each other and avoided all off-set contact. Lean was clearly in crisis, and tetchier than ever, treating actors with his customary discourtesy. Already overheated, he became embroiled in a long dispute with Guinness over how to play the role of Nicholson; Guinness hoped to inject humour, though Lean thought the character should be 'a bore'. In this rancid atmosphere, Lean also held a testy conversation with actor James Donald, who believed the film was anti-British.

To no one's surprise, Jack avoided the drama and found his happiest moments watching the female elephants toiling on the building of the bridge. Before the camera, he swung into action with a spectacular performance as Major Warden, while the imposing figure of William Holden added Hollywood glitter. Working on a percentage deal shrewdly negotiated in preference to a salary, Holden held out for big profits: 'Because I'm starred with Alec Guinness and Jack Hawkins, it's like getting a percentage of those internationally popular stars'. His deal was indeed remarkable: A $300,000 fee, plus 10 per cent of the gross receipts, payable at a maximum rate of $50,000.[7] Built like a rugby player, with broad shoulders, thick thighs, chestnut brown hair, and a clean-cut complexion, Holden had enormous charm but loved to drink. Legends grew about the filming. Though mosquitoes were a constant menace and source of sickness during the warm months, Holden once told the young actor Ryan O'Neil that he and Jack often found relief from the unbearable humidity by wading into a waterfall in the jungle deep in the Ceylon interior at Kitugala. One morning, they were perplexed as to why crew members began yelling at them from afar. The answer was soon evident. The crew was close enough to register the fact that they were both covered with bloodsucking leeches, sausage-sized parasitic worms. 'But not the kind you can get off with matches,' Holden recounted. 'These were big enough to require flamethrowers. Holden also recalled how ticks buried in his skin, causing agony, and swelling.[8] 'Ah, the glamorous life of a movie star,' he joked. 'Here I am on an island in the Indian Ocean, standing up to my naval in a filthy river, dodging elephant shit the size of cannonballs.'

Another oft-told account finds Alec Guinness in the make-up tent, watching Holden shave his chest because American ladies were supposed to be averse to seeing body hair, while Jack gummed on quantities of crepe hair to satisfy the English ladies.[9]

Some scenes were shot at the Mount Lavinia Hotel, a place Jack and Dee had visited in 1944 during their period at ENSA. For the film, the building was transformed to resemble a convalescent hospital with soldiers swathed in bandages, and plasters.

In general, other than a few bright moments, filming proved a terrible strain. Matters worsened when the continuity boy came down with chronic intestinal flu, while others suffered fever and dehydration. To make matters worse, Holden's ongoing battle with alcoholism—which became his legacy—was unleashed on several occasions. One memorable evening during dinner at the Galle face Hotel in Colombo, he threw a fit after Sam Spiegel bemoaned the discomforts of filming in Asia. Irritated that Sam was billeted in five-star luxury while he was in a native shack, the star even turned on Betty Spiegel, calling her 'a bitch', then, when Dee—sitting next to Bill's wife, Ardis—tried to intervene, he lashed out saying they 'were bitches as well'.[10] His energy spent, the American star stomped off to bed. The next morning, seeking redemption, he hand-delivered a hamper of fruit to Dee. 'He could be charming and then silent and sullen,' she remembered (Jack had refused to join the cast in Ceylon without Doreen, resulting in a lengthy spat with Spiegel, who eventually conceded).

The dinner incident was not Holden's only outburst. On another evening, he, Ardis, and a few others joined Jack and Dee in their suite for drinks. After several balloons of brandy, Bill was telling a story in a lively manner when—sweeping his hand for the punchline—he knocked the glass from Ardis's hand, ruining her dress. After she scoffed, Holden screamed, 'Goddammit, go out and buy six more dresses ... I'll pay for them.' Following an awkward silence, the party broke up. Again, Holden sent a note with champagne to Dee: 'If there's anything I hate, it's a nasty drunk—Bill' (Holden's biographer notes during the shoot 'he was closest to Jack Hawkins, who shared his love of booze and good times'). On the other end of the scale, Holden detested Spiegel. Speaking to the author, actor Michael Jayston related a conversation with Alec Guinness who once told him that Holden left Spiegel 'immensely upset' toward the end of shooting because of 'overage'—a daily fee paid when an actor is required after the contracted agreement: 'Holden was on something like US1,000 a day overage, and he did about ten days "over," so he gave a party which he dubbed "William Holden's overage party". This upset Sam so much, he was very distraught'.

Lean's final scenes seal the magnificence of *The Bridge on the River Kwai* as Jack's commando raid ends with the blowing up of the bridge, sending a Japanese troop train hurtling into the river below. After months under Asian skies, Jack arrived back in London 10 lb thinner, and despite all the on-set unpleasantness, the film proved a massive critical and financial hit, primarily due to Columbia's high production values: superb acting, Technicolor photography, and Carl Foreman's snappy script. After seeing the first preview, Alec Guinness sent a short note to David Lean. 'I was enormously impressed by Jack Hawkins,' he confessed. 'When I read it, I thought it was rather a map-pointing part such as he has often played—but his reality etc etc are remarkable. Bill [Holden] I liked too—I thought he was fine and made an almost over-sardonic character most likeable and intriguing.... A wonderful film. Thank you for having me. As ever, Alec'.[11] Funnily enough, Noël Coward—who had turned down a part in the movie—scribbled a note in his diary on 22 December 1957: 'A really magnificent picture,' he observed. 'Brilliantly directed by David and acted superbly by Alec, James Donald, Jack Hawkins, Sessue Hayakawa and Bill Holden. Really satisfying. I rather wish now that I had done it.'

Guinness went on to deservedly scoop the Best Actor Oscar for his performance, and business was brisk even before release with the picture heavily booked for major and provincial cinemas up and down Britain.[12] Jack joined Holden on a whirlwind tour of Germany, where the film premiered in Stuttgart and Frankfurt in early March and in Berlin a week later. In Frankfurt, Holden was greeted by young women in traditional Hessian folk costumes; in Berlin, Jack obliged fans with autographs while accompanied by a British military band playing Viennese waltzes and Bavarian polkas.

Returning to England, Jack was sent a rigorous schedule of promotional appearances before rolling up his sleeves and reporting to MGM-British Studios at Borehamwood for *Gideon's Day*, a tragicomic police drama about a day in the life of a Scotland Yard detective, directed by John Ford. Playing Gideon, a dogged police inspector, Jack manages to deal with a rapist, murderer, a prototypical conman, corrupt police officers, and three bank robbers all in the period of twenty-four hours. Subsidiary parts were filled by Dianne Foster and Cyril Cusack. Ford—known for his blockbusters *Stagecoach*, *The Searchers*, and *The Grapes of Wrath*—described Jack as 'the finest dramatic actor with whom I have worked'.[13] Likewise Jack got along wonderfully with Ford, whose quirky personality intrigued him. He praised the American as the 'perfect actor's director', a man who brooked no interference from accountants or management types. On set, Ford—who was on the wagon after a period of heavy boozing—became unusually specific about his cast refraining from drink but allowed Jack to slip off for a gin and tonic at lunchtime, provided he 'had one for me'.

After checking into Brown's Hotel, Ford completely embraced the project, soaking up bomb-scarred Britain. Though Michael Killanin, who produced *Gideon's Day*, was less enthusiastic about the 'corny' script, Ford was eager to take a break from Hollywood. 'I wanted to get away for a while,' he recounted. 'So, I said I'd like to do a Scotland Yard thing and we went over and did it.' Wearing an eyepatch and battered trilby, he wanted to know how people in London viewed the police, how they lived, what kind of people they were. He wanted to understand the daily routine of officers in Scotland Yard, what they wore, and what they thought—reality was his goal. Years later, Anna Massey, who played Jack's daughter Sally Gideon, remembered shooting under Ford turned out to be a crisp, clockwork affair. 'Having worked as an editor, he only shot what he needed,' she recounted. 'He never did more than one take. He edited as he filmed. His manner was easy and congenial.' When released, *Cahiers du Cinema*, the prestigious French journal, defined the picture as 'the freest, most direct, least fabricated film ever to spout from one of Her Majesty's studios.'

Once filming was completed, Jack continued his sporadic employment as a television actor by taking a lead role in Shaw's *The Apple Cart*, the play of his choice on BBC television featuring Moira Lister, Margaret Rawlings, Angela Baddeley, and Donald Price. 'It may not be acceptable to some, though I personally happen to like Shaw and revere most of his work,' Jack explained. 'It was probably his last big play. It's 29 years old, but so up to date it could have been written tomorrow. It's a play of brilliant talk. There was no modern play I felt entirely happy about.'

As it turned out, more time and thought seems to have been lavished on the ninety-minute telecast than many other productions at the BBC's Alexandra Palace studios. 'You can't really compare conditions. Rehearsals for a TV play are virtually the same as in the theatre,' Jack told Wilfrid Altman from *The Stage*. 'Now for filming I usually leave home at 7.15 in the morning and get back about the same time at night. For *The Apple Cart* we rehearse every day for three weeks from 9.30am till 2pm straight through, except for a ten-minute break. And I like it,' he explained. 'There's no looking at the clock for the lunch break and then doubling back far too heavily laden with food. No looking at watches for morning breaks either; I take a flask of lime juice with me!' With the transmission complete, August was spent playing a middle-aged test pilot in Michael Balcon's melodrama *Man in the Sky*, filmed on location in Wolverhampton, alongside Elizabeth Sellars, Eddie Byrne, and Megs Jenkins.[14] The first of the new Ealing films produced under the MGM banner, the film had all the qualities that made Balcon's team one of the most successful in British cinema. It told the story of a suburban family whose breadwinner (Jack) was a middle-aged test pilot and father of two young sons. Though desperate to take on mortgage repayments for a new house, he cannot secure a pay rise from the aircraft firm he works with, as it is almost bankrupt. In fact, it will go out of business if it cannot sell a new freighter which he was sent up to demonstrate to a ministry official and the prospective buyer's representative. The drama begins when one of the engines catches fire, the crew and inspectors bale out, and Jack is left to bring the aeroplane down. As the drama heightens, he is ordered to fly out to Liverpool Bay, bale out, and let the plane crash in the sea. But to do so would not only lose the plane and ruin the company, but also destroy the last remnants of his self-confidence. 'The role fits Jack Hawkins as one piece of a jigsaw fits another,' noted the *South Western Star*. 'But he really comes into his own towards the end when he arrives home after the ordeal to have a row with his wife over living such a life of danger.'

On returning from Wolverhampton, Jack kept up a remarkably crowded schedule. He became a sought-after guest star for variety shows and even hosted several episodes of the ITV extravaganza *Chelsea at Nine*, a live programme with all the possibilities for error and gaffes (for a £1,000 fee). He had, it seemed, no inhibitions whatever, but *Punch* described him as 'taut and theatrical as a juvenile lead in rep'. Unperturbed, his gaiety flowed over with guests such as Maggie Fitzgibbon and Bernard Cribbins and he even donned a topper and tails for a tap dance. 'I thought he was really courageous to tackle that side of television,' Dee confessed. 'If he had asked my advice about the dance routine, I might have tried to dissuade him. I'm not the bossy sort of wife who tries to dictate what her husband should do. However, he didn't ask—and of course he was right.' In this light, its little wonder that Jack gamely appeared in 'The Elocution Teacher', an episode of the iconic BBC comedy *Hancock's Half Hour*, alongside Tony Hancock and Sidney James. Sadly, like many episodes in the series, neither the film nor the audio has survived.[15] Needless to say, writers Ray Galton and Alan Simpson churned out a flawless script in which Jack engaged the shifty-eyed Sid James and incompetent Tony Hancock as agent and elocution teacher, respectively. Jack knew exactly when to pour it on and when to play it subtly. The role was notable as one of the few 'guest star' appearances on the show. Two weeks after Hancock aired, he resumed his globe-trotting on a *Kwai* promotional shindig to the USA. In Los Angeles, he joined the William Morris Agency, one of the oldest established and largest theatrical managers in the world, representing the *crème de la crème* of Hollywood. Almost immediately, agents began submitting his name as a candidate for roles in US television and film productions. Speaking to Joe Hyams of the *Herald Tribune*, Jack said he had avoided visiting 'tinsel town' for years because people in Europe kept saying he would not like it. 'I tried to get Alec Guinness to say what he thought of Hollywood, but oddly enough he drew a deep veil over his opinions,' he explained:

> All my other acting friends told me that Hollywood was a devourer of talent—a rat-race—and I would get there, receive a tremendous welcome and be knocked down and be used as a door mat. It was really quite a frightening description. Before I left England there were headlines in the papers saying, 'No Hollywood for Jack,' and that sort of thing. There is resentment in Britain about stars who leave the isles for Hollywood and I'm one of the last really reliable British stars. I resent terribly the people who over the years have said I wouldn't like it. They kept me from going there. I can only believe that those who have a tough time in Hollywood and complain so much about it must be slightly deficient in talent. I may be the odd fish, you know, but I must admit I liked Hollywood, and I can't wait to get back there to make a picture.

During that trip, he concluded negotiations with Hanna Weinstein, a TV producer with a long and illustrious string of credits, to join the cast of *The Four Just Men*, an Edgar Wallace mystery series. 'Jack met Mrs Weinstein, and of course, had long been an admirer of all the TV film series she had made ever since *Colonel March of Scotland Yard*,' Dee recounted. 'What worried Jack was this problem of character identification in a TV serial—you become "typed" in viewers' minds as a bandit or a detective or whatever the character is. When Jack came back to our hotel after meeting

Mrs. Weinstein, he was very pleased because the character identification problem had been overcome', meaning none of the stars were in danger of becoming typecast. More to the point, the money was good—£45,000 for nine episodes with a cut of the world distribution rights. Filming was to take place in a hurried manner throughout the early months of 1959. Jack would play a globe-trotting charmer, alongside Richard Conte, Dan Dailey, and Vittorio De Sica.

Returning to London shortly thereafter, Jack trooped over to the Elstree Associate British Studios to begin work on *The Two-Headed Spy*, a thin yarn in which he played General Alex Schottland, a man of German-English birth who spent twenty-five years in the German Army but never lost his loyalty to Britain.

He remained patient during final script amendments which were being done on a crash schedule by Michael Wilson, who had worked on *The Bridge on the River Kwai*. J. Alvin Kugelmass's scenario tells how Schottland, a British spy, became one of Hitler's favourite generals and kept London supplied with secrets and so altered the course of the war. When production started moving, Jack joined co-star Gia Scala and a small band traveling from London to Berlin on 6 March 1958 for intensive location shooting in the British sector. For two days, the crew closed off the one-way street near the Brandenburg Gate and filmed several sequences near Hitler's bombed-out bunker. Hungarian director Andre DeToth, famed for his noir flick *Pitfall*, took pains to make the film look historically authentic and even hired a bulletproof Mercedes used by Herman Goering at £20 a day, though the 7-ton hulk clocked only 5 miles to the gallon. There were other unforeseen expenses, too, according to editor Teddy Darvas. He never forgot endless retakes as Gia Scala muffed her lines: 'I think we went for more takes than I ever remember, it went up about sixty takes, she couldn't remember anything'. At one point, things got so awkward that the assistant director rolled out a blackboard and held a sweepstake on how many takes she would go for with Gia. 'She [Gia] was a very sad case because as it happens,' says Darvas, 'she was born in Liverpool when her Italian parents were on the way to America during the war. And she was at the Columbia Charm School, and she did one or two films when she looked very promising and then they found that she wasn't all that good.' However, critic Leonard Mosley (an author noted for his extensive writings on the Second World War) was generally impressed:

How far this is true few people, because of the Official Secrets Act, will ever know, though I can myself vouch for the fact that a tune played over the Nazi radio did once give us a vital secret. The trouble with this film, however, is that it manages to make its remarkable story look and sound like unbelievable melodrama. Except for Jack Hawkins as Colonel Schottland, and Alexander Knox as a Gestapo brass hat, its characters are wooden. When life imitates spy fiction it should add a little humour to make it more believable.[16]

From Berlin, Jack joined Kenneth More and Trevor Howard for an all-expenses jaunt to Paris for the premiere of Otto Preminger's *Saint Joan*, adapted from George Bernard Shaw's play (Jack had, in fact played Dunios's page in a 1923 Thorndike production of the same play). However, as More—a man with a treasure trove of stories—recounted, the screening proved so boring that all three 'escaped' the ordeal halfway through by tiptoeing off to a local bar, only to be met with a withering glance from a British tabloid journalist.

Back in London, time was spent with Gordon Harker who had been injured in a fall. On many afternoons, Jack was spotted pushing his wheelchair along Albert Bridge and around Battersea Park. This kind of gesture made Dee buzz about her husband's selfless loyalty, she often said he was 'so consistently and constantly the man I first fell in love with. Perhaps that is an experience which every wife does not enjoy and for that reason among many others, I am lucky. Jack—the real Jack Hawkins I alone know—does not change.' Giving a glimpse into family life, she explained how Andrew wanted to be an anthropologist, while Nicolas 'announced the other day he wanted to be an archaeologist. He is fascinated by anything old.' Baby Caroline was a 'budding dancer'.

Meanwhile, with several film projects competing for his attention, including an intriguing script titled *Ben-Hur*, Jack found time for media interviews. 'Love scenes are so dull and respectable in our films,' he complained, four years after his own unsuccessful stint as a romantic lead. 'Where is all the fire and fervor they generate in American and Continental pictures? Our people just don't seem to be able to manage these qualities. And this is the secret of big, international success these days.' *Picturegoer* teasingly remarked that 'tough guy Hawkins has a hankering to get a few love scenes himself but this, say our film makers, would be quite out of character.' Jack, who was then forty-eight, snapped: 'If I've got a kiss in the script they shudder, like a schoolmaster kissing a girl pupil'.[17]

Meanwhile, after dithering over several offers, Jack finally accepted £50,000 to play Roman consul, Quintus Arrius in the extravagant swords-and-sandals epic *Ben-Hur*, a likely hit given a rebirth of interest in biblical costume pieces. Based on Lew Wallace's bestselling novel, the plot concerns the adventures of a Jewish prince betrayed and sent into slavery by a Roman friend, who regains his freedom and comes back for revenge. Heavyweight performances were given by Charlton Heston in the coveted title role and Stephen Boyd as his enemy. Subtler ones came from Jack as Quintus Arrius—icy and sinister initially, though his character warmed as the story progressed. Another old acquaintance, Hugh Griffith, shone as an Arab horse dealer.

While some films invite myth, *Ben-Hur* was the real thing. At a cost of an estimated $15 million, it ranked as the most expensive action-adventure spectacle ever made. However, for the most part, shooting on nine sound stages at Rome's Cinecittà studios—a vast sprawling complex built by Mussolini to produce fascist propaganda—became a challenge. With filming lasting for twelve to fourteen hours a day, six days a week, a physician was brought onto the set to give a vitamin B complex shot to anyone who requested it (Director William Wyler and his family later speculated the doses may have contained amphetamines). Adding to the gruesome schedule, Jack loathed the endless frustrations of working in Italy, where the crew were intent on their own jobs: 'They couldn't care less about what's going on in front of the camera and it's the greatest difficulty to get any silence,' he said gruffly.

Despite such grumbles, Heston was delighted with his work. In a diary entry made on 30 August 1958, he noted: 'Today Jack and I worked hard doing the angles over our backs to the togaed and perfumed crowd listening to the speech where he adopts me. I found Jack very moving in it and consequently did well myself'.[18]

Meanwhile, Wyler seesawed back and forth over endless dialogue amendments. Some of the script—written on site by Gore Vidal, the accomplished American man of letters—incurred the director's wrath. As the story goes, Wyler was concerned that Vidal was unwilling or incapable of writing heterosexual characters realistically. As Heston's biographer Marc Elliot remarked, 'Having to put words into the super-straight Heston's mouth was not something Vidal enjoyed or was at all interested in doing.' However, in later years, Vidal rejoiced that some of his coded gay subtexts slipped through the net. In one scene, Jack practically drools when he sees the muscular Ben at the oars of a boat, and that whole scene and the ones following are all about his attraction to Heston. In another scene, Ben-Hur is marched into Quintus Arrius's apartments, perspiring and bare to the waist. When Ben-Hur questions why he has been summoned, Arrius said he was considering turning him into a gladiator. As Elliot notes, the dialogue and direction were heavy with implication and innuendo. In a later scene involving Jack, when Ben-Hur regains his freedom, 'he returns Arrius's ring, a scene with an oddly romantic tinge'. In a 1979 review of the film, Clive James wryly noted: 'Eyeing the muscular Ben as he toils at the oar, Quintus Arrius (Jack Hawkins) is plainly boiling with suppressed lust. Is Quint a queer quaestor?'[19] On set, Jack found Wyler could be equally taxing as he kept his crew and actors busy, although the shooting began to run behind schedule. On one occasion, when playing a scene with Stephen Boyd, Wyler (megaphone in hand) kept repeating:

'No, do it again'.
   Jack and Stephen said, 'What should we do differently?'
   Wyler said: 'Just do it again'.
   A few days later, when they had massed over 100 takes, Wyler finally said: 'Print it!'
   Jack, went bananas and yelled: 'That's the same way we've been doing it for the last 100 takes!'
   And Wyler replied: 'I know, but the construction of the next set wasn't ready'.

During the commotion of filming, Jack's temper was lifted by a letter from the prime minister inviting him to accept a CBE for services to the British theatre, the only public honour he ever received. At the same time, he was offered (and turned down) the lead role of Colonel Jock in *Tunes of Glory*, put off by the prospect of shooting in the drizzly Scottish Highlands (Alec Guinness took the role). However, to celebrate the CBE, Dee arrived in Rome mid-shoot, and the couple spent time with the Wylers and virtually lived in the stylish Passetto's restaurant, Excelsior lounge, and Harry's, the see-and-be-seen nightspot near the Colosseum, frequented by café society. During one boozy dinner, the evening turned sombre when a message arrived that *Ben-Hur*'s producer Sam Zimbalist had collapsed suddenly of a heart attack and was rushed to his villa, where he died. The second blow, more personal and devastating to Jack, came when Tyrone Power—one of his closest friends—died a few weeks later after being stricken by a massive heart attack while filming *Solomon and Sheba* in neighbouring Spain. Dee was also staggered by the news. 'He [Tyrone] had so many friends in London, as indeed he had everywhere,' she wrote in a private letter to Radie Harris, an aging but influential American showbiz columnist. 'How awful that a man loved by so many should be taken with so much to give to the world in talent and kindness. Heaven knows, there is little enough of the second virtue around. It is so hard to realise he has gone. Only a few days ago I came across his last letter to us. Full of plans for the future.' For Jack, in particular, it was an enormous personal tragedy. He found it incomprehensible how at just forty-four years old, such an outgoing, impulsive, fun-loving person could be felled in such a cut-and-dried manner.

When Tyrone's wife, Deborah, gave birth to a son on 22 January 1959, two months after her husband's death, Dee noted: 'I'm so happy that

Debbie had her son safely, but oh, the awful bitterness! How happy Ty would have been. How the poor girl has survived this ghastly nightmare I cannot think'.[20] It was hardly surprising that throughout this period in Rome, Jack held long conversations with William Wyler about mortality. Taking a mental inventory, they lamented the recent loss of friends and contemporaries, including Zimbalist, Power, Humphrey Bogart, and Robert Donat. 'It has been a long and arduous business making the film,' Jack told reporters on returning to London. 'I've lost a lot of weight inside a suit of armour all the summer.'[21] Typically, he took the opportunity to gripe about the taxman. 'There wasn't much left of that £50,000 by time it got to me,' he complained vociferously. 'The Italian tax people managed to grab some of it. I suppose as the Italians never pay their taxes the country's got to get money from somewhere.'[22]

The release of *Ben-Hur* was an eagerly anticipated event. After radio and TV specials, newsreel and magazine features, the film became a genuine phenomenon and not only saved MGM from financial disaster by making $20 million on its initial release but was also nominated for twelve Academy Awards, winning an unprecedented eleven. Sensitive to the fact that the script was questionable and the shoot miserable, Jack glossed over the film in his memoirs. His return to London in early 1959 coincided with a period of strange weather and peasouper fogs, setting off a series of sinus-related illnesses. According to Dee, he had been plagued by sniffles and a chesty cough. 'We have all climates this winter,' she informed Radie Harris in a gossipy letter. In it, she lauded the premier of William Wyler's *Big Country*, 'we loved it,' and the first showing of *Room at the Top*: 'It is wonderful to see a picture that treats sex in an adult fashion'. She also mentioned Kenneth More had arrived home from New York with jaundice and was duly comforted by Jack: 'Kenny and Bill (his wife) are off to France for ten days before he starts work on his film with Betty Bacall. It is nice to have her among us. Kenny is much better. He has to watch his diet still, and of course, no drink'. That winter, Jack continued to do his usual star turns, batting for the Lord's Taverners and participating in a charity football match. He found time to commission renowned modernist architect Patrick Gwynne to design a house on the outskirts of Bournemouth for his mother-in-law, a project he found particularly absorbing. 'I got to meet Jack through Laurence Harvey,' Gwynne recounted. 'It was a simple, quite small house with special requirements because the mother-in-law had to be downstairs because she was lame ... the [house] is not much like anything else in Bournemouth.' The foundation stone was laid just as shooting began on the first episodes of the *Four Just Men*, the TV serial deal agreed with Hanna Weinstein a year earlier. Sidney Cole, who was producing, remembered Weinstein had acquired a new husband and she had put him in charge of financial matters. 'Jack's agent had insisted on certain clauses in his agreement which they wanted to vary,' he said. 'This new financial wizard said leave it to me. He offered Jack an increased salary of £250 a week to give way on these other clauses. Jack told me afterwards and said, of course, I took the money but as long as it's you producing and Basil Dearden directing I've got no worries.'[23]

With budgets of £20,000 lavished on each episode, it became apparent the project was turning into the most ambitious film series ever made for British television. Leading directors, experienced in handling feature films, were engaged for individual episodes. The series presented the adventures of four men who had served together as Allied soldiers in Italy during the Second World War who then met again in the '50s and decided to fight for justice and against tyranny, using money donated by their late commanding officer. The bulk of the stories involved kidnap, murder, extortion, and espionage. Based on Edgar Wallace novels, the show was produced by Sapphire Films at Walton Studios in Surrey—a facility owned by Weinstein's production company. The series was unusual in having the four main actors appear alternately, one or occasionally two made a brief appearance in each other's episode. Jeff Ryder (Richard Conte) was a law professor at Columbia University in New York, Tim Collier (Dan Dailey) was an American journalist based in Paris, Ben Manfred (Jack) was a crusading independent politician in London, and Ricco Poccari (Vittorio De Sica) was an Italian hotelier based in Rome. It took nearly five months to shoot the series. By the time Weinstein finished editing, thirty-nine episodes, each twenty-five minutes long, were ready for distribution.

Broadcast globally, including behind the Iron Curtain, the show provided a quantum leap in the magnitude of Jack's international celebrity and proved an instant hit with television critics. Thus, he brushed off suggestions that his transition to TV was sacrificing quality to quantity. 'A lot of my film producer friends have told me that I'm doing wrong. But they're all mistaken,' he asserted.[24] 'Film production in this country has slowed down almost to a standstill. Actors must move with the times. And to survive, you've got to work in TV.'[25] Indeed, amid the crises and emergencies brought on by TV, Jack had watched the foundations of Rank studio crumble as film projects were ditched in favour of television production. 'It is a big gamble for me; if it works, I shall do more TV,' he explained. 'This is the way to pay for the future. And every actor needs to think of that.' Ironically, despite global distribution, the anticipated US network sale of *The Four Just Men* (to ABC, CBS, or NBC) was not to be. Blame was found with the scripts and the star roster, which, while big enough to impress viewers in the United Kingdom and Europe, appeared to have no great significance to sponsors in New York. Despite his disappointment, Jack was determined to divide his time between film and television. By this point, TV shooting schedules had been pared down to allow for a brief lunch, there was scant time for rehearsals, and re-takes were a luxury. Since 1956, over 1,200 TV films had been made in the UK, and although a long way from being the epics crafted at Pinewood, producers churned them out at the rate of one every five days. Occasionally, Jack displayed traces of his anger over the state of the film industry. Talking to Kenneth Passingham, he blurted that Doreen 'couldn't understand how Tommy Steele can earn twice as much as I can in a year. It is very sad.'[26] Adding to his consternation, the chief of the Film Finance Corporation launched a blistering attack accusing top film stars of being overpaid and contributing to the industry's 'precipitous decline'. He said cinema-going, once a habit, had become an occasion and extremely high fees paid to top producers and actors were 'driving up production costs'. Several stars stated they were willing to accept smaller pay and a share in any revenues.[27] In the face of such unexpected criticism, Jack replied in a half-angry statement by notifying the press that he was negotiating a £10,000 cut in salary for a new film, in return for which he would accept a share of the profits: 'I feel any scheme to reduce production costs must be equitable. The actor must be safeguarded—he should not be the only one to suffer.'[28] He shared his professional plight with Alec Guinness, who was also forced to take one-third of his salary in cash and the remainder from profits. 'I have done this with three previous films, but generally film companies do not like the idea,' Guinness claimed.[29] Even so, according to producer Roy Boulting, as many films did not make a profit, 'many actors were not keen' on profit sharing.[30] A favourite sport of writers at this time was to denounce the plight of the film business. Magazines were full of articles with such titles as 'Film industry moans and groans', 'British film industry faces a bleak future', and 'British film industry in its fight for survival'. Though harsh, this criticism had merit and Jack's forebodings were so intense that he prevailed upon the William Morris Agency to find more American work, and they duly delivered with an offer to reunite him with Jessica Tandy for a CBS television special of *The Fallen Idol* for *The DuPont Show of the Month* which saw him return to New York to take on the role of Baines, the part originally played by Ralph Richardson, with Jess portraying his domineering wife. Back home, after unsuccessfully negotiating with Columbia to form his own production company, he signed up as one of the founders of 'Allied Film Makers', a production-distribution co-operative composed of writers, actors, and directors set up in conjunction with the Rank Organisation. The outfit was headed by Michael Relph, Basil Dearden, Guy Green, Richard Attenborough, and

Bryan Forbes, and as *Kinematograph Weekly* reported, they announced an ambitious slate of productions:

> The group has the extensive financial backing of The Rank Organisation and has a working capital of one million for its confirmed programme of eight pictures which will be released through Rank. John Davis (Rank's MD) has allowed the group complete freedom in production and choice of subject matters. Future Allied productions will not necessarily involve all the members working together. Relph and Dearden will make films under the Allied banner and have already commissioned an original screenplay from Janet Green, who wrote *Sapphire*. Jack Hawkins plans to produce two of the eight productions and has commissioned screenplays from William Rose. Two more will be contributed by Attenborough and Forbes, and director Guy Green will himself supply a product.[31]

Jack took an enthusiastic part in the new group. For years, he had actively sought good material, plays and books that his experience and 'nouse' told him would be right for the big screen. So, he was enthused when Carl Foreman, writer of *The Bridge on the River Kwai*, sent him a copy of John Boland's bank caper *The League of Gentlemen*. 'I have bought a novel that deals with a bank robbery carried out according to the strictest military tactics,' Foreman announced in November 1958. 'It is an absolutely serious account of how it is done, which is why I think it is so funny.'[32] As it later transpired, Foreman tried, unsuccessfully, to recruit Cary Grant, Trevor Howard, John Mills, and Michael Redgrave; however, all refused, and along with casting troubles, he became bogged down in preproduction for the Peter Sellers comedy *The Mouse that Roared* and the action epic *Guns of Navarone*. Though Foreman was protective of the property, Jack convinced him to sell *The League of Gentlemen* to Allied Film Makers for their first venture, a deal sealed when Foreman 'kept a part of the action'.

Thus, Jack scored a coup, and *The League of Gentlemen* was handed to Allied on a silver platter—not only the story but a near complete screenplay by Bryan Forbes. In his 102-page script, Forbes crafted Jack's character, Lt-Col. Hyde, as an acerbic army officer, embittered by his enforced retirement after twenty-five years' unblemished service. Angry at the world, Hyde vowed to exact revenge by executing a million-pound bank robbery.

For the job, producer Michael Relph handpicked Nigel Patrick, Kieron Moore, Richard Attenborough, Terence Alexander, Norman Bird, and the husky-voiced Roger Livesey to play the group of army misfits who pull off the theft. Almost as an afterthought, Relph also cast Forbes in the role of Captain Martin Porthill, another member of Hyde's gang. The script evolved throughout the summer, reaching its final stage just as the film went before the cameras at Pinewood on Monday 9 November 1959, after months of preproduction chores.

In the final draft, oozing gritty texture, Forbes provided a captivating treatment of the cops-and-robbers theme. But instead of the crooks being razor-scarred goons, they were all ex-officers and seemingly gentlemen—although none of them left the army with any noticeable flourish of trumpets. As leader of the group, Hyde (Jack), called them together to outline his proposals for 'Co-operative Removals'—explaining that the country went to considerable trouble and expense to equip them with various specialised skills for which there was no longer demand. Regarding this as a waste of public money, he organised a bank robbery with the detail of a military operation. When the bank raid was on—with gas masks and tommy guns—the League of Gentlemen swung into action. In fact, so ingenious was the scheme that it is difficult not to feel a touch of sympathy when—as the final frame spun forward—the whole extravagant plan broke down, a victim of film code morality which dictated that 'crime does not pay', and so, a forced mischance led to their downfall.

Jack remembered the excitement of having 'real control' over the film as he moved through the shoot with astonishing ease. However, he recounted feeling off-kilter during a sequence requiring smoke to billow onto the set. Dryness, shooting throat pains, and a persistent cough saw him sucking on lozenges but to no avail. At first, he suspected laryngitis, but—immersed in the project—put off seeing a specialist. Bryan Forbes remembered several times Jack apologised for being hoarse, 'and then came the moment when his voice failed altogether, and he was forced to leave the film for a period'. Forbes pinpointed the scene, indeed the shot of Jack when he knew his magnificent voice was 'slipping away'.[33] Forbes's girlfriend, actress Nanette Newman, who was also in the film playing Elizabeth Rutland-Smith, recounted that despite his anxieties, Jack trooped on, 'he was the least actorish of all the men I ever worked with.' When filming wrapped, editing and postproduction went smoothly, and plans were made for a huge publicity campaign which began with the premiere at the Marble Arch Odeon, where model Laura Thurlow arrived in an armoured van wearing nothing but 350 new pound notes. Critics used the brightest phrases to express their awe. Ernest Betts of the *Sunday People* spoke of a dashing, spirited affair which put British pictures on the upbeat: 'It is carried out with schoolboy glee and it's a pleasure to see jolly Jack Hawkins swapping his usual rock-like honesty for polished villainy. He's never done so much dirty work so well'. The film was also released throughout the United States, where reviews were equally positive. 'Neatly written and expertly played,' wrote *The New York Times*, 'a devilishly inventive and amusing screen play by Mr. Forbes ... directed crisply and spinningly by Basil Dearden'.

Never one to miss an opportunity, Jack maximised the marketing possibilities by signing a lucrative tie-up deal with Standard Vignale automobiles (as used in the film) to feature on 2,500 posters distributed to the motor trade.

12

The Sixties

The League of Gentlemen provided Jack's last starring role. In the early
'60s, the decline in his popularity occurred for a variety of reasons. Firstly,
his veteran fanbase accumulated in the '50s began to wane as a different
style of film star emerged. Also, as he approached fifty years old, he
found himself, like other stars in the same age bracket, competing against
younger actors like Albert Finney, Tom Courtenay, and Laurence Harvey.
And unlike this modern wave of marquee names—all oozing charisma and
political opinions—Jack refused to air his views on civil rights, religion,
Apartheid, nuclear armaments, or politics. 'To remain a star,' he asserted
with bemused diplomacy, 'you have to be an actor and not a personality.
Otherwise, the audience soon tires of seeing the same performance.
You see it took me a long time to get where I have. I sometimes feel the
young stars who have achieved it overnight haven't learnt the necessary
discipline or professionalism.' In an earlier interview, he said the reason
for his grounding was the fact that his generation were 'just plain everyday
supporting actors in companies like Gielgud's for years before the war'. He
courteously mentioned Guinness, Redgrave, and Mills among them, before
adding: 'When we were small fry, the big fry set us a good example of how
to behave. And, you know, we're none of us like these young chaps in
Hollywood who get dragged from being a soda jerk or something and get
shot up into being a so-called star overnight'. Jack certainly did not look
like a modern movie star either donned in silk scarves, 'J.H.' embroidered
shirts, sharply pressed trousers, a red carnation in his buttonhole, and a
short-back-and-sides hairstyle.

Secondly, a trend was also developing in the film business away from
jut-jawed epics toward grimmer socially conscious cinema—a genre
neither admired by Jack nor suited to his style. More significantly, of the
studios that dominated the post-war period, only Rank at Pinewood and
Associated British at Elstree had survived the onslaught of television.

Both Ealing and London Films—which together had been integral to his career—had gone bust by 1958.

Predictably, by 1960, his interest in film had begun to wane as his thoughts turned more to theatre and television. As he was operating independently, not bound by any studio contract, *The Lizard on the Rock* seemed like the perfect project to usher him back onto the stage after a nine-year absence. Set in the Western Australian desert, the play sees Rockhart (Jack), a man of outward success and power, faced with the collapse of his lifetime achievements. Promoter Peter Bridge arranged a pre-London tour to open at the Opera House in Manchester followed by dates in Liverpool, Leeds, Oxford, and Brighton. 'Always when I have been offered a play, I have been tied up with a film,' Jack explained when indulging in a bit of pre-show publicity. 'Then, when the film was over, the play was gone. This pattern has repeated itself for nearly eight years!' Just prior to rehearsals in late January, John Woodvine, a heavy, dark-haired actor later famed for his role as Dr Hirschin in *An American Werewolf in London*, was released from his contract with the Old Vic to join the cast. He recalls theatre-land was changing as fluffy plays by Noël Coward and Terence Rattigan were being side-lined for social realism and so-called 'kitchen sink' dramas, like *Look Back in Anger* and *The Entertainer*. 'It was very exciting, a great opportunity. This was a period when poetic dramas were still popular, there was still a bit of highbrow playwriting going on,' he told the author. 'I thought this project was going to be very important for me.' With the contract signed, Woodvine never forgot climbing into his car to join the entire cast at Jack's house in Roehampton for drinks: 'This was just before rehearsals, it all seemed very jolly, and I remember being rather excited'. As usual on such occasions, as the house filled up, Dee served an elaborate buffet and drinks. When the cast retired to the drawing room, Jack, in an unusually candid moment, confessed to being scared that theatre critics might 'go after' him because he was a film star. 'It's a terrible problem because I want to do it. Yet I know I'm inviting being smacked on the head,' he explained.

Woodvine remembered, however, that less than a week later, the air of excitement changed abruptly: 'I believe we were in rehearsals for a couple of days when "they" said "Jack's got a bad throat … a sore throat, so we are going to pause for a couple of days"'. Woodvine continues: 'I had no idea his health was in a questionable state. The upshot was Hawkins never actually appeared. And of course, that was it. We heard nothing for a week or so, then we were told the project wouldn't be going ahead' (in fact, Jack did appear for a single script reading at the Scala theatre on Monday 1 February along with author John Hall).

Though in something of a quandary, Peter Bridge assured journalists the play would 'probably' materialise in 1961. 'Obviously, that never happened,' Woodvine adds. 'We all drifted off to other things' which put the kibosh on *The Lizard on the Rock*.

As this was happening, Jack continued to quietly consult specialists in Wimpole Street. In late February 1960, he was admitted to the Royal Marsden Hospital for an examination of his voice box. Under sedation, a laryngoscopy revealed a small cancerous growth, described as 'a condition' by his doctor. Radioactive cobalt treatment was advised, a newish procedure using radiotherapy machines to beam gamma rays into the body to kill tumour tissues. Jack agreed and under a veil of secrecy—so as not to alarm potential employers or friends and family—he underwent such intense treatment that it would have been fatal to have had any further therapy. There was no pain, but the fourteen-day procedure left him exhausted and depressed.

His voice returned but in a noticeably huskier monotone. He recuperated with a trip to Italy followed by bedrest at the family's well-furnished apartment at 34 Ennismore Gardens, a short walk from Harrods and the museums of South Kensington. Characteristically, when word seeped out of his ordeal, Jack played the whole thing down. 'No wonder people began clicking their tongues and shaking their heads,' he said, 'it did look pretty grim. I felt sorry enough for myself, but I felt even sorrier for poor Peter Bridge, the chap who was putting the play on.' 'Don't ask me what the trouble was,' Jack told journalist Cecil Wilson, 'These medical boys give it such tongue-twisting names. Anyway, in layman's language, it was the equivalent of a corn on the vocal cords. I'd never had anything wrong with me and this looked jolly serious.' To make things worse, Jack explained how he was put under a two-month treatment designed to stop him speaking: 'I couldn't answer the telephone and had to speak with everybody—even my own wife and children—in nods and scribbled notes'.

Calling the therapy 'a blessing in disguise', he said 'the gagging treatment' did the trick and he had been given the 'all clear': 'If they hadn't turned off my voice like a tap, I might have thrashed away at it until it was beyond repair'.

As time wore on, he experienced some slight weight gain, and although every cough, sore throat, or pain sparked fears, he was back at work within months. He was well-enough to join Kenneth More and David Niven in a sketch on the finale of *Night of 100 Stars* at the Palladium and even managed some gentle joshing and threw a few kisses. Soon after, he attended the British Film Academy awards at the Dorchester and made a flying visit to Paris for David Lean's wedding to Leila Devi, an Indian

Right: Jack aged twelve. He successfully auditioned for the role of 'page boy' in George Bernard Shaw's first production of *Saint Joan* where he found himself treading the boards with Sybil Thorndike, one of the outstanding figures in British theatre.

Below: Jack was born in the master bedroom of 45 Lyndhurst Road, a modest terraced house in the tight suburban community of Wood Green.

Left: In 1932, Jack secured the part of a naval officer in *While Parents Sleep* at the Royalty Theatre. He is pictured here with co-star Diana Beaumont.

Below: Jack in *Autumn* at St Martin's, which ran from 15 October 1937 to 5 March 1938.

Above: A theatrical sketch from *Autumn*. Jack's lover (pictured) was played by Flora Robson.

Right: Autumn Crocus led to Jack's first encounter with Jessica Tandy, a tiny, mousy-haired actress with pale blue eyes and dark lashes who exemplified the perfect theatrical all-rounder.

Left: A one-time poster-boy of British cinema, Ivor Novello had been panned by critics in the 1920s for his attempt to become the new Rudolph Valentino.

Below left: Jack understood the importance of physical appearance and became a publicist of immense skill, cultivating the press by associating himself with virile activity.

Below right: Jack in 1937. In this year, he starred in *The Frog*, a production packed full of shoot-ups, pyrotechnics, and mysterious disappearances.

Above: Jack, George Howe, Peggy Ashcroft, Margaret Rutherford, and John Gielgud in *The Importance of Being Ernest* at the Globe on Shaftsbury Avenue. The Second World War broke out during the second week of production.

Right: John Gielgud in 1937. An *Evening News* drama critic forecast that Gielgud and Ralph Richardson, a man admired for his calm and sanguine nature, were destined for stardom, but could be outstripped by Jack.

Above: In *Next of Kin*, Jack was full of energy and authority playing a British officer and giving an early display of the solid-sturdy temperament for which he later became famous.

Left: Doreen in ENSA. For a woman of twenty-five, Dee had acquired a wealth of theatrical experience. Born Doreen Mary Beadle in Southampton in 1919, she started her theatrical career as a child playing small parts at the city's Grand Theatre.

Above: On the set of *Bonnie Prince Charlie*. David Niven lamented the film was a 'huge, florid extravaganza that reeked of disaster from the start'.

Below: Jack and Betty Chancellor in *The Moon in the Yellow River* on 26 November 1947, at Arts Theatre, London.

LYRIC THEATRE – HAMMERSMITH

Lessees: Associated Theatre Seasons Ltd.   Licensee: J. Baxter Somerville

Telephone: RIVerside 4432

THURSDAY, SEPTEMBER 27th, 1951, at 7.15

Every Evening at 7.15   Mats.: Thurs. and Sat. at 3.0

TENNENT PRODUCTIONS LTD.
present

DIANA CHURCHILL   JACK HAWKINS

in

Two Plays by Christopher Fry

A PHOENIX TOO FREQUENT

with

GEORGE COLE and JESSIE EVANS

Decor by Loudon Sainthill

and

THOR, WITH ANGELS

GEORGE COLE   LYN EVANS
DOROTHY TUTIN   BARBARA CAVAN
MEREDITH EDWARDS   PHYLLIS MORRIS
ALAN TILVERN   ERIC PORTER
RICHARD WARNER   JOHN GLEN

Decor by Gurschner and W. Stanley Moore

The Plays directed by MICHAEL MACOWAN

A COMPANY OF FOUR PRODUCTION

Left: Jack embarked on a brief foray back to theatreland in Christopher Fry's plays *Thor, with Angels*, written for the Canterbury Festival in 1948, and *A Phoenix Too Frequent*, at the Lyric in Hammersmith, alongside Dorothy Tutin, George Cole, Jessie Evans and Winston Churchill's daughter, Diana.

Below: Though dreadfully miscast, Jack took the part of a high-testosteroned archer in *The Black Rose*, which offered him the chance to work with Hollywood A-lister Tyrone Power (pictured).

Above: Jack's second Korda feature, *Lost Illusion* (re-titled *The Fallen Idol*), was a stylish Graham Greene melodrama of domestic tragedy seen through the eyes of a little boy.

Right: Jack's face frequently appeared on the covers of film fanzines. Here seen in a 1955 edition of *Picture Show* promoting *Touch and Go* and in later issues from 1957 with Jack and Arlene Dahl in *Fortune is a Woman*, with Glynis Johns in *The Seekers* (1954), and with Claudette Colbert in *The Planter's Wife* (1952).

Above: Jack with Noel Purcell in *The Seekers*.

Left: A theatrical poster for the French release of *The Cruel Sea*.

In the '50s, Jack peddled everything from foodstuffs to stationery.

Jack with a young starlet outside the Italia Conti school, *circa* 1956.

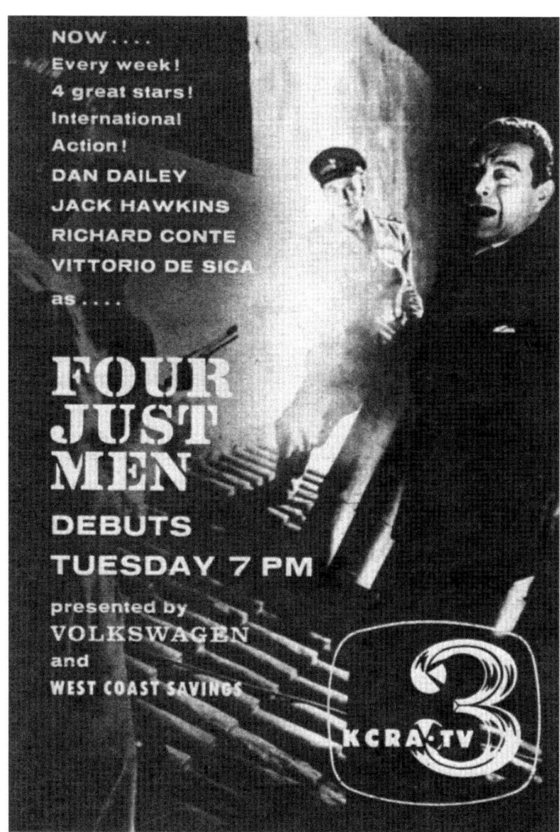

Left: Jack starred in *The Four Just Men*, a TV serial deal agreed with Hanna Weinstein in 1958.

Below: Dianne Foster and Jack in *Gideon of Scotland Yard* (1958).

Right: For the most part, *The Bridge on the River Kwai* was a tense, unhappy movie to make. Everything during production was difficult: relationships, living conditions, script, even Ceylon, where the story was filmed, proved inhospitable.

Below: Jack took a small part as General Cornwallis, a lordly and swaggering army officer in *Lafayette*, a Technicolor epic set in the American War of Independence, starring Orson Welles and Pascale Audret.

Above: Jack visits his old school. He was never academically accomplished nor received any formal qualifications.

Left: In *Masquerade*, Jack plays Colonel Drexel, an upstanding, pipe-smoking, double-dealer asked to abduct a young Arab prince (Christopher Witty, pictured).

Above: In 1968, Jack committed himself to play the part of a bandit chieftain in *The Adventures of Gerard,* a witty adventure starring Peter McEnery and Claudia Cardinale. (*Photo courtesy of Peter McEnery*)

Below: Jack put his salary aside to accept the nominal fee of $1 to join the cast of *The Poppy Is Also a Flower*, an anti-drug film financed by the United Nations.

Above: At the 'Men of the Year' luncheon in November 1967. After Sir Francis Chichester was honoured, Jack was praised for his courage in overcoming cancer, and Israeli actor, Topol, was feted for entertaining troops during the Middle East war.

Below: Portrait of Jack Hawkins taken in his apartment in Kensington, London 1973. (*Allen Warren*)

secretary who he met while filming *Bridge on the River Kwai* (it was his fourth marriage).

Though doctors advised him to slow down, Jack poured over potential projects for Allied Film Producers. 'As soon as possible,' he said, the company would activate *Whistle Down the Wind*, a comedy fantasy written by Mary Hayley Bell, the wife of John Mills, for her young daughter Hayley, who scored a personal triumph in Disney's *Pollyanna*. Another story in preparation was *The Man on the End of the Rope*, from a novel by Paul Townshend. 'This one,' he said, 'we'll have to make in colour in either Switzerland or Austria. It's a drama with a climbing background about an international playboy who quietly tries to scale one of the highest peaks in the Alps.'

Around this time, Jack fulfilled a long-held dream by accepting an invite to go to America to appear in *Two Loves*, his first ever Hollywood assignment. Based on the book *Spinster* by Sylvia Ashton-Warner, the film concerns four people connected with a school in rural New Zealand whose relationships were fraught with dramatic consequences. 'I thought I ought to make a picture before exerting my voice on the stage,' he explained, 'but finding the right script was another matter.' Then, he described how 'out of the blue came the irresistible chance of playing a school inspector in the picture with Shirley MacLaine ... it's the best script of its kind I have read since *Mandy*.'

In addition to MacLaine, the strong cast included Laurence Harvey and Japanese actress Nobu McCarthy. Jack thought MacLaine—who had just wrapped filming *The Apartment*—as being 'bright and honest' in a 'scatty' way, he especially appreciated her understated sense of humour and warmth. However, her sunny disposition was not enough to calm her fights with producer Hal Wallis (of *Casablanca* fame), she despised her role as a schoolteacher, and detested Harvey, to whom she was supposed to be romantically involved. Perhaps worst of all, Harvey, a talented but increasingly finnicky actor, loathed MacLaine and hated Wallis, whom he described as 'the Eichmann' of the film business.[1]

Regardless of the cheerful smile that Jack wore on set, he remained anxious about his health. 'I listen to myself all the time,' he told a friend. 'Sometimes my voice would let me down a bit, although no one but me noticed. I would find myself wondering if something nasty was happening.'[2] Despite his personal worries, he was impressed at American film production. The efficiency, he opined, was due to their technicians, 'even quite lowly ones, like focus-pullers, staying in their jobs into middle-age so knowing them right inside out.' As an example, he recounted a scene where he had to give a Māori boy a sixpence coin:

I took a handful of my own sixpences along. The propman was insulted. 'Do you mind?' he said showing me a draw filled with halfpennies, pennies, three-penny bits, sixpences, shillings, everything.

Although his voice held out and shooting wrapped without a hitch, *Two Loves* received grouchy reviews. Speaking about the ordeal to author Jonathan Freedland, Jack quipped that, 'every now and then an actor realises that he is in business to make money and you hope you'll draw your cheque without anyone even noticing the film came out.'[3]

MacLaine, too, disliked the picture and sourly referred to it as 'a terrible movie' that no one had ever heard of.[4] But on the upside, Jack welcomed his first experience of filmmaking in the USA. Off-set, his days were uncrowded, and he enjoyed a full roster of events, including lunches at La Scala, perched on the corner of Rodeo and Santa Monica, and schmoozing with members of the British colony, an important part of the social life of the town. He observed the 'too-luxurious houses, the too-lavish parties' where hosts hankered after Hollywood's evaporating 'golden age'. Although past its halcyon days, he adored the Beverly Hills Hotel, a legendary institution providing a hideaway for the Hollywood elite. 'It was decked out in its signature pink and green colours and became my absolutely favourite hotel in America,' he explained when recounting how Frank Sinatra, John Wayne, and Elizabeth Taylor used it as a hideaway. 'While I was there the jewellery shop in the lobby of the hotel closed down,' he remembered, retelling a conversation with the man who ran it:

'There was a time,' he said, 'when a fellow would come in and spend a fortune on a pair of ear-clips before taking a girl out to dinner. But nobody here ever buys anything anymore. I'm all right,' he added. 'I've got a business in Las Vegas'.

When the Hollywood whirlwind ended, Jack took several weeks of idle, unsalaried time, broken by an appearance on *The Sid James Show*, where, according to one critic, he gave a 'surprising but proficient performance as a comedian, rather than the big, tough, stiff-upper-lip type we are used to seeing.' More significantly, during that same week, he met with Sam Spiegel to discuss an offer to join the cast of *Lawrence of Arabia*, a military adventure about T. E. Lawrence—a lonely and shy British officer—who attempted to unite the Arab factions in revolt against the Turks in the First World War.

Spiegel's finances were gold plated, and the project thick with the cream of international cinema. Lawrence was to be played by newcomer Peter O'Toole, a young actor with a well-earned reputation as the mightiest drinker in London. The cast included Alec Guinness, Omar Sharif, and Anthony Quinn. At first, Jack was asked to play Colonel Williams, and then in typical fashion, Spiegel became delayed in post-production and requested he play Allenby, a shrewd old general and commander of the British Forces in the Middle East.

Noteworthy was the fact that when Spiegel hosted the stars of *Lawrence* for a pre-shoot dinner, it was revealed that Cary Grant and Laurence Olivier had been tapped for the Allenby role, but both showed little interest (in fact, David Lean had been wooing Grant for a year, and later wrote, 'bugger and blast to the star system' after losing his patience and advised Columbia Pictures that Jack 'would make a mighty good stab at the Allenby part'). Moreover, guests learned that Spiegel also tried to cajole Marlon Brando, the oft hammy, always fascinating actor, to take the part of Lawrence.

Unsurprisingly, negotiations waxed and waned before Jack finally accepted third billing (after Guinness and Quinn) to play Allenby, even though he was effectively third choice for the role. In preparation for the part, his first call was at the famous 'Hawkes' tailor shop where he was fitted by a courtly old man who had proudly served Allenby during the First World War. 'This kind of encounter was obviously very good in preparing my role,' he recounted. A further coincidence occurred at the bootmaker 'Fosters' in St James where they still had an original pair of the general's button-up boots in the storeroom.

Thirty years after his first screen appearance, shooting commenced in southern Jordan. Jack did not appreciate some of the contract's fine print, especially a clause stipulating he shave his head. A bald pate and drooping moustache were, according to Lean, key in creating the Allenby character. However, when Alec Guinness encountered Jack at the beginning of filming, he was surprised at his fragility. 'He's so very shaky,' he wrote to his wife, Merula. 'His hands tremble all the time and having the top of his head shaven he looks wounded in his pride.'[5] To make matters worse, David Lean took exception when Jack struck up a bond with O'Toole. 'I think you should be careful that your friendship does not intrude on your performance,' Lean advised. From Jack's perspective this 'extraordinary observation' overstepped the mark. Alec Guinness—who feuded furiously with Lean in *Kwai*—never forgot Jack being reprimanded for celebrating the end of a day's filming with an impromptu dance. Guinness was also privately appalled at O'Toole's penchant for boozing, brawling, and public buffoonery. In numerous interviews after Jack's death, O'Toole appeared to delight in telling how he nipped off with Jack 'in the middle of boring setups to have a light ale and keep the tonsils healthy. I have never seen Jack worse for drink on set, mind you though, I have seen him taken drunk off-set! But he had a reputation, and I had a reputation and none of it was ill deserved.'

Though Lean exasperated everyone, the atmosphere gradually improved, and the Hawkins/O'Toole friendship endured. He was attractive to the young actor for reasons other than camaraderie. As well as finding a kindred soul, Jack represented a living connection to the golden age of British theatre and cinema. 'There never was a man who was so much on top of his material ... on top of himself,' O'Toole once said. 'And yet his sense of humour was just so rich.' Jack, too, had a great affection for O'Toole, whom he considered one of his protégées. Although just thirty years old, O'Toole's dyed blonde hair made him seem younger (Noël Coward cattily observed that if O'Toole had been any prettier in the title role, they would have had to call it *Florence of Arabia*). The Irishman often romanticised about the sandstorms engulfing the cast in dust, 'and the magic of the desert dawn before the thermometer starts going sky-high, and the rays of the setting sun backlighting the blowing sand with pink and purple hues.' Typically, Spiegel—a man happiest when conducting business on a comfy sofa—huffily complained filming was like waging war: 'The places we were shooting—it was 100 degrees in the winter. We worked in different countries, different hemispheres, in Jordan, Morocco, Spain'. As filming progressed, Jack, too, lamented a torturous production filled with embroidered facts and 'Hollywood distortions' as history was sacrificed for drama. Eyebrows were raised at an over-the-top depiction of the attack on Aqaba—a nonsensical scene involving the Arab Council, and the implication that the Bedouin abandoned Lawrence once the opportunity for plundering dried up. Much to his horror, Jack later received a scathing letter from Allenby's daughter-in-law who was incensed that his portrayal showed 'a monster ... not a great man. It is most distressing for the family, who loved and respected him to know that his character is distorted in this way.' With some awkwardness, Jack publicly retorted the film was 'about Lawrence, not the Field Marshall.'

All things told, *Lawrence of Arabia* was a surprisingly tight production and, when edited, ran for three hours and forty-one minutes. The film was handsomely mounted and beautifully acted, giving way to a flood of spectacular reviews. 'Jack Hawkins as General Allenby rises like a barbed old fish to bite hard on some of the best lines in Robert Bolt's beautifully baited script,' gushed the *Daily Herald*. Likewise, the *Birmingham Daily Post* was equally beguiled: 'Peter O'Toole gives a magnificent performance as Lawrence, supported with fine appropriateness by Jack Hawkins as Allenby'. Dilys Powell went as far as saying it was the first time the cinema had communicated 'ecstasy'.

Feeling happy and revitalised, Jack returned to London where he declined an offer of the lead in *Victim*, Basil Dearden's ground-breaking film examining the persecution and extortion of gay men. 'The legality of homosexuality was very much in the forefront at the time, and it was really a major evil that people were being blackmailed,' producer Michael Relph recalled. After the success of *The League of Gentlemen*, Allied Films struck a vein making serious sociological thrillers. In *Victim*, Jack had been offered the part of Melville Farr, a gay barrister, but refused, fearful it might compromise his masculine image. Dirk Bogarde, who eventually played Farr, suggested it was Dee who scotched the idea, fearing Jack would 'prejudice his chances of a knighthood' (compounding the irony, Bogarde was knighted by the queen in 1992).

Despite such sensitive content, the film proved surprisingly successful with audiences and provided a boost to Bogarde's career. 'At that time, he was the sort of young matinee idol—and a romantic lead—it was very courageous of him to do it,' said Relph. 'It was really the beginning of him playing serious parts. It was really a very important step to take.'

'Actually,' says Derren Nesbitt, who played the sinister blackmailer 'Sandy' in the film, 'it helped change the law. It was a very brave move on Dirk's part because everybody in the business knew he was homosexual.' Speaking to the author, Nesbitt added: 'I'm not surprised Jack refused the role; in my mind's eye, I just can't see that would have worked'. Nesbitt recounted how homosexual acts between males were illegal in England and Wales until 1967. The fact that willing participants in consensual homosexual acts could be prosecuted made them vulnerable to entrapment, and the criminalisation of homosexuality was known as the 'blackmailer's charter'.

Peter McEnery played Jack 'Boy' Barrett, a young working-class gay man who fell prey to Nesbitt's blackmail in *Victim*. 'That film was discussed at length in the press,' he told the author. 'Remember, it was five years before the law was passed making it [homosexuality] legal. It was interesting because those Allied films in the late fifties and early sixties were pretty good stuff—I thought Jack's *League of Gentleman* one of the best.'

In the end, Bogarde's performance was praised as his finest but despite critical success, *Victim* was not a hit and Allied Film Makers began winding down. 'It didn't last very long because everybody went their own ways,' Relph recalled, 'but while it did it was a sort of cooperative effort, and we made one or two good films.' With the demise of Allied, Jack finalised a deal with Guy Hamilton and American impresario Jules Buck to form Tricastle Pictures to produce 'low-budget films of high quality'. Their first effort, *The Party's Over*, directed by Hamilton on the streets of Chelsea, featured a cast including Ann Lynn, Oliver Reed, and Louise Sorrel. The official promotional blurb from Tricastle stated:

> It's the sort of party where anyone who has any inhibitions to lose, loses them quickly … where pot (a type of drug) is smoked coolly in corners … and where, if you happen to pass out, you are liable to have a ban-the-bomb sign painted on your face or be stripped.

Predictably, the film touched off a storm of controversy when the aforementioned party depicted a drunken girl stumble headlong down a flight of stairs, only to be set upon by two other women and stripped naked. What caused a wave of revulsion was when one teen had sex with her as she lay apparently unconscious, but she was, in fact, dead. For all the uproar, Hamilton delivered a sound movie, but sex was the main headache for the censors, with necrophilia a close second, leading to the refusal of an 'X Certificate'. John Trevelyan, the secretary of the board of the BBFC, called the movie 'unpleasant, tasteless and rather offensive'. By the time it was finally approved for release, two years after completion, Jack had removed his name from the credits and wound-up Tricastle.

13

Jack of All Trades

Jack Hawkins remained an itinerant worker through much of 1961, accepting offers from all directions. At the time, Dee made this prophetic comment: 'The life of a star is pretty short lived. What can you do once the hair and teeth have gone? And even if you earn great sums of money, you can't save anything for yourself, so the only thing to do is to try and provide something for the children'. Indeed, Jack had been so overwhelmed by 'creating a nest egg' that a previous scheme aimed at saving money came back to haunt him. That summer, after a three-round bout with the Inland Revenue, three appeal court judges ruled that £500 he paid in dividends to his three children under 'Roehampton Productions', the trust company he established in the mid-'50s, should be regarded as his own income and was liable to surtax. 'Now I don't know what to do,' Jack declared after the ruling. 'I've got leave to appeal to the House of Lords, but heaven knows what that'll cost. Naturally, deep down, I want to take the fight to the end because, after all, a principal is involved—yes, this definitely is a principal, not a fiddle ... I'm not a person who has ever evaded my tax. If I wanted to dodge taxes, there are easier ways than this ... like leaving the country' (it seems worth mentioning that Tom Hawkins, who had always existed in the shadow of his younger brother's success, was also listed as a director at Roehampton Productions. Since the 1950s, Tom had been caretaker at St Michael's Primary School in Bounds Green Road and later the verger at St Michael's Church in Wood Green. He remained a close confidant). It bothered Jack that he was being scrutinised and there was more than a hint of exasperation when he dramatized his grievance to columnist Patricia Lewis of the *Daily Express*, positioning himself as a man wronged. In a stagey moment, he passed his thumb wearily across his temple, turned to Dee, and 'privately' remarked: 'By the way darling ... I'm afraid we'll have to reconsider plans for the children's education'. Then, fixing a gaze on Lewis, he added: 'I was going to send them abroad to learn languages. Public school means they've got to slog through so much that's no use to them later, whereas a few years travelling is a good grounding ... but that may not be possible now'.

In the event, a few melodic variations of the tax debacle followed before Jack was distracted by a cable from French director Jean Dréville urging him to consider a small part as General Cornwallis, a lordly and swaggering army officer in *Lafayette*, a Technicolor epic set in the American War of Independence, starring Orson Welles and Pascale Audret. While relishing the idea of working with Welles in France, his eye was firmly on the offer of second billing. Even better, the shoot promised an opportunity for Doreen to visit the Riviera and indulge in a spot of house hunting, after having set her sights on owning a Mediterranean villa. The original plan had been to finish *Lafayette* in four weeks, but it took far longer to complete than Dréville had planned as shooting became weighed down by showy displays. In the end, Jack had virtually nothing to do in the movie, and only appeared toward the finale, drinking punch on a horse, feigning bonhomie, and pointing at a battlefield. 'I only did the film for the money,' he later admitted. Remarkably, as shooting chugged along, Dee found a property in France, but during foreclosure, Jack left her to finalise details after being tapped for a part in the Columbia Pictures feature *Five Finger Exercise*, alongside Rosalind Russell, the actress famed for her role as a fast-talking reporter in Howard Hawks's screwball comedy *His Girl Friday*. Written by Peter Shaffer, the film deals with the emotional entanglements of a Californian family. However, Jack seemed sadly miscast as a bewildered American father with a 'transatlantic' accent. Indeed, certain scenes had an almost soap-opera quality. 'There are not all that number of mature leading men about,' Jack said when explaining why he was essentially playing an American:

At least that's what we're finding in England. There seems to be a generation missing. A lot of them drifted out during the war. And when the war was over, it was difficult for them to get back in the theatre. I have friends who were promising actors before the war, but they never got back. They became merchants, real estate men and insurance salesmen.

Five Finger Exercise challenged him only in the sense that he had to keep up the strained accent, which occasionally lapsed back into British. As far as characterisation went, some moviegoers might have sensed a similarity to Jim Fletcher from *Touch and Go*. Away from the set, LA's social life kept him busy as he was 'lionised' in the closed community of Hollywood society and escorted from party to party by Rosalind Russell, a woman he described as one of the 'reigning queens of Hollywood'.

From Los Angeles, Jack flew to New York and then to London where *Lafayette* was released to poor reviews. Writing in the *Daily Express*, critic Clive Barnes thought the trouble with the picture was the girlish-looking hero: 'Michel Le Royer as Lafayette hardly looks as if he could buckle a swash to save his life. We are left with a smoke laden spectacle and a few brief character sketches, such as Orson Welles bumbling amiably as Benjamin Franklin, and Jack Hawkins as General Cornwallis'. Meanwhile, Jack continued to see Peter O'Toole from time to time; the pair made an appearance, but not to bid, at a sale of modern paintings of the late film magnate Alexander Korda at Sotheby's. Peter also encouraged Jack to join Roger Moore, one of the more colourful characters of the British film industry, to judge the star-studded final heat of the Miss United Kingdom contest. By this point, the title deeds for a small villa at Cap Ferret on the French Riviera had been processed, and Dee was thrilled when she took possession of 'our corner of paradise', a second home, rather than a holiday retreat to be visited during the summer months (Jack was astute enough to have kept his French Franc salary from *Lafayette* and paid for the property in local currency).

As there were precious few reasons, professionally or personally, to stay in London, the couple began work on the property at Saint Jean, located a mile outside Nice, heading east towards Monte Carlo. Set behind pine trees, the villa had been converted with panache from what was then the huge playroom of the sprawling estate of the Duchess de Talleyrand, an American railroad heiress. With its whitewashed walls, terracotta roof, and sloping manicured garden leading to a private beach, it was homely rather than ostentatious. Jack tended the rockery in a garden complete with a wrought iron sundial and lush with bougainvillaea, lavender, mimosa, roses, and grapefruit trees jutting out on stilts over the sapphire bay of Ville Franche.

But the real draw of Cap Ferret was the little social set—David Niven, Rex Harrison, Somerset Maugham, Véronique and Gregory Peck, Leslie Bricusse, and screenwriter Jack Davies all lived nearby. Jack once remarked this A-list lifestyle left him pleasantly unaffected: 'I've always been fortunate in being able to tread the whole razzmatazz of stardom at worst with a kind of cynicism and at best with achievement'.[1] As well as offering precious privacy, the French bolthole was easily in reach of home comforts. 'Pork sausages and smoked haddock—we import 'em into France,' Jack told a visiting reporter when advising that Mediterranean Langouste was a 'poor, cotton-woolly substitute for Scottish or Irish lobsters'. He was proud to be able to enjoy France, yet English at his core. 'I could never live permanently abroad,' he said puffing on his pipe, looking out onto the ocean. 'I am only at home in England.'[2] In contrast, Dee often remarked that the British weather 'doesn't agree with either of us. Jack gets bad throats ... and I get fibrositis. I'd be perfectly happy living abroad as long as all the family were together.' The next few months were idyllic—rising mid-morning, walking the beach, eating extravagantly. 'We all drank a lot in the South of France in those days,' Dee said, reminiscing about a life of swimming, sailing, fishing, socialising, tennis, and poker. 'We were always getting a bottle out of the fridge. It was difficult to draw the line.'

Donald Sinden was a regular visitor, but never too keen on the property which he once described as being 'a famously ugly villa opposite where David Niven had a place.' Lunchtimes were often spent at the 'African Queen' in Beaulieu where Jack weighed offers, he had little interest in accepting, including rejecting an advance to write an autobiography.[3] Financial necessity, however, did see him join Robert Mitchum in Hawaii for *Rampage*, a tortuous yarn about tensions in the Malaysian jungle. Although billed second and produced by Mitchum's own Talbot Productions, Jack was never happy with the project. His character, Otto Abbot, is a big-game hunter with unresolved emotional issues and a thirst for blood. It was a slow-going production, combating Mitchum as 'the catcher' against Jack as 'the killer'. While the dialogue was crisp and quotable, it was littered with ludicrous lines such as: 'Prayers are reserved for the weak who wish to inherit the earth'. The project did little for Mitchum's angst, and he described *Rampage* as 'a lot of dancing girls, banjo playing and bull'. The film also took flak from the *Daily Mirror*'s mean-spirited critic who lamented a 'remarkably poor film' and questioned how Jack managed to get involved in it: 'The reliable Hawkins rarely gives a bad performance, but this time he has dropped a clanger and the poor screenplay is the reason'. As if that was not bad enough, the *Monthly Film Bulletin* baulked that 'one of the remarkable things about [it] is that it is possible to see animals act badly'. Although *Rampage* is far from vintage Hawkins, his relationship with Mitchum survived and the pair became occasional drinking partners, when circumstances allowed.

By 1963, Jack had wide experience in most branches of the media. As a television actor, he was in constant demand especially from the American networks NBC, ABC, and CBS. That summer, he accepted a part in a courtroom drama produced jointly by Associated-Rediffusion in London and NBC in New York, given a large cheque was more or less guaranteed (£5,000). *To Bury a Caesar*, directed by Wielder Cook—whose later film *The Homecoming: A Christmas Story* spawned *The Waltons*—told the story of a member of parliament who was repeatedly passed over for a cabinet post because of a rumour of cowardice in wartime. NBC network paid the fees of the all-British cast, while Associated-Rediffusion provided the technical facilities at their Wembley studios. 'I think there is a great future in these co-productions,' Cook explained. 'By splitting the cost, you get a better result than with one company alone.' When it aired, the production was praised on both sides of the Atlantic, with reviewer Jack Gould noting 'its chief virtue was excellent acting in the small parts as well as in the leads. Jack Hawkins and Pamela Brown imparted dimension into their roles.'

Throughout this period, Jack was busily preparing for a long shoot playing a missionary full of self-contempt in *Zulu*, Cy Endfield's all-star affair bristling with stiff upper lips and bayonets. The story relates the historic battle of Rorke's Drift in 1879 when a handful of men from 'B' Company, 2nd Battalion, the 24th Regiment of Foot, South Wales Borderers, defended a mission against 4,000 disciplined and fearless Zulu warriors. Speaking to the *Illustrated London News*, Jack remarked that both sides showed a courage that 'can be denied neither by contemporaries nor by posterity'.

Endfield, a stiff-looking Pennsylvanian and imposing forty-nine-year-old, had arrived in Britain a decade earlier after being blacklisted by the House Un-American Activities Committee. His previous three films—*Sea Fury*, *Jet Storm*, and *Mysterious Island*—had been popular successes but *Zulu*, one of the year's biggest, most expensive epics was a much more formidable enterprise.

Money, as always, was of vital importance. In addition to a flat fee of £30,000 and second billing, Jack was cheered at the prospect of working with Stanley Baker, who had played the frightful Bennett in *The Cruel Sea* (and delivered the immortal line: 'Snorkers! Good-oh!'). In a masterstroke of casting, Michael Caine—then earning a crust playing bit parts in budget movies—was given the part of the laconic Lieutenant Gonville Bromhead. Noting his cockney twang, Caine remained forever thankful that Endfield was an American 'because no English director would've cast me as an officer, I promise you, not one.'[4]

It had taken more than a year to shape the screenplay, and although writers were still tinkering with a few scenes, they had finished work on Jack's character Otto Witt, a stiff-necked Swedish missionary with a taste for brandy who sees his inner power fade under the tension of war. Endfield thought it generous of Jack to take what was, essentially, a smallish role, but one he enthusiastically threw himself into. 'It's a challenging part,' Jack explained on location in June 1963, 'because, although the missionary is a weak man, he must be portrayed with strength.'[5] There was a ghoulish quality about Witt. Clean shaven and wearing a pulpit gown, he begins spouting holy writ and delivering epic rants: 'You're all going to die,' he screamed at British troops. 'Don't you realize? Can't you see? You're all going to die! Death awaits you all.' Adapting to rural Natal made *Zulu* a punishing experience, as the cast and crew endured a hostile landscape plagued by reptiles and insects. 'Filming there was tough,' says Muirne Mathieson, daughter of the famed musical director Muir, who acted as continuity assistant on the film. 'The set of Rorke's Drift was actually built in the Drakensberg Mountains—the Amphitheatre, I think was the name of the section below which we filmed. It was more scenically impressive than the very flat area in which the Battle of Rorke's Drift had originally been fought.' Away from the location, the cast stayed at what was then a lovely hotel: the Royal Natal National Park Hotel. 'It all seemed pretty cushy and amazing to me,' Mathieson adds.

Other than socialising, entertainment came via the BBC overseas service, board games and a shelf stacked with dog-eared paperbacks. 'I've only been here a little while, not like Stan and the rest. But frankly I won't be sorry to get home,' Jack complained after a couple of days in the wilderness.[6] Despite the hardships, Mathieson told the author that Jack was always able to channel energy into his performance, even in such bleak surroundings: 'He was an incredibly good and consistent actor— so easy and polite to work with. He was delightful and carried out his performance in the most professional manner'.[7] However, she still retains clear memories that 'he had a problem with his throat which couldn't have made his life easy'—an early sign that despite the cobalt treatment administered three years earlier, his health was on the wane.

On the credit side, he was able to stay in touch with Dee by wire, and found solace in the company of Baker, Caine, and Nigel Green. On a brief visit to the shoot, journalist William Hall remembered spotting Jack ducking in and out of the chill night air, flapping over the threshold in a flowing cloak and pastor's hat: 'He took my arm in an iron grip and hustled me towards the bar.... Britain's own favourite screen man o' war, was this time oddly cast as a fire-and-brimstone preacher, a role in which he never seemed entirely happy'.[8] A month later, with the first unit still way off in the hills of rural Natal, Baker praised Jack's commitment: 'He has never given a really bad performance in his entire career. In all his films, he has always been a pillar of strength'.[9] Prior to release, Paramount's publicity hyperventilated. 'Dwarfing the mightiest! Towering over the greatest! The supreme spectacle that had to come thundering out of the most thrilling continent!' Though publicity was extensive and early trade notices superb, Jack was incensed by the editing which, he thought, made Witt look buffoonish. Too aggrieved to laugh the matter off, he even walked out of the premiere of *Zulu* in London on 22 January 1964, though, he was sufficiently composed to show his face at an afterparty. However, most critics agreed in every sequence, he gave a gritty, lucid, and engrossing performance. The only dissenting voice came from the film critic of the *Liverpool Echo*, who was not impressed: 'For once Jack Hawkins, as a hysterical clergyman, fails to convince possibly because this is the one really fictitious character in the story'.[10] Though *Zulu* was regarded as one of the best films of 1964 and was even nominated for a BAFTA, Jack hated it and later lamented that he was 'cheated out of a good performance'.

During *Zulu*, there was some talk of work on a planned epic of Joseph Conrad's novel *Lord Jim*. Back in London, Jack received a phone call— followed by a hand-delivered draft screenplay—from Peter O'Toole, who was acting as an associate producer. Duly, he signed to play 'Marlow', Conrad's famous narrator in a picture set in the latter half of the nineteenth century. The story tells how Jim—played by O'Toole, by then a hot commodity—deserted a wrecked ship at sea, and after being stripped of his officer's rank, wanders about the Far East, searching for a way of vindicating his honour. A strong cast had been put together, which featured Eli Wallach, James Mason, Noel Purcell, and Curt Jurgens. The picture was being produced by Richard Brooks, husband of actress Jean Simmons, who had spent much of 1963 looking for an authentic backdrop to the story, before deciding to film in the Far East, where much of the novel had taken place.

Again, like *Kwai*, the location provided Jack and Dee an opportunity to visit their beloved Asia, and on 6 December 1963, accompanied by Jack McGowran, they touched down in Hong Kong for six weeks' filming. 'I must say I'm beginning to feel like part, of the British export programme,' Jack told the press at the airport. 'My children should learn more geography from my travels than from their school lessons.'

Though the temperature was warm, the hotel luxurious, and the food delicious, there were some frustrations such as when filming started without a complete script—the final tangle of pages was handed to Jack hours before shooting. That said, he was needed only occasionally and seemed to consider his time on the movie as something of a vacation. His mood was further cheered by Noel Purcell—a sort of gentle giant, half-covered by a grizzled beard—who arrived well-lubricated. Waving a dog-eared script, he told reporters he had flown halfway around the world to read a few lines of dialogue. By any measure, the presence of O'Toole, McGowan, and Purcell propping up the hotel bar made it inevitable that, as day follows night, the drinks flowed freely. Jack could often be found firing up a cigarette in the saloon, and despite enduring a hacking cough and dry throat, he remained a militant smoker, puffing through at least sixty a day.

Still under British rule, Hong Kong back then was like a gargantuan amusement park—an exciting, vibrant city bursting with energy. James Mason thought the best thing about the whole experience was 'that we all got to visit the Far East in a style consistent with the demands of our respective agents.' In many ways, Hong Kong reminded Dee of her ENSA days in Asia and luckily for the film crew, parts of the harbour front were so unchanged from its appearance in the 1880s that little dressing had to be done.

After a month, before the production moved to Cambodia, Jack and Dee returned to London and missed the horrors of jungle filming, where the crew were threatened by dysentery, heat rash, snakes, and stinging insects. 'The three months we spent in Cambodia were dreadful,' O'Toole remembered. 'Sheer hell. A nightmare. There we were, all of us, knee deep in lizards and all kinds of horrible insects. And everyone hating us. Awful.'[11]

The movie did well enough to be chosen for the Royal Film Performance and received generally positive reviews—some even gave glowing praise. Always prone to sentiment, *The Sun*'s critic said it was 'magnificent, vast, teeming, colourful, spectacular, strong, dignified, breath-taking, superb, splendid, beautiful, touching, big, alive, and exciting'. The *Mail* described it as full-blooded and stirring, it had 'just about everything for the occasion'. *The Guardian* put O'Toole through the mincer by rejecting his 'quavering voice, the watery blue-eyed look, the panting, and the sweating'. Their critic reckoned the star looked as if he was 'building himself up to play the lead in all four Gospels at once'.

Back in London, Jack went to the dog track, played golf, and gave interviews focusing on *Lord Jim* before joining the cast of *Guns at Batasi* at Pinewood with Richard Attenborough, Flora Robson, John Leyton, and the blond Scandinavian starlet Britt Ekland. The film depicts an erupting world where newly empowered forces, both black and white, embrace the realpolitik of post-colonial times. A group of veteran British NCOs, headed by upright Regimental Sergeant Major Lauderdale (Attenborough), becomes entangled with a coup in a recently independent African state dogged by political intrigue.

Shot on the stage next to *Goldfinger* between February and April 1964, the project became legendary for Peter Sellers behaviour—a remarkable feat, considering he was not even involved with the film. Having just married Ekland, Sellers was so paranoid about her having an affair with the dashing young Leyton that he asked his old friends, David Lodge and Graham Stark, who were co-starring in the picture, to spy on his new wife. Although Ekland found her husband's suspicion ludicrous, she told the author that she remained 'on set for less than three weeks' before pulling out of the production.[12] As Graham Stark remembered, *Batasi* shut down for two days before a 'very young, very long-haired girl came timidly on the set. She'd been flown in from New York to replace Britt'—the girl was Mia Farrow.

Amid all this upheaval, another private drama was being played out at Pinewood. Throughout filming, Jack's voice began audibly fraying; apart from one relapse, it was the first serious discomfort since location shooting on *Zulu*. Terrified the cobalt treatment administered in 1960 was failing, he found a ray of hope, however faint, from a divinely inspired faith healer, who, friends said, genuinely seemed to work miracles. Although not enthusiastic, it was a straw to clutch at, given there was no prospect of another course of cobalt therapy—one treatment was as much as the human body could handle. Frightened of receiving a more deadly diagnosis, Jack was fully aware that should the cancer return, surgery to remove his vocal cords was the only option left. The faith healer prayed, meditated, and provided encouragement, which, remarkably, not only made him feel mentally better, his voice, albeit still weak, returned clearer and audible.

Though he could sense Jack's insecurity, Attenborough remembered he remained a trooper on set and even helped him craft an outstanding performance as the RSM by advising he visit Wellington Barracks to watch the parade ground mannerism of the sergeant major. To round-off the tuition, Jack arranged for 'Tibby' Brittain, owner of the most-feared voice the British Army had ever known, to provide military elocution lessons. With no big-name epics competing against it, the *Guns of Batasi* performed well, taking $1.8 million at the box-office, a profit of $445,000. For his efforts, Attenborough won a BAFTA Film Award.

As the sets were dismantled (and replaced with interiors for *Those Magnificent Men in Their Flying Machines*), Jack was already learning lines for a comedy-thriller, *Masquerade*, slated to be filmed in Spain. The project, put together by Michael Relph and Basil Dearden, featured Cliff Robertson, Marisa Mell, and Christopher Witty and was based on a clever story by William Goldman. In it, Jack plays Colonel Drexel, an upstanding, pipe-smoking, double-dealer asked to abduct the young Arab Prince Jamil (Witty), heir to the throne of a Near East kingdom after oil concession talks between the state and Britain collapse. 'It was an unforgettable experience,' says Witty. 'We were located in Benidorm; this was before tourism when people could get on a plane and go somewhere quite cheaply ... there was also a lot of shooting at a dam which was under construction.'

Throughout the shoot, Jack looked jowly and pasty. The throat issue also weighed heavily on his mind. 'Actually, he seemed fine. Jack was a very affable, pleasant man,' Witty recounts. 'He was very helpful to me as a young actor. The film was directed by Basil Dearden, who was a bit of a tyrant—he wasn't terribly engaging, so I was always a little bit nervous of him in contrast to Jack who made everything very easy. The other star, Cliff Robertson, wasn't as welcoming. He was American and much more matter-of-fact.'

By way of letters and phone calls, Dee kept her husband posted with news from the home front. Like most kids, Andrew and Nicholas were taking a healthy interest in pop music. At Westminster school, Andrew led a group called the *Runabouts*, while Nicholas directed another group at the equally exclusive Millfield School, Somerset. 'When they are at home, Jack and I put in earplugs if the din gets too great,' Dee joked. 'Otherwise, we go out.' By this point, Andrew was taking a keen interest in acting and starred with Richard Attenborough's son, Michael, in Westminster school's production of *Bartholomew Fayre*.[13]

Back from Spain, Jack received a call from ITV with an unusual offer. Would he be interested in the challenge of playing against type as an out-of-work family man lamenting his lot in Robert Storey's *Putty Medal*, an ABC sixty-minute *Armchair Theatre* drama? His answer was an immediate 'yes'. Ostensibly a kitchen sink-type production, it was described as 'one of the few successful contemporary visits to a middle-class home paid by TV drama'. 'It was a good script, touching and credible,' co-star, Barry MacGregor told the author. 'This was a complete departure for Jack, a real change of tempo ... an affectingly simple character.' Although the production was delayed by the death of Winston Churchill, which disrupted rehearsals, performances were uniformly first-rate. And though critics praised the characters, situation, and dialogue, the play was always unlikely to appeal to viewers who preferred to see Jack in tougher roles—his stardom still depended on an amalgam of bullishness and bravery. 'Whoever cast Jack Hawkins as Len Driver in the ITV play, *Putty Medal*?' asked Mrs Grant of Derby in the *Sunday Mirror*. 'He acted the part superbly as only he could—but I like him as a man of iron, not as a simpering old man doing jigsaws. Still, I hope we see more of him.'[14] For MacGregor, the opportunity of working with Jack again was a welcome pleasure. He remembered his quick sense of fun and enthusiastic nature:

I thought he was wonderful to talk to. He was part of the life that you were creating, he was also listening to you and interested in you as a person. I happened to mention that I had just done a play at the Westminster Theatre, which was then heavily influenced by the Moral Re-Armament movement. It was not a club, its not a cult—it's a group of people who believed very strongly that you shouldn't wear suede, you mustn't swear, homosexuality was very wrong, and you look after each other. There was a hierarchy which was based on wherever you're born or whatever you're born into: stay there, don't try to get out of it because that's what the creator wanted. Jack took me aside and said: 'For God's sake Barry, don't get caught up—they are the most evil group of people you'll ever work with, they were after me in the 30s.'

Early 1965 would be devoted to a single project. During January and February, Jack worked principally in Israel playing the role of a British major in *Judith*, a rambling Lawrence Durrell suspense story of one woman's personal vendetta against a background of the turbulent politics of the 1947 Arab-Israel war. A three-page synopsis prepared by 'Cumulus Productions' concisely described key scenes involving Peter Finch—among the most intense actors of his day—playing a kibbutz leader, Aaron Stein. Sophia Loren took on the unlikely role of Judith, an Austrian Jew who arrived in Israel to track down her former Nazi husband, Schiller, who left her and their child to die in a German concentration camp.

Set just before the British mandate ended, the film centres on a band of underground fighters planning to capture Schiller—who is thought to be in Syria and planning an Arab invasion of Palestine when the British move out. In the absence of photographic evidence, they smuggle in Judith as she is the only person able to recognise him. Amid the tension and danger of Israel's fight for freedom, Stein (Finch) is just as intent on saving him so as he can obtain information about the invasion of Palestine by the Arab countries. Jack played Major Lawton, a British officer, who unofficially aids Judith on the trail of her ex-husband.

'Sophia is so professional,' Jack said during an on-set interview. 'She does her job with no fuss or bother. Up at four in the morning, never late, never bad-tempered. Magnificent. I have some really torrid love scenes in this film with Sophia. And get paid for it—one thing I might have done for nothing!' During filming, a tense truce existed between Israel and the Arab countries, overseen by United Nations peacekeepers since the ceasefire following earlier hostilities. Finch took the step of going and working on an Israeli kibbutz for a month to get the feel of things before shooting started. 'Open air living suits me best,' he told journalists. 'And in the atmosphere of the kibbutz, anyone with problems get straightened out. In a community that is fighting for its existence, whose people are working for the community as a whole rather than for their individual needs, personal needs seem suddenly very simple.' However, Finch's own needs saw him struggling with a painful divorce and embarking on a series of mighty benders. One biographer noted, when not filming, he would be rolling around sozzled or feverishly painting, using every atom of energy. Hungover and shielding his eyes from the light, 'he would shove his artwork under people's noses saying, "Look at that. It's the saddest and cruellest picture I've ever painted in my whole life. That's how I feel tonight. A clown's face in savage torment."'

This unrelenting soap opera was too much even for Jack who tried to be sympathetic, but then immersed himself in his reading. In his spare time, he drove through the hilly roads to Jerusalem, visited fruit markets, and bathed in the Mediterranean. He was glad at the experience in Israel but genuinely disappointed when *Judith* brought protests of 'Israeli propaganda' from Arab countries. To his apparently genuine bewilderment, Jack was appalled when the powerful Arab League denounced Sophia Loren and barred all her films—old and new—from being played in the Orient. As if that was not bad enough, *Judith*'s premier at New York's Radio City Music Hall was panned by American critics—one cruelly stated that Jack gave a performance of 'worrying ambiguity'. In Britain, *The Tatler* casually remarked it was 'a hollow, unconvincing piece'. Critic David Adams mused why he found such a 'second rate film' so entertaining. 'Was it just Miss Loren, flitting about the kibbutz in skin-tight shorts and a shirt several sizes too small?' And although Finch knew perfectly well that he had hardly behaved during the shoot, the hostile press led him to claim he no longer cared about the size of a part: 'I'm only interested in the quality of the script. I think this has finally taught me the lesson that if the film is stupid, I'm going to look twice as stupid if I have a big part in it'. Even Loren, who was dismayed by jokes about the film, refused to mention it in her memoirs, *Yesterday, Today, Tomorrow: My Life*.

Curiously, Jack managed to avoid the *Judith* promotional hullabaloo but never wavered in his support for Loren and her performance. Back in Britain, he set his established salary aside to accept the nominal fee of $1 to join the cast of *The Poppy Is Also a Flower*, an anti-drug film financed by the United Nations, produced by Edgar Rosenberg, the gentlemanly husband of Joan Rivers. Featuring Yul Brynner, Omar Sharif, Trevor Howard, and Rita Hayworth, the movie tells the story of UN narcotics agents tracing heroin shipments from the Afghanistan-Iran border to a European distributor. Still photos show Jack in army uniform—belt tied around his tunic and a 'Sam Browne' leather strap across his shoulder, a file in one hand, and the inevitable cigarette in the other. Though smiling broadly, Trevor Howard recounted Jack was positively glum during most of the shoot. 'I remember one day on the set Jack's voice just sort of gave out, and it distressed him clearly,' Howard reminisced:

Later, I took him for a drink, and he looked quite ashen, and I said, 'What is it, *amigo*?' although I knew what was troubling him. He was afraid the cancer had returned but he was trying to be optimistic. He said, 'Nothing to worry about. The doctors gave me the all-clear. Besides,' he said, 'I've been to a faith healer and since then I've been fine.' But I think he knew. Just didn't want it to be true, but he was worried, and I was worried.[15]

Indeed, Jack admitted he 'somehow managed to get through it', before continuing his gruelling pace which included shooting in New York for the Bob Hope Theatre in *Back to Back* with Shelley Winters and in London, he was the leading man in the BBC production of *The Trial and Torture of Sir John Rampayne*, playing a former diplomat kidnapped at Heathrow by a young showbusiness impresario played by Ian McKellan. Rehearsing at a drafty old building in Wandsworth, Jack lamented a tortuous experience made worse after a severe coughing fit when he was left with a mouthful of blood. Doctors thought the bleeding was caused by a ruptured blood vessel. 'Cancer,' they said, 'doesn't behave like this.'

Meanwhile, Jack accepted an offer to appear in six episodes of *Dr Kildare*, a syrupy American TV medical drama. Though he had just finished an arduous year, it preyed on his mind that, somehow, he needed to remain the family breadwinner. 'I tend to feel insecure about my work— all actors do—and I now think it is necessary to keep on one's toes,' he confided. 'And I've given up my status cars like the Bentley. It takes far too long to park and maneuver.'[16]

Financed by CBS, *Dr Kildare* promised a good payday and the chance to relax under the Californian sun. Starring alongside Richard Chamberlain and Raymond Massey, Jack played an outspoken atheist admitted to Blair Hospital at the same time as an evangelist. The show had a large cast including Diane Baker playing his daughter, Bradford Dillan as the evangelist, and John Napier making a cameo appearance as a patient. In many ways, the job doubled-up as a holiday, as there was enough time to enjoy a busy social calendar and spend time with Massey, a laid-back old Canadian character actor with whom he had been friends since working together in the Thorndike troupe in 1924.

At the Metro-Goldwyn-Mayer studios, Jack's hair was dyed pepper-grey but close-ups in 'Metrocolor' made him look tired and flabby. The scripts were very good, if not spectacular, and all seemed to be going well until, without warning, his gravelly voice began to fade 'like a radio with a draining battery'. In the middle of a scene, after uttering a mouthful of dialogue, he was terrified to discover he could muster little more than a croak. Consequently, after a local doctor detected nothing suspicious, the producers—eager for haste and economy—said the croaky voice added 'realism' to the performance.

Tapes of *Dr Kildare* survive and show a remote, distant performance as Jack endured his private crisis on the plywood set of a soap opera hospital. Remarkably in Hollywood, where conversation consisted solely of shoptalk, the lid was kept tight on his condition. Even Richard Chamberlain remembered none of the real-life drama other than he 'enjoyed working with Jack Hawkins'.

Prophetically—and we will never know if Jack realised or not—his last lines in Hollywood using his own voice were delivered on Stage 2 at the MGM studios on Washington Blvd; in a tear-filled close-up, he said: 'It was God's will … never doubt that. Remember me as I am at this moment … please. Never have I felt so whole or so happy'.

Back in London, doctors confirmed he had suffered a haemorrhage and the cancer had returned, sending Jack on a lengthy journey that he had no desire to be on. 'We both knew the ultimate was facing us and that unless some miracle occurred, he would have to have his larynx removed,' Dee recalled. But there was no miracle or last-ditch alternatives, as radium could not be used because of complications, meaning the only course of action was to remove the entire larynx and silence his celebrated voice forever. It was either that, doctors said, or face certain death within months.

Theo Hartley, a journalist who knew the family, claimed Jack was fully aware he had performed his 'last true speaking part' and confided that had he not had Dee and the kids, he would have let nature 'take its course'. Remarkably, during this particularly traumatic period, Jack managed to record a performance of *The Open Door* with Rachel Gurney, a production for ITV's *Mystery and Imagination*. Filming went smoothly; so smoothly that, on set, he told the crew his hoarse-sounding voice was due to laryngitis and gave no indication of the turmoil within.

However, after the taping, he called a family meeting. Standing with his back to the fireplace, he bluntly told the kids that he had cancer, and if he did not have an operation to remove his larynx, he would die. Nicholas remembered there was no emotion, 'he just made the statement'. 'We went through all degrees of despair,' Doreen confessed, but prayer sustained them both. 'I am a great believer in thinking positively,' she explained. 'We took the same attitude to his illness. There was never a moment when we both sat down and said: "Oh God, isn't it awful? What are we going to do? We count our blessings for what we have and what we are now."' During this period, she also turned to Betty Bacall, 'for we had so much in common. She helped me so enormously in so many ways. The warmth and fun of her tremendous personality are part of my life.'

On a drizzly Friday evening in late January, Doreen drove Jack to the University College Hospital for the operation which would change his life. During that journey, a car cutting out of a side street nearly collided with them, prompting Jack to wind down the window and yell, 'You Bastard!'—his last public statement using his own voice.

The four-hour operation was a success.

As Dee later told the syndicated press, Jack came through the operation remarkably well:

It was a long operation on Saturday. When I saw him on Sunday he was out of bed and last night he was walking around. Now it is mainly discomfort. He is not able to use his throat and has to be drip fed. Already he is taking physiotherapy for breathing and he finds this a bit exhausting. After he comes out of hospital to continue the therapy we shall go to France. After that we shall discuss the future. He may be doing some production. I should say he will be out of action for about three months. The important thing is that the malignant growth was in a place which was operable, and I am pleased to say it was successful.[17]

14

Picking Up the Pieces

Surgery had left a hole the size of a halfpenny in Jack's throat by his Adam's apple—it went straight down to the windpipe and lungs. As Dee alluded to, his time in hospital was upsetting and he groused at the frustrations and irritations, only made easier by two no-nonsense Australian nurses.

As he could not eat orally, feeding was by tube; hard massages kept his lungs clear, and a bed pan was required to avoid any 'undue strain'. He was finally discharged on Thursday 10 February 1966. A bit unsteady, he was supported by Dee and managed to wave as a group of well-wishers looked on. From here on, a long and challenging period of adjustment began. Close friends like David Niven helped revive his spirits as he embarked on breathing and speech therapy at home. 'David was wonderful all through Jack's illness,' Dee remembered. He had 'an infectious gaiety, and an extremely colourful sense of humour, both of which buoyed me up immensely.' By 15 February, Jack felt well enough to pen a letter to columnist Radie Harris:

> I arrived at home on Thursday night having made a rather rapid recovery from surgery—now a long haul with the speech therapist. It has been very moving; we have had thousands of letters and cards from all over the world—particularly—which is very nice, the USA![1]

However, in addition to post-surgery pain, Jack tired easily and suffered from a continuous runny nose—that brought on a persistent melancholy. 'The operation cut off communication between my throat and my lungs,' he explained, in a croak of short sentences. 'I breathe through the hole in my throat. It is entirely different, and the sounds are different from normal talking.'[2] The first months were difficult. Doreen admitted Jack's attitude to life had changed as some of the 'striving went out of him'. As well as changing physically, there were, understandably, mental strains. 'I think he was amazed to find himself still alive and able to lead a very full life,' Dee said. 'He hadn't believed that would happen.'

Though it took months to adequately communicate, efforts slowly began to yield results as he learned to speak by using air controlled by the stomach muscles to vibrate the oesophagus. 'It was a bloody nuisance at first. I couldn't speak. I didn't know what I was going to do. I had to go around with a pen and a notepad,' he explained. 'But I was lucky. My doctor took the notepad and threw it out the window.'[3] A few members of the press were inquisitive about the state of his health. In a melancholy moment, he confided to journalist William Hall, 'Of course, I'll never act again. I'm resigned to that. There's no point thinking about the past, in regretting anything.' For a while, he used a portable voice box—like the type used by Stephen Hawkings, the physicist. 'I don't like using this damn thing,' he complained, brushing aside the bulky microphone and amplifier.

Amid the struggles, his mood was frequently lifted by pleasant encounters. Among friends who dropped in to see him were Bernard Lee, Laurence Olivier, and Ralph Richardson. In the years to come, Jack's 'little parties' would take on a legendary atmosphere. 'They were usually at his flat in Kensington,' says Michael Jayston. 'It was always aswarm with people. Everyone was there, John Mills, Rex Harrison, Ava Gardner, Peter O'Toole … the world and his wife was there. It was quite unbelievable; you could have cast King Lear out of the guests.'

After several months confined to home, Jack's emotional temperature was raised when Virginia McKenna invited him as a surprise guest at the Royal Film Performance of *Born Free*. That night, a single spotlight found him—prompting a truly loving standing ovation. 'He was never defeated,' says McKenna. Queen Elizabeth led the applause which thundered through the theatre. 'It's marvellous to have so many friends and get such a welcome back,' Jack said. 'It was a most warming and moving reception.'[4] Speaking to journalists, Dee said Jack had made a remarkable recovery 'and we go out almost every other day. He is living a normal life.'[5] Indeed, using a neck scarf to cover the hole in his throat, he attended all the important theatre shows in the West End, enjoyed golf, fishing, and accepted invitations to attend industry events.

By summer, his daily schedule—breathing exercises, therapy, and endless free time—had become routine. 'Once it was off to the studios, into town, always on the move,' he explained. 'Now, suddenly, I've got time to appreciate this other side to life, to stop and stare.' He insisted he was not particularly courageous and said wartime experiences may have helped him cope: 'I want to work at something. Over the next two or three years I hope to develop some new interest but I'm not sure what yet. It won't be painting or gardening. Something more active'. He still had many unfulfilled ambitions and persisted with a long-held desire to direct a film. Dee had also been urging him to switch gears and turn his attention to life behind the camera. Jack asked journalist William Hall to inform his readers 'not to worry about me,' adding: 'I went to Vienna the other day, and everyone fussed around me like bees round a jar of honey. They're very kind—but I didn't want them to'.

Escaping the bleak British climate, which Dee had always detested, the Hawkinses ensconced themselves in France that summer, hopeful that the change of scenery would make life easier. But before they had even unpacked, a bitter fight with the National Health Service (NHS) failed to sweeten Jack's disposition. 'They don't seem to think you can be sick here as you can in England,' he scowled.[6] 'They [the NHS] asked me why can't you continue with your employment? I wrote back: "I have no vocal chords and it is generally considered useful for an actor to be able to speak." I told them I'm only out here to try to get fit in order to get back to work in the shortest possible time.'

Despite the endless emotional turmoil, he soon settled into Riviera life, enjoying quiet evenings at home and the simple pleasures of gardening and fishing. Though unable to swim, he could bob about the Mediterranean perched in an inflatable ring. 'I'm not supposed to go swimming because if the water got through the hole, it would go straight into my lungs and knock me off,' he joked. 'I've taught myself to go paddling with a rubber tube. I have to be wary of waves and tell everyone that if they see me catch a big one, they would be doing me a kindness to turn me upside down and let the water drain out.' 'Actually, it was worse than that,' recalled Michael Jayston. 'He once told me he couldn't even take a bath, or he might drown.'[7] Unsurprisingly, Jack was more than ever dependent on his relationship with Dee, who during that long summer, played nursemaid and housekeeper—clattering around the kitchen and coordinating medication. A woman of untamed energies, she remembered feeding Jack remained messy. And despite his lost sense of smell, sausages and haddock continued to arrive by courier from Blighty.

A few months later, Jack seems to have delighted in welcoming Ivor Herbert, a journalist invited to observe his recovery. Sipping cocktails on the veranda, he watched his subject staring into the sun, 'his great chin jutting; filmed a thousand times, paintable certainly but sculptable more so ... clefts in chin, between brown owl-coloured eyes, beaky nose: round sunburnt neck, a gold St Christopher medallion obscuring the place where only four months ago he had the operation for cancer in the throat.' Though Herbert was usually an especially observant spectator, he failed to notice any melancholy or anxiety in Jack's manner, or even suggest the operation had taken a terrible toll of him, 'he was more-than-humorous, bubbling funny, happy man.' Washing down lunch with champagne, Jack spoke in measured tones about everyday life: 'The kids often come out here—they help to liven up the place'.

Finally, when the summer ended, the couple were both exhilarated to return to Britain and lunch with Queen Elizabeth II in the gilt exuberance of Buckingham Palace. Covering his mouth with a napkin, Jack apologised for 'speaking in this funny voice.' With a wave of her hand, the queen allayed his anxiety by brushing off the remark, saying, 'I can understand every word you have said, and am pleased you are talking so well,' to which he timidly quipped, 'I am hoping for the return of silent films.'[8]

For the first time in memory, both Jack and Dee saw a clear horizon—with no obligations of any kind. They jumped at the chance of taking a sojourn to Mexico with Peter O'Toole and his partner Sian Phillips, where O'Toole announced he was to make a movie directed by Jack called *St Patrick's Battalion*, and he proceeded to scout locations in the pouring rain. However, Jack was struck by a case of double pneumonia and the film became one of O'Toole's long-gestating, never-completed projects.

Back in Europe, Jack renewed old friendships. He was put on intensive display after joining Richard Burton, Elizabeth Taylor, and Yul Brynner in Sicily for the Taormina Film Festival, a top-ranking movie junket. In London, he waved a miniature Union Jack at the World Cup at Wembley and joined Douglas Fairbanks in presiding over a special draw for blind children. Amid this activity, he also crossed paths with journalist Michael Parkinson, who was then working on regional television. 'Jack walked into the room and in a casual manner opened a packet of cigarettes and put one to his lips,' Parkinson told the author, when recounting a 'Green Room encounter' at Thames Television. 'He did it in nonchalant fashion and you could feel a sense of shock in the room. He didn't of course light the cigarette but started laughing at the consternation he caused.' Weakened though he was after the operation, Jack was still puffing around twenty cigarettes a day (down from sixty). 'The fact that he still smoked was extraordinary,' says actor Peter McEnery:

I watched him doing it. He couldn't draw on the cigarette because he was breathing through the hole in his throat and yet he still smoked. It was about the whole motion of putting the cigarette to his lips. The hole in his throat was the size of a half crown. It was an enormous hole which he covered up with a medallion and a scarf. But he had to be very careful; he would cough, for instance, by holding a handkerchief to his throat.[9]

An American journalist once asked Jack: 'Isn't it crazy to smoke after what you've been through?' He replied philosophically. 'It's a bit late to worry about that now. I like smoking, so I'm going to continue doing it. It was a sister at the hospital who started me off smoking again. After the operation she offered me a cigarette and I took it up again. It's just a silly habit.'[10]

As if by providence, as Jack's thoughts turned again and again to work, Henry Hathaway came knocking in the autumn of 1966, eager to use him as an associate producer on a tale of a hunter out to shoot an elephant that killed his friend. Jack loved the basic idea—Dee went a long way toward assuring him he could do the job—and Hathaway promised an 'exciting shoot'. On paper, *Last Safari* was just what the doctor ordered, and Jack arrived in Nairobi on 23 November 1966 and headed for the snow-capped Mount Kenya for a short rest at William Holden's exclusive safari club at Nanyuki, before facing an intense month of work. His contribution to the project, though not taxing, was performing as a go-between with the actors and film crew. It was a great boost to his confidence; however, the project was put together in a hurry, and although trailers advertised 'an epic adventure', its star, the burly Stuart Granger, called it the 'worst film ever made in Africa' and a downright clinker. Nevertheless, the experience rejuvenated Jack's spirits. 'I thoroughly enjoyed myself,' he beamed on arriving at Heathrow, looking tanned and healthy. 'I never thought a year ago I'd live to get back into the swim. It's been fun and I'm so grateful to all the people that made it possible.'[11] In the same breath, he declared, 'you soon find out who really cares two-pence for you. Glenn Ford, Peter O'Toole, David Niven—they never leave me alone. Well, let me admit at the beginning I was convinced I was finished. That I'd never make another picture.'

Around this time, Jack had other irons in the fire. After abandoning *St Patrick's Battalion*, O'Toole offered him the deceptively simple role of the British ambassador in Shaw's *Great Catherine*; the offer, O'Toole said, was made out of 'charity in the name of love, in the terms of a hand-out, no'. Though his ailment made him difficult to cast, Dee pointed to the 'fantastic progress' Jack had made getting his voice back during the year. 'In *Great Catherine* he has only a line or two to say. He might be able to keep on acting if he could get parts requiring practically no talking.'[12] Filmed at Shepperton, the story tells how a British officer, Captain Charles Edstaston, is sent to the Russian court of Catherine the Great as an envoy, where he must contend with the crafty machinations of her chief minister, Potemkin, played with brassy style by Zero Mostel. 'It was a marvellous part,' Jack enthused. 'Absolutely tailor made for me. You see, every time this ambassador fellow opened his mouth to speak, someone interrupted him. In the entire film the ambassador was only allowed one line to speak!'

However, continuity girl Tilly Day remembered a low moment when 'some words or other had to come forth that he had to say, and he suddenly put the script down and walked away.' She recounted: 'Tears were coursing down his face. I went up to him later because time was allowed to pass. I said, "What's the matter, Jack?" He said, "It's the words, they're so beautiful and I can't say them." It was some Shakespearean thing he'd got to quote. It was a shame."'[13] Despite his lack of voice, O'Toole stated Jack was not a craftsman without tools—he could act with his eyes, or even a glance, registered by sharper, more clarified Panavision photography. Film critic Gillian Franks noted, 'one vintage Hawkins glance is worth pages of dialogue. His close friends would seem to agree with that. Since his operation, they say he is acting better than ever.'[14]

Even today, *Great Catherine* sparkles, polished by a beautifully realised visual style bestowed by art directors John Bryan and William Hutchinson, Oswald Morris's unmatched camera work, and Dimitri Tiomkin's exceptional musical score.

With filming complete by the end of April, Jack was again free to accept another offer, this time from Euan Lloyd to feature in *Shalako*, a British-German production capitalising on the trend of popular spaghetti Westerns. 'I've known Jack for years,' said Lloyd. 'But don't think he got the part because we are old buddies. He is still one of the most capable actors. He can convey as much with a glance as someone else with a page full of dialogue. We all consider it a privilege to work with him.'[15]

Though burpy-gulps were sufficient for delivering brief lines, when longer speaking parts were called for, Jack would mime the parts and another actor's voice was dubbed for him because it took time and visible effort for him to produce the words. 'Charles Gray was the voice of Jack from then on,' says John Woodvine. 'He sounded a bit like Jack, you see, maybe a bit lighter. He was also quite a character.'[16] (Grey was later known for his portrayal of the villainous, cat-loving Ernst Blofeld in *Diamond's Are Forever*.) On a visit to Roehampton before *Shalako* went into production, journalist Donald Zec noted:

> Jack had mastered the art of talking from the stomach via the oesophageal by-pass. Admittedly, that familiar voice loses considerable volume on its windy detour from midriff to mouth. The trick is to fill the stomach with air (Jack has managed to work bottled beer into the act) and then shape the words around the burps. At the moment, the result leans more towards flatulence than eloquence.

Jack told Zec he could not sound his aitches though. 'Call myself "Jack 'awkins"—the surgeons have turned me into a ruddy cockney.' Laughing, too, could be painful. 'Which is a pity because some very funny things have happened since the operation,' he joked:

> … there was this chap I answered on the phone the other day. 'Blimey, guvnor,' he said, 'you ain't arf got a shockin' cold!' And then there are those people who, having seen some of my old films on television recently, imagine that they were made after the surgical job. Several have written to say things like: 'We just want you to know that we think your voice is as good as it ever was.'

Jack told the 'shockin' cold' anecdote at the 'Men of the Year' luncheon in November 1967. After Sir Francis Chichester was honoured, Jack was praised for his courage in overcoming cancer, and Israeli actor Topol was feted for entertaining troops during the Middle East war. 'It would only be half a life without acting,' Jack told the gathering. 'So, I am happy that moviemakers had enough confidence in me to give me another chance … even without the voice.'

Meanwhile, with *Shalako* looming, Jack packed for a three-week stint in Almeria, Spain, a setting with plenty of atmosphere and dusty mountain scenery. Though 'timidly working his way back into acting', he was awarded fourth billing in this tale of a group of European aristocrats traveling to New Mexico in 1880 to hunt big game but, after violating Indian Territory, found themselves the target of angry Apaches. The picture starred Brigitte Bardot and Sean Connery, who took the flamboyant central role. When the cameras were rolling, Jack was in fine fettle playing Sir Charles Daggett, the cuckolded husband of Lady Julia Daggett (Honor Blackman), a seedy Sydney Greenstreet-like role with several meaty scenes, including a shoot-out with Indian attackers. The experience had a tremendous effect on his morale and affirmed he could construct a new career without a voice.

One afternoon, after a full day's slog, news spread around that Bardot's dog had died—a development which brought the entire production briefly to a halt. 'She was actually bereaved,' a crew member noted. 'It was a personal tragedy.' At this moment, Connery perched himself beside Bardot in the 'executive tent'. Watching from afar, a Frenchman sitting next to Jack asked uneasily, 'What is Connery going to say to her? He must be careful what he says!' 'Don't worry,' Jack whispered, 'He is only conveying the condolences of Her Majesty the Queen.'[17] The Frenchman was not amused.

After twenty-one days on location, the cast and crew returned to London to shoot interiors at Shepperton where Charles Gray was preparing to dub Jack's voice, an event, he recalled, which turned out to be an unforgettable experience:

Jack loaded us up with Black Velvet, I remember, and we had a run at it, but it wasn't entirely successful—a lot to do with the Black Velvet I think—and we had to do it again. Part of the trouble was that Jack had been saying the lines in his own voice and therefor gulping. So, we came to a sort of arrangement. I said, 'In future, could you possibly try not to vocalize but just mime the words?' which is an awful thing to say to an actor. It's like, you know, telling a dog not to bark when it hears the doorbell go. But afterwards it was much easier because there weren't those unnatural lulls between words.[18]

Although now considered a classic Western, Connery had doubts about the film when director Edward Dmytryk delivered his final cut. However, critics generally agreed that *Shalako* was a fine picture. Jack's next venture, though, was determined by a large paycheque, which he was in no position to refuse, given 1967 was one of his leanest years ever. When the National Council of the Churches of Christ in the United States thought America needed spiritual renewal, they bankrolled a religious short, titled *Stalked*, for the Lutheran Churches of America. For some reason, Jack was chosen to portray a man alienated and withdrawn from the world trying to escape God by travelling abroad but, as the production notes detail, 'finds he is unable to escape God's love'. Skilfully directed by prolific Christian filmmaker Rolf Forsberg, shooting took the form of a monthlong itinerary at locations in Amsterdam, London, and Madrid.[19] (Other than the financial reward, the reasoning that underlay his choice to do the film is difficult to discern. However, Dee added a familial mood with an extended visit to Amsterdam.)

A more 'traditional' assignment followed in September 1968, when he committed himself to play the part of a bandit chieftain in *The Adventures of Gerard*, a witty adventure starring Peter McEnery, Claudia Cardinale, and Eli Wallach, based on satirical short stories by Sir Arthur Conan Doyle. McEnery played the egotistical Etienne Gerard, a fatuous, strutting hussar, serving during the Napoleonic Wars who thinks he is the best soldier and lover that ever lived and intended to prove it during a merry chase through Spain. 'I think Jack was in Rome for only a week,' recalls McEnery, who remembered a physically challenging shoot, complicated by a diverse crew. 'Playing those kinds of heroes is very demanding … very tiring,' he told the author. 'It was quite challenging, in fact, because the director was Polish and didn't speak a word of English. We were filming in Italy with an Italian crew, Polish cameraman and lighting guy and it was very difficult. I don't think the director fully understood the wit—the tongue in cheek humour—of Conan Doyle, of which it is based.' Even so, despite all the pressures, filming was relatively trouble-free. McEnery never forgot a sequence in which Jack's character captured him then planned a grizzly death. 'He was the leader of a band of brigands living in the mountains,' he explained:

> I'm tied to trees and the idea was to catapult me over this chasm. And what happens is that Jack must cut a rope and the two trees spring apart and I'm torn in half—well, that was the sort of macabre idea. However, what happened was when he cut the rope, the trees whiffed back, and they just pulled my boots off. Amid the noise and the dust, I thought Jack was admirable in his behaviour ... putting up with all that.

McEnery lamented that there was no publicity swing for *Gerard*, and 'it sank without a trace ... the film really didn't do anything at all. I don't think they could edit it when they got back to Hollywood, and they even had a lot of problems with marketing it. Remarkable, because it had a stellar cast.'

For his next film, Jack turned his focus to a small part in Sam Spiegel's *Nicholas and Alexandra*, a picture hyped as the first truly accurate account of the last ruling Russian monarch, Tsar Nicholas II, and his wife, Tsarina Alexandra. The role of Vladimir, the minister of the Imperial Court, was almost negligible, but he accepted the part not only for the decent salary but also the opportunity to work with Michael Jayston (playing Nicholas), one of the shining lights of the Royal Shakespeare Company. 'The Russians didn't want us to film in the Soviet Union, obviously, so we filmed in Spain, which can look like Yorkshire or anywhere,' Jayston told the author. 'We spent nearly five months on it.' Unlike Jack, who had grown used to Spiegel's methods, Jayston judged him 'an appalling human being ... one of the nastiest people I ever met in my life':

> I've never met anybody who liked the man. The first person who was offered Rasputin was Max von Sydow, and Sam turned him down because he had an accent. Rasputin was a peasant, and he could have easily played it. The next person up for it was Peter O'Toole and I was in Sam Spiegel's office when he got a message from Peter saying 'I'm not going to do it' written on a roll of toilet paper. Sam went berserk. Sam also turned down Liv Ullmann—such a great actress—because she had an accent! That was the stupidity of the man. I mean Alexandra was German, she could have quite easily have had an accent.

Away from the cameras, Jayston remembers spending 'a hell of a lot of time together with Jack' in Madrid: 'He was incredibly generous; the generosity was unbelievable. We'd be drinking champagne—but never got drunk—we were eating the most incredible food'. He never forgot one scene where Jack was struggling with his voice, trying to get out words, which were dubbed later: 'It was so moving; it was one of those few occasions that I got quite emotional about it. I didn't say anything afterwards. He had to do it about four or five times. It was just the effort that it took him … remarkable'.

Immediately after *Nicholas and Alexandra*, Jack found himself in Paris with Brigitte Bardot for the premiere of *Shalako* where the media—in typical tabloid fashion—were more interested in Bardot's monkey skin 'flapper' jacket. In a brief interview outside the Ambassador Theatre, Jack said the fact that producers were still offering him work was the source of much gratitude: 'I flatter myself that when they cast me in a part it's me Jack Hawkins they want and not the person who was once Jack Hawkins … if you know what I mean. And I'm perfectly honest with anyone who hires me. I tell them exactly what they're letting themselves in for'.

On the home front, he was thrilled to see his eldest son, Nicholas, gaining experience working in the theatre. Having spent eighteen months at art college, he found work as the stage manager for *Cinderella* at Liverpool's Royal Court. 'I've gone into the theatre off my own bat, really, for although we talked about it a lot together, Dad has never tried to influence me one way or the other,' he explained at the time. 'I had a yen for acting at school, probably because, as the son of a famous actor, I felt I ought to. But my first love was painting. Then I began feeling the pull of the theatre and I started looking around for jobs.' In an effort to earn extra pocket money, his training as a painter of portraits and landscapes came in handy with the weekly budget: 'My latest portrait was of actor David Niven's two children. His wife Hjordis asked me to do it as a birthday present for David'.

Meanwhile, Jack enjoyed a brief rest in France before shooting a small part in the darkly comic *Oh! What a Lovely War* as Emperor Franz Joseph, a project for which Richard Attenborough, in his directorial debut, recruited many old acquaintances—among them Dirk Bogarde, John Gielgud, John Mills, Kenneth More, and Laurence Olivier. Jack, Attenborough said, was cast for 'his great personality and stature'.[20] The film provides a theatrical and musical chronicle of the First World War, told through the songs and documents of the period. In one scene, John Gielgud remembered Jack hardly spoke but had to weep 'which he did most beautifully with great skill. He was absolutely master of his technique. But I could see that he was under tremendous strain.'[21] One well-known reviewer thought *Oh! What a Lovely War* was worth 'a million peace demonstrations' and kicked the hell out of jingoism.

Unlike the Attenborough picture, there was not much laughter on the set of Ken Annakin's thirty-third film *Monte Carlo or Bust*, a comedy about intrigues and personal battles during a vintage automobile race. Jack had accepted the role of Count Levinovitch, the head of a ring smuggling stolen jewels, but the project proved an unhappy experience. Filming took place in Rome, and starred American screen idol Tony Curtis, Peter Cook, Dudley Moore, and Terry-Thomas playing a conman, accompanied by Eric Sykes.

Much to Annakin's annoyance, Curtis proved 'brittle, self-centred and a bully … his embarrassing performance [was] utterly selfish as I had feared and not in key with the rest of the cast or story.' The director never forgot the first time Curtis sidled onto the set where Susan Hampshire stood waiting. She smiled at him and reached out her hand:

> 'Oh, Mr. Curtis, I am so happy to be working with you. I feel I will learn so much.' And from that moment, he gave her hell—shat on her, ridiculed her in rehearsals, so much so that the poor girl used to pull me aside and cry desperately. 'What shall I do, Ken?' she cried. 'I've worked on the London stage, I know I'm a good, competent actress but this man rewrites the script, changes his lines and I'm left without a cue—looking a complete idiot!!' Even Terry-Thomas, the hardened old pro that he was, would often look askance at some of Tony's antics, especially in one garage-scene where Tony went into a kind of belly-dance, then rushed over and planted a wet kiss on Terry's lips! Occasionally, he used to do the same to me.[22]

Another negative factor was Curtis's enthusiasm for narcotics, easily obtainable in Rome. 'Apparently, Tony had been on coke for years.… Thus; in the mornings he was bright, exuberant, and apparently very eager to give me his best,' Annakin recounted. 'But after lunch I would come back and find him sprawled in a chair, scowling, and looking ten years older. At these times, as a conscientious director, I would have to decide whether he was genuinely depressed with the scene we had shot, or whether it was just that the drug had worn off.'

'Mr. Hawkins never seemed interested in squabbles and politics,' says Derren Nesbitt, who played Waleska, Jack's villainous sidekick. While respectful attention was showered on Curtis, Nesbitt was left astonished when no one would sit with Jack at lunch, 'that is, except me.… I think the others were just uncomfortable. He was basically on his own with his ever-present cigarette in his own unassuming way … but I sat with him.' Nesbitt thought the best thing about Jack was his relaxed manner: 'He once offered me a morsel of advice. He said do you want to learn how to screen act, young man? And I said, yes, I would. He said: "Find a chair and fall asleep!" I never forgot that and still quote it!'

In the few scenes they shared, Nesbitt recounted the mechanics were sometimes a struggle because, 'you know, you speak but Jack doesn't. So, you don't know what level to get to.' As Jack later explained: 'There were problems when I came to the end of my lines because other actors had to have a cue to reply. But I worked out a system with the others beforehand. Sometimes I would scratch my nose or brush a fly from my face. Or I would pull out my handkerchief. When the signal came, the other actor would start his lines.'[23] He admitted that he sometimes 'got depressed' about his voice but said 'people have been wonderful to me, particularly my fellow actors. They've been patient. No sympathy as such, just understanding and not making a fuss because of my handicap. Just how I wanted them to be.'[24] He recounted—and said he loved—the occasional jokey comments like, 'speak up Jack,' 'Got a cold Jack?', or 'I can't hear a word you're saying'.

When released, *Monte Carlo or Bust!* was positively received by critics alike and won a legion of fans, including the recording star, Joe Brown, known for his hit *A Picture of You*. 'I've always loved British comedy in films and *Monty Carlo* says it all,' he told the author. 'Terry-Thomas playing his typical villain and Eric Sykes as his long-suffering side kick. Peter Cook and Dudley Moore with their Heath Robinson inventions and British army snobbery. Jack Hawkins and Gert Frobe also providing some kind of side plot. The whole film is a comedy classic.'[25]

When his last frame was shot, Jack returned home to a remarkably busy schedule, beginning with an appearance on Simon Dee's BBC TV chat show. 'I think we were reacting to a newspaper article, which described Jack's condition,' recalls producer Roger Ordish. 'We approached his agent, who said that Jack was keen to spread the word that laryngectomy did not mean you could no longer speak.' During the broadcast, cameras caught the intensity of Jack's plight as he spoke by inhaling air into his windpipe and then 'belching' his replies. 'The result sounded better than you might imagine,' Ordish recounted. 'In "hospitality" after the live transmission, he had several of us learning how to do this strange 'belch talk' with much laughter. What a marvellous man. Unforgettable.' Mrs E. M. Barrett from Welwyn Garden City was so moved by the interview that she wrote to the *Daily Mirror*: 'After seeing actor Jack Hawkins on Simon Dee's show, I would like to nominate him as the *Man of the Year* for his courage and determination'.[26]

From here on, the cancer which had touched Jack's life in such a brutal way gave impetus and new purpose to his charity work. 'We have our sense of values all wrong, particularly our attitude towards research into diseases,' he complained when opening a cancer laboratory at Mount

Vernon Hospital, near London. 'Naturally, I have great personal interest in the efforts being made in research. Let's face it, it is a tragic experience for an actor to face life without a voice, but it may be in a few years the result of what is being done will prevent the larynx having to be removed.' He went on to say that in Britain 'our values were all wrong,' as millions were spent on modern aircraft in prestige projects (a barbed reference to Concorde): 'Our prestige would be much higher in this country if we made a real attack on cancer'. It was his clearest message on the subject.[27]

Though Jack worked steadily, his career lacked the incandescence of his earlier years. However, in *Waterloo*, he gave a dose of fire and bluster as General Picton in this historical pageant recreating Napoleon's final defeat at the hands of the duke of Wellington. Director Sergei Bondarchuk, wearing a floppy hat and cravat, engaged a magnificent cast including Rod Steiger, Christopher Plummer, Virginia McKenna, Michael Wilding, and Orson Welles, playing Louis XVIII, 'grotesquely swaddled in his own fat' (the description of one unkind critic). Shot in the summer of 1969, *Waterloo* 'was an immense undertaking', according to Ian Ogivly, who played Colonel Sir William Howe De Lancey. In his autobiography, Ogivly gave a vivid snapshot of filming in Rome, Ukraine, and Hungary where everything was beyond human scale with thousands of extras and oversized sets. To recreate the battlefield faithfully, workers laid 5 miles of roads, transplanted 5,000 trees, sowed fields of rye, barley, and wildflowers, and recreated four historic buildings.

As all this was happening, the cast arrived at Budapest airport where customs officers unearthed a copy of *Playboy* in Jack's suitcase. Within minutes, a crowd of officials entered the fray. 'Jack looked quite pleased at the attention his light reading matter was attracting,' Ogivly recalled:

> Once all the naked ladies had been checked over, with the magazine being turned this way and that to get all possible alternative views, the rest of the pages were then examined with painstaking thoroughness. When Jack asked for his magazine back, we heard for the first time the word that came to symbolize Soviet society for us: 'Nyet'.

After a rough first week, Michael Wilding—an actor known for his unintelligible mumble—found himself in a Russian hospital after tripping during a battleground scene. Hearing of his predicament, Jack proceeded to his bedside and, after sustained garbling, managed to affect his release. 'I was concussed, you see,' Michael related to Bryan Forbes, 'and dear old Jack said it was the only time in his life he could understand what I was saying. The moment I recovered; it was back to the old mumble.' Virginia McKenna, playing the waiflike duchess of Richmond, remembered the mood of the cast lightened in Italy: 'I had the greatest privilege of seeing Jack, and his beautiful wife Doreen, and these are memories from the past that I have never forgotten'. In Rome, the Hawkinses returned to Passetto's, the Excelsior lounge, and other old haunts such as Harry's. 'My husband, Bill Travers, Jack, and I, and one or two others, always had dinner together and exchanged stories,' McKenna remembers, 'Wonderful times.' During this period in Rome, ensconced in a suite at the Eden for the balance of the shoot, Dee prevailed on Jack to put pen to paper and embark on writing his autobiography—a work largely built from warmed-over press interviews and clippings. He enjoyed the experience and wrote in longhand, Dee corrected spelling and punctuation. Back home, he was photographed celebrating Noël Coward's seventieth birthday at the Savoy Hotel, with John Gielgud, Laurence Olivier, and Kenneth More before returning to Pinewood for *When Eight Bells Toll*, an Alistair Maclean adventure starring Anthony Hopkins and Robert Morley. Playing Skouros, a Greek villain, he hung his performance on Aristotle Onasis, enhanced by the addition of a spivvy moustache, rouge-tinged cheeks, garish smoking jacket, and a little pinkie ring.

During July 1970, he was back at Pinewood to play the sadistic Mr Brocklehurst, a minor antagonist in a made-for-television movie of Charlotte Brontë's classic *Jane Eyre*, alongside Susannah York who portrayed Jane dressed in a black coif with curls. The historical Brocklehurst—the supervisor of a boarding school for orphaned girls—was a brutal figure, who behaved in the most appalling manner toward his young charges. Jack depicted his character with harshness and cruelty (if the role required the audience to hate him, then he made them hate him). Though a clone of Robert Stevenson's 1943 Fox production, the film enjoyed a long life in China after being dubbed into Mandarin and endlessly repeated on television. There was also a brief visit to South Africa for *The Last Lion*, a low-budget local production in which Jack played an ailing millionaire out for one last hunt. It was Wilbur Smith's first film script, and as he later recalled, the British film industry was 'up in arms over what they saw as us condoning South Africa's apartheid policies by working in the country.' For the most part, Jack avoided any direct flak, a remarkable feat, given Equity, the British actors' union, frequently castigated members working in South Africa and offered little support or protection to performers. Interestingly, Nicholas Hawkins, who had been honing his theatrical skills, had shown some interest in film production, and helped with second-unit work on the picture. From the tension of South Africa, Jack flew to join the cast of *Sin* in Cyprus, an island enduring its own national problems as friction between Greeks and Turks continued to escalate. Though he was not an obvious choice for the part of a village priest, only his love of travel can possibly explain why he chose to feature in this woeful American-Cypriot-British drama starring Richard Johnson and porcelain-skinned Raquel Welch, then cinema's biggest female attraction. Doreen described Jack's part as a 'bit of an Archbishop Makarios role'. He was offered the part by Patrick Curtis, Welch's husband and head of Curtwel Productions, which had a stake in the movie. Curtis described the project as a 'modern drama with Greek tragedy overtones'. Welch played a married woman with a stifled life in a sleepy Cypriot village embarking on an affair with a friend of her husband, and the story had a classically blood-soaked ending. 'This is the first time I've had the opportunity to play a real live woman, a woman of the earth—not just a celluloid character,' Welch told a London columnist. Jack enjoyed a genuine rapport with Welch and was coaxed into the PR circus which saw her literally stop the traffic in Nicosia. He was also pleasantly surprised to encounter a flock of film fans holding up little pads for his autograph and an invite to appear on the British Forces Broadcasting Service (at the officers' mess, he was treated with the respect befitting a military dignitary).

Back home, anxious to settle on a new project, he committed to a picture called *Kidnapped*. But before that, he joined Dame Peggy Ashcroft, Richard Attenborough, and Cicely Courtneidge to petition parliament on the issue of actors working on Sunday, something he felt passionate about. The plea read: 'Actors and Actresses earnestly and humbly beg that the House of Commons will not allow them to be compelled, in the interest of commercial managements, to work on Sundays, but will preserve to them the liberty which the law provides to work only six days in each week and to have their day of rest in their own homes'[28] (in April 1972, the Sunday Theatres Bill, introduced by Baroness Lee of Asheridge to allow performances on Sundays, passed its remaining stages in the House of Commons).

Jack also put his name to an advertisement in *The Times* supporting Britain's accession to the Common Market (the forerunner of the European Union), along with Henry Cooper, Adrian Boult, and Benjamin Britten.

Work eventually began on *Kidnapped* in the spring of 1971. Loosely based on the Robert Louis Stevenson novels *Kidnapped* and *Catriona*, Jack played the oily 'Hoseason,' a burned-out, cigar-chomping, seadog set on robbing Alan Breck, a heroic highlander (Michael Caine) and enslaving David Balfour (Lawrence Douglas). The lavish Technicolor affair set during the Jacobite Revolution plucked Douglas from repertory theatre and into the national spotlight. 'I came from nowhere, literally,' he told the author. 'We had ten weeks filming in Scotland, and the weather was glorious when we actually wanted rain and thunder!' The photographic unit was based at Oban on the West Coast of Scotland, with other locations on the Isle of Mull, Loch Awe, and Stirling Castle. Early in the shoot, Douglas remembered being invited to Jack's dressing room to familiarize himself with lip movements and what to expect on set:

> He was obviously in a lot of difficulty, which he bore tremendously well. He did try to articulate and project; he knew the importance of that. He did his best to keep up the pace of the scene by producing as much sound as he could which I was able to hear and could anticipate when it was my cue to speak. He was charming, professional, and stoic throughout, despite his obvious difficulties.

Produced by Frederick Brogger and directed by Delbert Mann, some accounts have contended the movie ran out of money halfway through shooting, and only just managed to wobble to a conclusion. Caine later snapped, 'I never got paid for it, so I refuse to discuss it. It was an absolute and utter disaster from beginning to end.'[29] Critics were equally unimpressed. '*Kidnapped* comes out as a somewhat tedious tale and its 107 minutes screening is awful long,' John Krier noted in a dispiriting review. 'Jack Hawkins makes an all too brief appearance as a sort of Scots Long John Silver, though his voice is painfully obviously dubbed.'[30]

Jack's next move was more surprising, when he made an emotional appearance on *The Dick Cavett Show*, a national American talk show filming at Elstree in London. During a fifteen-minute interview, he described his life without real speech, hoping to give encouragement to those with a similar ailment.[31] 'The most I can hope for is to vary the pitch of the sounds,' he said. 'The actual croaking quality, I'm afraid is here to stay. It's a damned nuisance, but there you are.' This appearance, though, was somewhat overshadowed by a visibly inebriated George Brown, the politician who served as deputy leader of the Labour Party, who, after a marathon bender, slurred his way through an excruciating interview. To make matters worse, his late arrival kept Jack, Kenneth Tynan, the theatrical critic, and the studio audience waiting two hours. 'To think this wet brained clown was once the Foreign Secretary!' Tynan scowled in his diary.

The most important enterprise, without a doubt, during this period was when Peter O'Toole invited Jack to co-produce *The Ruling Class*, a film version of Peter Barnes satirical attack on the aristocracy and establishment in which O'Toole appears as a long-haired oddball who imagines himself as the Holy Trinity all in one and demands to be called by any of the 9 billion names of God.

Reminiscing to the author, Hungarian-born director Peter Medak remembered decamping with the cast—including Alistair Sim, Arthur Lowe, Graham Crowden, and Caroline Seymore—at Harlaxton manor near Grantham in Lincolnshire. O'Toole stayed in an old schoolhouse, while Jack moved to a nearby cottage. 'All through the shoot they were very connected and great friends ... kindred spirits,' Medak explained. 'When Jack lost his voice, Peter took him immediately under his wing and because of that; he thought it would be a good idea if he were to become one of the producers of *The Ruling Class*.'

Until then, Medak had only directed two pictures, but he had been catapulted to notoriety with his second feature *A Day in the Death of Joe Egg*. From their first meeting, Medak hit it off with Jack: 'I met him at his home in Knightsbridge, he was a refreshingly earthy person and made me feel incredibly at ease—you see, I had this terrible accent and was quite conscious of it around all those actors speaking impeccable English. Jack said to me, "don't fret dear boy ... I have never passed an exam in my life!"' As it turned out, Jack was an asset to the project, and rolled up his shirtsleeves and cracked on. 'He was an enormous part of the film,' says Medak. 'It was a sixteen-week shoot, which is a long time for a movie. He was at the reading of the script; he was at some of the rehearsals in Covent Garden and he was incredibly helpful because Peter O'Toole and I had a relationship which had gone very sour during the movie.'

In fact, during production, the Hungarian was forced to suffer the occasional humiliation when O'Toole staged tantrums and sulks. 'I was working under strain. Jack became a wonderful troubleshooter between Peter and me because we started fighting and arguing,' he explained. 'If Peter didn't like something I wanted him to do, he just walked off the set at Twickenham studios.' On one occasion, Jack's patience was tested after a typical infantile O'Toole outburst: 'Jack was standing next to me after Pete stormed off to his upstairs dressing room. Jack started swearing and cursing ... he said I'm gonna go up and get that fucker! So, he went up and got Peter down again and we did the shot. That was typical Jack ... we became great friends during the movie'. After a successful screening at Cannes, Medak returned to London with the intention of chipping away twenty minutes from the film, a decision which raised O'Toole's emotional thermometer. 'Peter didn't want to cut one single line of the movie ... Jack was very much on my side,' Medak recalls. 'The film was over two and a half hours! Jack was very active in negotiating during the arguments between O'Toole. It was a bit of a nightmare situation which seemed to continue forever.'

When released, the film succeeded as a shocker for the older generation, and anyone seeking controversy was supremely rewarded. In fact, after a short clip was shown on BBC TV, a flurry of angry correspondence poured into *The Times* complaining of blasphemy. Catherine Bramwell Booth, a descendant of the founder of the Salvation Army, asked: 'Is there, Sir, no power in all the land, able to prevent the intrusion into any programme of such a beastly travesty of Him Whom I hold most Holy?'

During the shoot, O'Toole—who continued to enjoy a camaraderie and affection for Jack—observed his friend was going into retreat mode and could be tetchy: 'He [Jack] lost what he was on earth for, which was to act. He became isolated, he was a man who thrived on company and conversation and communication. He became sad, really, and depressed'.

A brief distraction came with a visit to West Berlin in April 1972 for *Escape to the Sun,* a mediocre French-German-Israeli production based on a story about a group of Jews attempting to escape from the USSR. It was not a picture that Jack wanted to make (and the budget was shoestring), but he was persuaded by Laurence Harvey, who had signed up to star in the film (and hoped it would revive his career. It did not). Sadly, throughout the shoot, off-set, Harvey (playing a KGB officer) was already displaying signs of illness and would succumb to stomach cancer two years later at the age of forty-five.

In his solo moment in *Escape to the Sun*, Jack (playing an idealistic novelist) mimes a long, impassioned address to his Soviet persecutors condemning the scourge of communism:

> You say that I'm mad! It is you who will make me mad. How is it possible for the state to claim that for medical and human reasons they have to power to take away from a man the right to think and express himself. I know where you are sending me, these 'institutions' of yours are as helpful as the Nazi's gas chambers. You call it help; it is not help. It is destruction—destruction of the spirit. It's worse than the death penalty!

It took six months of postproduction before *Escape to the Sun* was ready for release. Following the lukewarm reception, Jack's mood was further darkened by the death of Noël Coward on 26 March 1973 of heart failure. After the funeral, diversion came with a part in the low-budget gore-flick *Theatre of Blood*, followed by the hopelessly hack assignment *Tales That Witness Madness*, a horror produced by Norman Priggen. 'Jack and I hardly said anything about that production because I think we were a bit ashamed we were doing it because we needed the money, I suppose,' says Michael Jayston. 'It was a load of absolute garbage. Amazing cast … garbage script…. I remember Joan Collins saying to me, "why are you doing this?"'

Curtain Falls

Despite his growing mastery in using his 'oesophagus voice', Jack came to loathe what he disdainfully called 'the gulp'. He despised the flat tone and lack of inflection and having to swallow air, which, he complained, ruined the timing of everything. And all the time, in the midst of his busy life, he constantly sought a cure. It was just after being persuaded to take the part of a Russian general alongside Julie Andrews in *The Tamarind Seed*, slated to begin shooting in Paris in July, that news of an artificial voice-box developed in New York changed everything. Invented by Dr Stanley Taub, the little instrument, weighing just 3 ounces, promised the immediate restoration of 'effortless speech' for a person whose larynx, or voice box, had been removed in surgery. At last, the possibility of a return to normality presented itself. Or so it seemed.

From that point on events took on the character of a fast-moving drama as Jack applied himself to finding out more and, on impulse, flew to New York. 'It was all very sudden,' Taub told the author. 'I met him at my office and invited him to have dinner at my home in Brooklyn Heights, which he did.' As they ate, he explained that to install the instrument (known as a VoiceBak), a surgeon would cut a second opening through the side of the neck into the oesophagus, leading to the stomach. The instrument would then be fitted into the two openings for daytime use and could be removed before sleeping. The only downside was that just ten operations had so far been conducted, meaning it was still considered experimental.

Interestingly, James Glenn, a columnist with *The People*, claimed that after meeting forty-six-year-old Taub, Jack still could not make up his mind about the procedure. What changed things, according to Glenn, was a recorded interview with a BBC reporter in New York, 'Jack started with I'm not certain whether I shall go ahead or not'. However, after the interview, he asked for the recording to be played back. 'That had convinced me,' Jack reportedly said. 'I sound dreadful compared with patients who have had the operation for a new voice. I am going ahead.' Shortly after, he phoned home. 'It's marvellous,' he told Dee during a long-distance call from the Flower Fifth Avenue Hospital. 'I'm going to have it done.' Dee noted the change in his mood from depression to elation. 'He was determined to go ahead,' she recounted, and was 'absolutely certain about what he wanted. It was a very courageous act on Jack's part.'

With the emotions of the previous week having drained from him, Jack prepared for the first step of surgery on the evening of 16 April. 'He knew what he was going to have, and I was as reassuring as I could be,' Taub recalled. 'After that, Jack was admitted to the hospital and proceeded to get prepared for surgical procedure.' However, as he lay on the operating table, it soon became evident that things were not going smoothly. 'He got an infection in the flap that was put into the neck area,' Taub glumly noted. 'And he had a carotid leak because the vessels were near the area where we were operating on, they are next to the oesophagus.' According to Taub, Jack was lifted aboard a trolley and returned to a ward. 'I did have a chance to put the device in him during the phase of healing,' Taub recounted: 'I hooked him up to the VoiceBak and he spoke! My God, it was so clear but a little on the gruff side. And he heard himself talk—he was saying something from Shakespeare—it was really quite thrilling to hear him talk. Here was Jack Hawkins ... talking! It was emotional for all of us'. That same afternoon, Jack posed for pictures—one shows him looking down on Central Park from his hospital room, in another photo he has his arm around a doctor's shoulder and Taub is seen talking animatedly with another patient. Despite these encouraging signs, six long days passed before Jack was moved from the Flower to Lauren Bacall's apartment at the Dakota building on Central Park West, where Doreen was waiting. Talking to Mark Sennet of the *Daily Express* on 23 April, Jack was still full of confidence: 'I have tremendous faith in the surgeons and the men who have invented this device. I could have kept pondering about my decision and then maybe I would not have gone ahead'. Dee added: 'It will be so nice to be together here—take things easy and wait for the time when Jack is ready to receive his new voice. I am so happy for him'. However, still unhealed, and very much under the weather (he was also taking painkillers to numb the effects of the surgery), Dee nursed her husband and fed him wet foods through a tube. Receiving nourishment intravenously was messy, finicky, and always left him hungry. Soon after, as Taub recalls, things took a turn for the worse: Jack was pale and in terrible pain: 'I got a phone call at some point that he [Jack] was bleeding, so I rushed over to the Dakota apartment—I remember racing through Central Park—and I saw that he was having some bleeding through the neck'. A private ambulance arrived, followed by another doctor. 'We rushed him to the hospital where he underwent emergency surgery,' Taub explained. 'He recovered from that operation. He had a little weakness on one side, I believe, because of the interruption of the flow of blood to that side of the brain.' With the wound unhealed and the threat of more bleeding, plans to insert the VoiceBak were completely abandoned. 'I remember him leaving the hospital, raising his hand and saying goodbye and he went back to the Dakota,' says Taub. By this point, Nicholas had arrived in New York and accompanied his parents back to London on 10 May. But after a week recuperating at Roehampton, the wounds from the exploratory operation still failed to heal. On 17 May, he entered East Grinstead's Queen Victoria Hospital for a short stay which he tolerated well. Interestingly, Kenneth Williams makes a candid note in his diary on Friday 8 June after his doctor, John Musgrove, who was based at East Grinstead, told him he had got Jack Hawkins in as a patient and did not 'think he'll last much longer than a fortnight'.[1]

Remarkably, Jack pulled through and with Dee at his side told journalists he was optimistic of making a recovery. A few close friends were invited for drinks, David Niven among them. Wrapped in a cardigan and woolly scarf, Jack restricted his exercise to morning and evening walks in the garden and was fitted for costumes for *The Tamarind Seed*, which was slated to start shooting. And then, quite suddenly, on 10 June 1973, he was rushed to St Stephens Hospital in Fulham for a second emergency operation after blood began spurting from throat while was bathing—it was another severe haemorrhage. Dee covered the wound with towels, dialled 999, and waited for help. The ordeal began a month-long fight for life. 'Jack has been very ill indeed,' Dee told reporters: 'He appears to have come through the operation successfully and his condition when I left him this morning was certainly better. But he can't talk and must rest. Now we have to just wait and hope that the operation will have succeeded in clearing the trouble for good'. The next massive hit to his system came a few weeks later, on 2 July, with yet another haemorrhage, when doctors admitted he was 'not so well'. His condition was even mentioned in parliament by Laurie Pavitt, MP for Willesden West, who said the house would be wishing good luck to 'that marvellous British actor who is struggling for his life at the moment.'[2]

Frightened but poised, Doreen had a vivid memory of her last conversation at Jack's bedside in the intensive care ward of St Stephens, located in a darker part of the hospital. Despite his frail condition, the atmosphere was far from morose; in fact, the couple spent an hour laughing and joking. Jack sipped orange juice laced with a splash of vodka. He was 'so marvellous', that day, Dee remembered. That night, she left St Stephens 'feeling happy', as Jack dozed, apparently without discomfort.

The next day, he lapsed into a coma. The 'long tale of horror', as Doreen described it, wiping away tears, ended at 12:10 on Wednesday 18 July 1973, when Jack died. He was sixty-two years old.

His death certificate gives as first causes of death as a stroke (cerebrovascular accident) and a damaged main artery in the neck leading to the brain and continuous bleeding. It also records as a secondary cause of death cancer of the throat. Friends found it impossible not to share Doreen's tremendous grief. 'He was so brave I just can't tell you,' Dee told journalists, valiantly maintaining her composure: 'It was remarkable. He never complained and it was that that broke my heart. It was Jack's decision to go ahead with the voice box operation. It was very courageous of him, and I backed his decision'. She went on to say: 'I think about nine of these operations had been done before and it was very courageous of him to act as a guinea pig. It would have been marvellous for fellow sufferers if he had recovered. I am so sorry it did not work. One just regrets that such a brave heart should have to go'.

Peter O'Toole, his eyes welling up, was inconsolable. 'He had been warned how dangerous the operation was,' he told a journalist from the syndicated press. 'He put everything on one throw and lost. But the compromise he'd had to live with for the last decade of his life was simply not enough for him. He wanted a full life again for himself and for his family. That was enough for him to take the ultimate gamble.'[3]

When the news of Jack's death broke, Stanley Taub was in Greece with his wife and son. 'We were vacationing on an island there; I don't know if it was Mykonos or Corfu,' he told the author:

> And when I heard the news, I got a chisel and a hammer and went out and chiseled his name on a rock—Jack Hawkins. There is nothing worse than losing a patient. It was like a war experience for me. I had post traumatic syndrome—it bothered me for many years afterwards what happened to Jack. I think about that, and I get instantly depressed.

Obituaries appeared worldwide as condolences, flowers, letters, and telegrams came from all directions. 'Jack Hawkins may be dead, but his greatness, as a man and an actor who endeared himself to millions, will live on for many more years in his talking pictures,' the *Liverpool Echo* noted.[4] A few close friends were invited to the funeral on Saturday 21 July 1973, David Niven, Peter O'Toole, Richard Green, Lauren Bacall, and Dinah Sheridan among them. After the short, simple service at Golders Green Crematorium, the BBC's Michael Barratt talked to Niven about Jack, and as one newspaper observed, 'the essential goodness and courage of the man came out'.[5] Over the following month, Dee remained in shock. 'My main drawback had been lack of sleep,' she wrote to Radie Harris. 'This has been going on for some time, but since Jack's death nothing seemed to bring relief. However, I finally have a prescription that works—and maybe I am at the turning point.' She enjoyed the assurance of knowing friends, including David Niven, provided support. 'David was marvellous,' she recounted. 'He was filming in England, and he'd ring me two or three times a day. He was very good about anyone who was in trouble.' Characteristically for a man who forcefully protected his family, Jack bequeathed his property and gross estate of £13,019 to Doreen, and established a trust fund for Nicholas, Andrew, and Caroline. 'I suppose everyone expected Jack to leave half-a-million,' Dee said. 'But people don't realize that English actors are never rich because they pay such enormous taxes.'

There was a faint whiff of controversy after the funeral, when Donald Harrison, an ear, nose, and throat professor at London University and one of the most respected men in his field, told the media he was deeply unhappy with the American VoiceBak procedure. 'The operation, in my view, was dangerous on a patient that had received radiation therapy as Jack Hawkins had,' he asserted, adding that British medical thinking was such that radiation treatment weakened the tissue to such an extent that it made future surgery critically dangerous: 'We do not do it because it makes a hole in the oesophagus and this is the thing we try to avoid'.[6]

A fulsome memorial service took place on what would have been Jack's sixty-third birthday on 14 September at St Martin-in-the-Fields. Doreen, along with Andrew, Nicholas, and Caroline, was joined by Dame Sybil Thorndike, Lauren Bacall, Dame Anna Neagle, Rex Harrison, Stanley Baker, Robert Morley, Sir Alec Guinness, Douglas Fairbanks, Michael Caine, Dame Edith Evans, and Derek Nimmo. In one last act of duty and friendship, Kenneth More read a heartfelt and unscripted address. 'He lost a gallant fight to recapture an actor's most precious gift,' More said. 'He stands as an example to us all. And he earned the unstinted admiration of the world. The man who gave ... he was always ready to help, listen, sympathize, advise and he always picked up the chips. He was popular and loved by the British public, and he earned and held their respect'. After some quiet prayers, Richard Attenborough movingly delivered the lesson. Soon after, Dee informed Radie Harris, 'I have finally begun to get myself together again. The service was quite lovely, and the church was crammed—everyone was there. After such a period of awful strain, grief, and misery of losing Jack the feeling of loneliness and desolation settled upon me.'[7] Remarking on a visit to the villa in France, Dee wrote there were, 'too many happy memories and things from last year still around ... I simply could not believe what had happened. The weather was beautiful, and I had lots of my friends there being so wonderfully kind and helpful and yet I was alone.'[8] She returned to London for two events celebrating her husband's extraordinary life. Firstly, a tribute at Kensington Odeon in aid of the Cinema and Television Benevolent Fund and the National Society for Cancer Relief, attended by Princess Alexandra. Music was provided by the band of the Royal Welch Fusiliers, while John Mills introduced a screening of *The Cruel Sea*. Mills said the war films epitomising bravery, energy, and pluck, 'would always be his enduring memorial'. The second event was the publication of Jack's memoirs, for which Dee threw herself into penning a postscript describing his last ten weeks. Given he had lived a life free of scandal—tax affairs exempted—the manuscript contains no tawdry revelations. Critic Peter McGarry thought the book 'should be studied and absorbed, if only to persuade the reader to count his blessings'. Another reviewer remarked '*Anything for a Quiet Life* is a fine quiet book. Names are mentioned in it, but it seems these names are mentioned to honour the person remembered. The tone nowhere is at all boastful'.[9]

Half a century on, Jack's cinematic achievements remain his legacy. In all, he made fifty-six films, but *The Cruel Sea* alone would have ensured his place in cinema history. 'Who could forget him?' asks Bobby Henrey, the child star of *The Fallen Idol*. 'He was the living embodiment of that unshakable, sturdy British spirit which touched the lives of others.' Indeed, in his smooth effortless style, Jack helped save Malta, helped win the battle of the Atlantic, command pilots in the Battle of Britain, outwit the Japanese army, and as luck would have it, single-handedly spy for Churchill in the heart of Nazi Germany. Small wonder that no one, not even John Mills, ever made as much money out of being a celluloid officer as Jack Hawkins. But the last word must remain with the late Peter O'Toole, who said: 'Jack more than any other man put the stamp of English acting at its most red-blooded and clear and passionate and gave a different interpretation of the cliché Englishman with his stiff upper lip'.[10]

Not long after Jack's death, Dee moved to a grand red-brick apartment in Pont Street, Knightsbridge. 'I am frequently asked about my reaction to Jack's films on television,' she revealed in 1980:

I don't always watch; it depends very much on my state of mind. Mostly it makes me happy to see him again and hear his voice—before that terrible time of beginning to lose the timbre and the harshness creeping in. As with *Ben-Hur*, I lose myself very quickly into the life we were living during the making of the film. What age the children were, the people Jack was working with. I am completely transported. Afterwards, I sometimes wish rather practically that there was some money to come from all these re-runs. Alas no.

She complained that, apart from the obvious worries, one of the problems facing a woman alone was boredom:

> It does not matter how busy you keep, how much you fill your spare time—it is always there. It is difficult not to look back to the happiness and companionship I shared with Jack, but my involvement must be with the present. The tussle with life is always a challenge and, you never know, sometimes there is a victory.[11]

Dee outlived her husband by another forty years, passing away at the age of ninety-three in June 2013. In her twilight years, she penned a memoir of her time in ENSA titled *Drury Lane to Dinapur*. As for Jessica Tandy, in 1990, at eighty-years-old, she was crowned queen of Hollywood after becoming the oldest performer to win an Oscar for her appearance in *Driving Miss Daisy*. She died in 1994.

Filmography

Birds of Prey (1930) as Alfred, *The Lodger* (1932) as John Martin, *The Good Companions* (1933) as Albert, *The Lost Chord* (1933) as Sr. Jim Selby, *I Lived with You* (1933) as Mort, *The Jewel* (1933) as Peter Roberts, *A Shot in the Dark* (1933) as Norman Paull, *Autumn Crocus* (1934) as Alaric, *Death at Broadcasting House* (1934) as Herbert Evans, *Lorna Doone* (1934) as Member of the Court (uncredited), *Peg of Old Drury* (1935) as Michael O'Taffe, *Beauty and the Barge* (1937) as Lt Seton Boyne, *The Frog* (1937) as Capt. Gordon, *Who Goes Next?* (1938) as Capt. Beck, *A Royal Divorce* (1938) as Capt. Charles, *Murder Will Out* (1939) as Stamp, *The Flying Squad* (1940) as Mark McGill, *The Next of Kin* (1942) as Brigade Major Harcourt, *The Fallen Idol* (1948) as Detective Ames, *Bonnie Prince Charlie* (1948) as Lord George Murray, *The Small Back Room* (1949) as R. B. Waring, *State Secret* (1950) as Colonel Galcon, *The Black Rose* (1950) as Tristram Griffen, *The Elusive Pimpernel* (1950) as Prince of Wales/Footpad attacking Lord Anthony, *The Adventurers* (1951) as Pieter Brandt, *No Highway in the Sky* (1951) as Dennis Scott, *Home at Seven* (1952) as Dr Sparling, *Angels One Five* (1952) as Group Capt. 'Tiger' Small, *Mandy* (1952) as Dick Searle, *The Planter's Wife* (1952) as Jim Frazer, *The Cruel Sea* (1953) as Ericson, *Malta Story* (1953) as Air Vice Marshal Frank, *Twice Upon a Time* (1953) as Dr Mathews, *The Intruder* (1953) as Wolf Merton, Front Page Story (1954) as Grant, *The Seekers* (1954) as Phillip Wayne, *The Prisoner* (1955) as the Interrogator, *Land of the Pharaohs* (1955) as Pharaoh Khufu, *Touch and Go* (1955) as Jim Fletcher, *The Long Arm* (1956) as Detective-Superintendent Tom Halliday, *The Man in the Sky* (1957) as John Mitchell, *Fortune Is a Woman* (1957) as Oliver Branwell, *The Bridge on the River Kwai* (1957) as Major Warden, *Gideon's Day* (1958) as DCI George Gideon, *The Two-Headed Spy* (1958) as Gen. Alex Schottland, *Ben-Hur* (1959) as Quintus Arrius, *The League of Gentlemen* (1960) as Col. Norman Hyde, *Lafayette* (1961) as General Cornwallis, *Two Loves* (1961) as William W.J. Abercrombie, *Five Finger Exercise* (1962) as Stanley Harrington, *Lawrence of Arabia* (1962) as General Allenby, *Rampage* (1963) as Otto Abbot, Zulu (1964) as Otto Witt, *The Third Secret* (1964) as Sir Frederick Belline, *Guns at Batasi* (1964) as Colonel Deal, *Lord Jim* (1965) as Marlow, *Masquerade* (1965) as Colonel Drexel, *Judith* (1966) as Major Lawton, *The Poppy Is Also a Flower* (1966) as General Bahar, Stalked (short) (1968) as the Man, Shalako (1968) as Sir Charles Daggett, *Great Catherine* (1968) as the British Ambassador, *Oh! What a Lovely War* (1969) as Emperor Franz Joseph, *Monte Carlo or Bust* (1969) as Count Levinovitch, *Twinky* (1970) as Judge Millington-Draper, *The Adventures of Gerard* (1970) as Marshal Millefleurs, *Waterloo* (1970) as General Sir Thomas Picton, *Jane Eyre* (1970) as Mr Brocklehurst, *The Beloved* (1971) as Father Nicholas, *When Eight Bells Toll* (1971) as Sir Anthony Skouras, *Nicholas and Alexandra* (1971) as Count Fredericks, *The Last Lion* (1972) as Ryk Mannering, *Young Winston* (1972) as Mr Welldon, *Escape to the Sun* (1972) as Baburin, *Kidnapped* (1973) as Captain Hoseason, *Theatre of Blood* (1973) as Solomon Psaltery, *Tales That Witness Madness* (1973) as Dr Nicholas.

On Stage

This chronology is compiled largely from the biographical dictionary of actors, actresses, directors, playwrights, and producers of the English-speaking theatre published by the Gale Research Co., USA (1978) and constructed from *Who's Who in the Theatre*, volumes 1–15 (1912–1972).

1923–1929

Jack Hawkins made his debut appearance at the Holborn Empire, 26 December 1923, in *Where the Rainbow Ends*; at the New Theatre, from March 1924, he played Dunois' Page in *Saint Joan*; Holborn Empire, December 1924, Crispian Carey in *Where the Rainbow Ends*; played the Page in *Saint Joan* at the Regent, January 1925, and on tour, September 1925; Empire, March 1926, Bernardo in *The Cenci*; Lyceum, May, 1926, the Page in *Saint Joan*; Prince's, December 1926, Fleance in *Macbeth*; Q, June, 1927, he played Derrick in *The Price*, and later toured in *Interference*; Holborn Empire, December 1927, M. Bertrand and Saint George in *Where the Rainbow Ends*; New, February 1928, and Savoy, March 1928, Ainger in *Young Woodley*; His Majesty's, January 1929, John in *Beau Geste*; he then sailed for New York and at the Henry Miller Theatre, 22 March 1929, played 2Lt Hibberd in *Journey's End*.

1930–1940

On returning to the United Kingdom, Jack appeared at the Vaudeville, London, September 1930, playing Patrick Battle in *The Breadwinner*; Lyric, April 1931, Alaric Craven in *Autumn Crocus*; Wyndham's, November 1931, David Frankiss in *Port Said*; Savoy, December 1931,

Dan in *The Traveller in the Dark*; Phoenix (for Repertory Players), January 1932, Lieut. Heath in *Below the Surface*; Royalty, January 1932, Jerry Hammond in *While Parents Sleep*; Savoy, April 1932, Guy Treherne in *Red Triangle*; Wyndham's, October 1932, Michael Service in *Service*; Gaiety (for Repertory Players), January 1933, Charles Griffon in *One of Us; Cambridge*, March 1933 (for the Jewish Drama League), Lorenzo in *The Lady of Belmont*; Embassy, May, 1933, Dick Gable in *Sometimes Even Now*; Open Air Theatre, June, 1933, Orlando in *As You Like It*; Open Air Theatre, August 1933 Oberon in *A Midsummer Night's Dream*; Queen's, November 1933, played George in *Sunshine Sisters*; Aldwych, March 1934, Marquis of Yore in *Indoor Fireworks*. He returned to the Open Air Theatre, 1934, as Orlando, Orsino in *Twelfth Night*, the First Brother in *Comus*, Wyndham's, July 1934, Jack Maitland in The Maitland's, New, November 1934, Horatio in *Hamlet*, Shaftsbury, June 1935, Lucien Cambolle in Accidentally Yours, Aldwych, September 1935, Joe Kelly in *The World Waits*; St Martin's, November 1935, Peter Crayshaw in *Coincidence*; Prince's, April, 1936, Richard Gordon in *The Frog*; Ring, Blackfriars, January 1937, Benedick in *Much Ado About Nothing*; Open Air, July, 1937, Comus in *Comus*, and August, 1937, Leontes in *The Winter's Tale*; St Martin's, October, 1937, Mark Seeley in *Autumn*; toured, March 1938, as Sir Brian Brooke in the same play; New, September, 1938, Sir Thomas Hollick in *Can We Tell?* King's, Hammersmith, October, 1938, Sir Thomas More in *Traitor's Gate*; Broadhurst, New York, January, 1939, Nicholas Randolph in *Dear Octopus*; Globe, London, April, 1939, Ahasuerus in *Scandal in Assyria*; Lyceum, June, 1939, The Ghost and Claudius in *Hamlet*, subsequently playing the same parts at Kronborg Castle, Elsinore (Denmark); Globe, August, 1939, Algernon Moncrieffe in *The Importance of Being Earnest*; provincial tour in the same part, and again played it at the Globe, December, 1939; at the Old Vic, April–May, 1940, played Edmund in *King Lear*, and Caliban in *The Tempest*.

1945–1951

After the Second World War, Jack returned to the London stage at the Arts Theatre in August 1946, as King Magnus in *The Apple Cart*; toured on the continent for the British Council, 1946–7, as Claudius in *Hamlet*, *Othello*, and Morell in *Candida*; at the Piccadilly, March, 1947, played Othello, and the Rev. James Mavor-Morell in *Candida*; Arts, November, 1947, Dobelle in *The Moon in the Yellow River*; March, 1948, directed *The Lady's Not For Burning*; Covent Garden, July, 1948, appeared as

Faithful in *The Pilgrim's Progress*; Whitehall, September 1948, directed *Against the Tide*; Piccadilly, February, 1950, played Jacques Breval in *The Purple Fig-Tree*; toured the USA, and appeared at the Broadhurst, New York, March, 1951, as Mercutio in *Romeo and Juliet*; appeared at the Lyric, Hammersmith, September, 1951, as Cymen in *Thor, With Angels*.

Endnotes

Chapter 1

1 *Liverpool Echo and Evening Express*, 4 July 1966.
2 BBC Archives Transcript, BBC *Desert Island Discs*—Recorded 8 May 1953.
3 *Vogue*; New York, 1 May 1956.
4 *The New York Times*, 4 April 1954.
5 Unknown, *Further Letters from A Man of No Importance* (1914–1929), p. 226.
6 Mills, J., *Up in the Clouds* (Weidenfeld and Nicolson: London, 1980), p. 57.
7 Granger, S., *Sparks Fly Upward* (Granada: London, 1981), p. 41.
8 *The Era*, 14 March 1928.
9 *Picturegoer*, 21 March 1953.
10 *Illustrated Sporting and Dramatic News*, 9 February 1929.

Chapter 2

1 *Graphic*, 9 February 1929.
2 BBC Archives Transcript, BBC *Desert Island Discs*—Recorded 8 May 1953.

Chapter 3

1 *The Stage*, 21 June 1979.
2 Although from Swansea, Jay got his schooling in London, before joining a group of Japanese jugglers. He was invalided out of the Navy during the First World War and, as his disability prevented him getting stage work, he found employment as a film extra. Not long after, he was acting as an agent specialising in 'extras' at a time that film production was slowly climbing up from the lowest rungs of the show business ladder.
3 *The New York Times*, 26 December 1982.
4 Norman, B., *Hollywood Greats* (Hodder & Stoughton: London, 1979), p. 111.
5 *Ibid.*
6 Beckett, F., *John Gielgud to the Rescue* (Laurence Olivier, Haus Publishing: 2005), pp. 33–53.
7 *Picturegoer*, 23 March 1953.
8 *The New York Times*, 4 April 1954.
9 *Picturegoer*, 23 March 1953.
10 *Ibid.*
11 *Modern Weekly*, 3 December 1932.
12 Jessica Tandy biographical notes (Berlin Public Library), p. 50.

13   *The New York Times*, 4 April 1954

14   *Picturegoer*, 23 March 1953.

15   Quayle, A., *A Time to Speak* (Barrie & Jenkins: London, 1990), p. 79.

16   *Daily Herald*, 9 November 1933.

17   A reference to *Perfect Understanding*, a 1933 British comedy film directed by Cyril Gardner and starring Laurence Olivier, Gloria Swanson, and John Halliday.

18   Kiernan, T., *Sir Larry: The life of Laurence Olivier* (Times Books: London, 1981), p. 93.

19   Tandy, J., *Men You Know*. Cited from *Jessica Tandy: A Twentieth Century Acting Career*. Dissertation by Tonia Kreuger (Ohio State University: 2002), p. 62.

20   Saint-Denis, M., *John Gielgud* (Geoffrey Bles: London, 1938), p. 54.

21   *Sunday Post*, 27 January 1935.

22   *Liverpool Echo*, 10 May 1955.

23   *Kensington News* and *West London Times*, 14 June 1935.

24   *Picturegoer*, 23 March 1953.

25   *Picturegoer*, 28 March 1953.

26   *Daily Mirror*, 19 January 1935.

27   22 June 1935.

Chapter 4

1   Grissom, J., *Follies of God: Tennessee Williams and the Women of the Fog* (Vintage Books: New York, 2016), pp. 116-117.

2   *Fleetwood Chronicle*, 30 July 1937.

3   *Picturegoer*, 7 April 1951.

4   *Daily News* (London), 16 June 1938.

5   Neame, R., *Straight from the Horse's Mouth* (Scarecrow Press: London, 2002), p. 35.

6   *Daily Herald*, 8 September 1938.

7   *Daily News* (London), 8 September 1938.

8   *West London Observer*, 28 October 1938.

9   *Daily News* (London), 16 January 1939.

10   *Weekly Dispatch* (London), 30 April 1939.

11   *Ibid.*

12   *Daily Herald*, 15 September 1939.

Chapter 5

1   Jess phoned Jack from Liverpool. Hannen Swaffer, the improbably named reporter known by detractors as a toffee-nosed bastard, overheard Jack speaking to Jess on the phone at the Savage Club in St James's. He earwigged as she shouted down a crackly line informing that she had 'a dozen eggs and some bacon and butter'. The 'scoop', which highlighted the severity of rationing, was enough for Swaffer to chronicle it in the *Daily Herald*.

2   *The Tatler*, 15 May 1940.

3   Guinness, A., *My Name Escapes Me* (Penguin: London, 1997), p. 197.

4   *The Bystander*, 12 June 1940.

5   Sanderson, M., *From Irving to Olivier: a social history of the acting profession in England, 1880–1983* (Athlone Press, 1984).

6   Email from Harriet Cruickshank to Nathan Morley, 11 October 2021, citing her father's memoirs.

7   *Ibid.*

8   *Daily Mirror*, 23 September 1992.

9   Interestingly, according to the memoirs of Dee Lawrence—who would become Jack's second wife seven years later—the couple sold their matrimonial house and everything to pay for the voyage and accommodation in the USA.

10   Beckett, F., *John Gielgud to the Rescue* (Laurence Olivier, Haus Publishing: 2005), p. 287

11   Guinness, A., *Positively a Final Appearance* (Hamish Hamilton: London, 1999), p. 222.
12   *Strathearn Herald*, 18 April 1942.
13   According to the *Kensington Post*'s cinema critic.
14   *Daily Herald*, 21 February 1942.
15   *Daily Mirror*, 23 September 1992.
16   *Ibid.*
17   *Burton Daily Mail*, 13 August 1980.

Chapter 6

1   BBC Archives Transcript, BBC *Desert Island Discs*—Recorded 8 May 1953.
2   *Holloway Press*, 11 August 1944.
3   *Evening Despatch*, 18 July 1953. Tapes in the Imperial War Museum also contain accounts from Fred Rolleston who served as comedian with Cross Keys, specialising in Max Miller impersonations. He never forgot 'Captain Jack Hawkins and his insistence on professional standards'. Likewise, saxophonist Dennis Boast recalled Jack was involved in the writing of stage material; 'supervising dress rehearsals; overseeing special costumes made by Indian civilians; the design of mobile stages; development of scripts and much more'.
4   Dean, B., *The Theatre at War* (London: Harrap, 1956), p. 424.
5   *The Stage*, 17 August 1944.
6   *Daily Dispatch* (Manchester), 10 January 1945.

Chapter 7

1   *The People*, 30 June 1957.
2   *Aberdeen Evening Express*, 14 August 1961.
3   *Daily News* (London), 14 November 1944.
4   *TV Mirror*, 1958.
5   Interview with Howard Thompson, 4 April 1954.
6   *The Stage*, 31 August 1989.

Chapter 8

1   *The Stage*, 5 December 1946.
2   *The Stage*, 15 August 1946.
3   *Daily News* (London), 9 August 1946.
4   Morley, N., *Disney's British Gentleman: The Life and Career of David Tomlinson* (History Press: Cheltenham, 2021), p. 81.
5   Morley, S., *The Other Side of the Moon* (Harper: London, 1985), p. 114.
6   *The Australian Women's Weekly*, 15 September 1971.
7   *Ibid.*
8   *Ibid.*
9   P146.
10   *The Sketch*, 16 February 1949.
11   *Warwick and Warwickshire Advertiser*, 22 July 1949.
12   *Bradford Observer*, 4 May 1949.
13   British Film Institute, 1977, p. 126.
14   *Marylebone Mercury*, 2 December 1949.

Chapter 9

1   Higham, C., *Sisters: The story of Olivia de Havilland and Joan Fontaine* (Coward McCann: London, 1984), p. 182.
2   12 March 1951.
3   *Ibid.*, p. 183.
4   *Theatre Arts 1951*: Volume 35 Issue 5.
5   *Herald Tribune*, 11 March 1956.
6   Quill, J., *Spitfire: A Test Pilot's Story* (Crecy Publishing: London, 2002), p.190.
7   *Truth*, Friday 28 March 1952.
8   Gielgud, J., *Sir John Gielgud: A Life in Letters* (Arcade Publishing: New York, 2004), p. 153. (A decade later, Diana Churchill ended her life after taking an overdose of barbiturates.)
9   Cole, G., *The World Was My Lobster* (John Blake Publishing: London, 2014), p. 68.
10 Berliner Zeitung, *Das Mädchen Mandy.*
11 *Chelsea News and General Advertiser*, 12 September 1952.
12 *Ibid.*

Chapter 10

1   Donald Sinden radio interview, Radio Napa, August 2004.
2   Vincent Kane, BBC interview, 1975.
3   *Holloway Press*, 7 October 1955.
4   *North Wales Weekly News*, 15 January 1981.
5   *Illustrated*, 16 July 1955.
6   Monsarrat, N., *Life is a Four-Letter Word* (Macmillan: London, 1969), p. 286.
7   *The New York Times*, 11 August 1953.
8   Desmond Carrington interview with Nathan Morley, March 2013.
9   *Picturegoer*, 13 December 1952.
10 *Dundee Courier*, 27 March 1953.
11 *Daily Mirror*, 27 March 1953.
12 *Picturegoer*, March 1953.
13 *Daily Herald*, 3 October 1953.
14 *Picturegoer*, March 1953.
15 *TV Mirror*, December 1958.
16 Munn, M., *Trevor Howard, The Man and his Films* (Robson Books: London, 1998), p. 106.
17 *Daily Herald*, 6 April 1953.
18 *Picturegoer*, February 1954.
19 *Daily Express*, 30 October 1954.
20 *Daily Herald*, 25 July 1953.
21 *Daily Express*, 30 October 1964.
22 *Picturegoer*, 14 September 1957.
23 *Tele views and News*. Titbits Magazine, 3 October 1953.
24 *Picturegoer*, 23 March 1953.
25 *Aberdeen Evening Express*, 3 March 1955.
26 Donald Sinden, *Film Festivals*, in Eric Warman (ed.), (Preview: London, 1957), pp. 5-10.
27 *Daily Mirror*, 31 December 1953.
28 *The Australian Women's Weekly*, 3 February 1954.
29 Annakin, K., *So You Want to be a Director?* (Tomahawk Press: London, 2001), p. 67.
30 Davis, R., (ed)., *The Kenneth Williams Diaries* (Harper Collins: London, 1994), p. 93.
31 Each evening a different celebrity introduced her. The roster included Noël Coward, Alec Guinness, and David Niven.

32   The leading British stars that appeared in local films were: 1 Jack Hawkins. 2 Dirk
      Bogarde. 3 Norman Wisdom. 4 Glynis Johns. 5 Kenneth More. 6 Alec Guinness. 7
      Anthony Steel. 8 Ronald Shiner. 9 Richard Todd. 10 John Mills.

33   Foot, D., *40 Years On: The story of the Lord's Tavern*ers (Good Books: London, 1990),
      p. 31.

34   *Picturegoer*, May 1958.

35   *Bradford Observer*, 22 April 1955.

36   Born in Birmingham in 1896, Balcon began his career in films just after the First
      World War. It was in 1938 that he went to Ealing, where he enjoyed its golden
      years—synonymous with a particular brand of wry humour called 'Ealing Comedy'.
      Much of this must be credited to Balcon, for he chose the directors, writers, actors,
      and technicians. Films included: *Whiskey Galore, Kind Hearts and Coronets, The
      Ladykillers, Hue and Cry*, and *Passport to Pimlico*.

37   *Daily Gazette*, 7 November 1955.

38   *Daily Herald*, 25 April 1955.

39   *Sunday Mirror*, 21 November 1954.

40   In fact, it was a joint christening at the Church of the Annunciation, Bryanston Street.
      The children—Nicholas John, aged six; Andrew Robert George, aged four; and
      three-month-old Caroline Mary—were christened together owing to Jack's filming all
      over the world. Elizabeth Allan was one of the godparents.

41   *Britannia and Eve* ,1 March 1955.

42   Sykes, E., *If I Don't Write It, Nobody Else Will* (Fourth Estate: London, 2005), p. 348.

43   *The Stage*, 25 July 1957.

Chapter 11

1   Email from Joan Collins agent Barry Langford to Nathan Morley, 15 June 2021.

2   *Times of Cyprus*, 12 October 1957.

3   *Picturegoer*, 14 July 1956.

4   *The Sketch*, 1 August 1956.

5   3 January 1957.

6   Hayakawa, S., *Zen Showed Me the Way* (Bobbs-Merrill: New York, 1960), p. 21.

7   *Torbay Express* and *South Devon Echo*, 28 January 1957.

8   Thomas, B., *William Holden, Golden Boy* (St Martins: London, 1983), p. 177.

9   Guinness, A., *Blessings in Disguise* (Hamish Hamilton: London, 1984), p. 224.

10   Phillips, G., *Beyond the Epic: The Life and Films of David Lean* (University Press of
      Kentucky, 2006).

11   Brownlow, K., *David Lean, A Biography* (Macmillan: London, 1996), p. 384.

12   It was the highest-grossing film of 1957 and received overwhelmingly positive reviews
      from critics.

13   Peary, G., *John Ford: Interviews* (University Press of Mississippi, 2002), p. 39.

14   It was the first Ealing production to be made at MGM-British Studios in Borehamwood,
      just north of London.

15   Episode: *The Elocution Teacher*. Transmitted on BBC television on 25 November 1957.

16   *Daily Express*, 21 November 1955.

17   *Picturegoer*, 26 April 1958.

18   Heston, C., *The Actor's Life: Journals 1956–1976* (Pocket Books: New York, 1979),
      p. 56.

19   *Observer*, 30 December 1979.

20   Letter from Dee Hawkins to Radie Harris, dated 29 January 1959.

21   *Daily Mirror*, 10 November 1958.

22   *Daily News* (London), 2 February 1960.

23   Sidney Cole, *The History Project*.

24   *Weekly Dispatch* (London), 29 December 1957.

25   *Ibid.*

26   *Weekly Dispatch* (London), 18 January 1959.
27   *Daily News* (London), 16 July 1959.
28   *Ibid.*
29   *Ibid.*
30   *Ibid.*
31   *Kinematograph Weekly*, 5 November 1959.
32   *Aberdeen Evening Express*, 21 November 1958.
33   Forbes, B., *Notes for a Life* (Harper Collins: London, 1974), p. 239.

Chapter 12

1   Sinai, A., *Reach for the Top: The Turbulent Life of Laurence Harvey* (Scarecrow Press: London, 2003), p. 260.
2   *South China Morning Post*, 28 February 1962
3   Freedland, M., *Shirley MacLaine* (Salem House: Manchester, 1986), p. 74.
4   The picture was a ghastly flop at the box office—public attendance was so sparse that it racked up a loss of $1.7 million.
5   Read, P. P., *Alec Guinness: The Authorized Biography*. (Pocket Books: London, 2004), p. 355.

Chapter 13

1   *The Stage*, 28 June 2001.
2   *Daily Express*, 30 October 1964.
3   Signed letter from Jack Hawkins to Catherine O'Brien, thanking her for sending stills, and asking her to inform Jack Aitken that he is turning down the offer of his [Hawkins'] life story, dated 30 September 1963.
4   *60 Minutes*, TV interview, recorded 20 December 2015.
5   *Marylebone Mercury*, 26 July 1963.
6   *Liverpool Echo*, 21 June 1963.
7   Letter to Nathan Morley, 24 October 2022.
8   Hall, W., *Raising Caine: The authorized biography* (Sidgwick & Jackson: London, 1981), p. 77.
9   *Marylebone Mercury*, 26 July 1963.
10   *Liverpool Echo*, 25 January 1964.
11   *Photoplay Film Monthly*, February 1977, O'Toole, speaking with Ken Johns.
12   Britt Ekland, note to Nathan Morley, 10 October 2021.
13   *Daily Mirror*, 24 March 1966.
14   *Sunday Mirror*, 28 February 1965.
15   Munn, M., *Trevor Howard, The Man and his Films* (Robson Books: London, 1998), p. 106.
16   *Daily Express,* 30 October 1964.
17   *Torbay Express* and *South Devon Echo,* 25 January 1966.

Chapter 14

1   Handwritten letter from Jack Hawkins to Radie Harris, 15 February 1966.
2   *National Enquirer*, 28 December 1969.
3   *Ibid.*
4   *Washington Post*, 19 July 1973.
5   *Liverpool Echo*, 15 March 1966.
6   To reporter Ivor Herbert, who observed the terrible strain.
7   Interview with Nathan Morley, 18 March 2022.

8   *Liverpool Echo*, 16 May 1966 and *Liverpool Echo*, 18 July 1973.
9   Peter McEnery interview with Nathan Morley, 8 March 2021.
10   *The People*, 8 April 1973.
11   *Daily Express*, 12 December 1966.
12   *Sunday Mirror*, 26 March 1967.
13   The History Project, retrieved from: historyproject.org.uk/interview/tilly-day.
14   *South China Sunday Post*, 11 April 1971.
15   *National Enquirer*, 28 December 1969.
16   In fact, Gray and Jack were old chums, and neighbours.
17   Evans, P., *Bardot: Eternal Sex Goddess*. (Leslie Frewin: London, 1972), p. 123.
18   Norman, B., *Hollywood Greats* (Hodder & Stoughton: London, 1979), p. 123.
19   Although destined for a limited reception in closed church groups, the film was
     uploaded to the internet decades later.
20   Dux, S., *New Directions: Oh! What a Lovely War (1969)*, in Richard Attenborough,
     pp. 37–61. (Manchester University Press, 2013).
21   Norman, B., *Hollywood Greats* (Hodder & Stoughton: London, 1979), p. 124
22   Annakin, K., *So You Want to be a Director?* (Tomahawk Press: London, 2001), p. 227.
23   *National Enquirer*, 28 December 1969.
24   *Ibid.*
25   Interview with Nathan Morley, 29 September 2022.
26   *Daily Mirror*, 4 January 1969.
27   *Harrow Observer*, 23 November 1971.
28   House of Commons. Volume 821: debated on Friday 23 July 1971.
29   Hall, W., *Raising Caine: The authorized biography* (Sidgwick & Jackson: London,
     1981), p. 255.
30   *Alderley & Wilmslow Advertiser*, 20 July 1972.
31   6 May 1971.

Chapter 15

1   Davis, R., (ed)., *The Kenneth Williams Diaries* (Harper Collins: London, 1994), p. 451.
2   House of Commons. Volume 859: Debated on Friday 6 July 1973.
3   *South China Morning Post*, 28 February 1982.
4   18 July 1973.
5   A week after the funeral, Stanley Taub's *VoiceBak* received its Patent 3,747,127 and
     went into production by LaBarge Incorporated in St Louis as the first commercially
     available fistula prosthesis.
6   22 July 1973.
7   Letter from Doreen Hawkins to Radie Harris, 10 October 1973.
8   *Ibid.*
9   *Bay Area Reporter*, 26 December 1974.
10   *Burton Daily Mail*, 13 August 1980.
11   *Echo*, 4 June 1980.

Bibliography

Annakin, K., *So You Want to be a Director?* (Tomahawk Press: London, 2001)

Beckett, F., *John Gielgud to the Rescue* (Laurence Olivier, Haus Publishing: 2005)

Brownlow, K., *David Lean, A Biography* (Macmillan: London, 1996)

Cole, G., *The World Was My Lobster* (John Blake Publishing: London, 2014)

Davis, R., (ed)., *The Kenneth Williams Diaries* (Harper Collins: London, 1994)

Dean, B., *The Theatre at War* (London: Harrap, 1956)

Evans, P., *Bardot: Eternal Sex Goddess* (Leslie Frewin: London, 1972)

Foot, D., *40 Years On: The story of the Lord's Taverners* (Good Books: London, 1990)

Forbes, B., *Notes for a Life* (Harper Collins: London, 1974)

Freedland, M., *Shirley MacLaine* (Salem House: Manchester, 1986)

Gielgud, J., *Sir John Gielgud: A Life in Letters* (Arcade Publishing: New York, 2004)

Granger, S., *Sparks Fly Upward* (Granada: London, 1981)

Grissom, J., *Follies of God: Tennessee Williams and the Women of the Fog* (Vintage Books: New York, 2016)

Guinness, A., *Blessings in Disguise* (Hamish Hamilton: London, 1984); *My Name Escapes Me* (Penguin: London, 1997); *Positively a Final Appearance* (Hamish Hamilton: London, 1999)

Hall, W., *Raising Caine: The authorized biography* (Sidgwick & Jackson: London, 1981)

Hayakawa, S., *Zen Showed Me the Way* (Bobbs-Merrill: New York, 1960)

Heston, C., *The Actor's Life: Journals 1956–1976* (Pocket Books: New York, 1979)

Higham, C., *Sisters: The story of Olivia de Havilland and Joan Fontaine* (Coward McCann: London, 1984)

Kiernan, T., *Sir Larry: The life of Laurence Olivier* (Times Books: London, 1981)

Mills, J., *Up in the Clouds* (Weidenfeld and Nicolson: London, 1980)

Monsarrat, N., *Life is a Four-Letter Word* (Macmillan: London, 1969)

Morley, N., *Disney's British Gentleman: The Life and Career of David Tomlinson* (History Press: Cheltenham, 2021)

Morley, S., *The Other Side of the Moon* (Harper: London, 1985)

Munn, M., *Trevor Howard, The Man and his Films* (Robson Books: London, 1998)

Neame, R., *Straight from the Horse's Mouth* (Scarecrow Press: London, 2002)

Norman, B., *Hollywood Greats* (Hodder & Stoughton: London, 1979)

Peary, G., *John Ford: Interviews* (University Press of Mississippi, 2002)

Phillips, G., *Beyond the Epic: The Life and Films of David Lean* (University Press of Kentucky, 2006)
Quayle, A., *A Time to Speak* (Barrie & Jenkins: London, 1990)
Quill, J., *Spitfire: A Test Pilot's Story* (Crecy Publishing: London, 2002)
Read, P. P., *Alec Guinness: The Authorized Biography* (Pocket Books: London, 2004)
Sinai, A., *Reach for the Top: The Turbulent Life of Laurence Harvey* (Scarecrow Press: London, 2003)
Saint-Denis, M., *John Gielgud* (Geoffrey Bles: London, 1938)
Sanderson, M., *From Irving to Olivier: a social history of the acting profession in England, 1880–1983* (Athlone Press, 1984)
Sykes, E., *If I Don't Write It, Nobody Else Will* (Fourth Estate: London, 2005)
Thomas, B., *William Holden, Golden Boy* (St Martins: London, 1983)
Unknown, *Further Letters from A Man of No Importance* (1914–1929)